KU-308-900

Routledge Revivals

Browning

Routledge Author Guides

GENERAL EDITOR: B. C. SOUTHAM, M.A. B.LITT. (OXON)
Formerly Department of English, Westfield College, University of London

Titles in the series

Byron by J. D. Jump, *Professor of English, University of Manchester*

Tolstoy by Ernest J. Simmons, *sometime Professor of Russian Literature, Harvard University*

Browning by Roy E. Gridley, *Associate Professor of English, University of Kansas*

Routledge Author Guides

Browning

by

Roy E. Gridley

Associate Professor of English
University of Kansas

STIRLING
DISTRICT
LIBRARY

Routledge & Kegan Paul
London and Boston

B

First published 1972
by Routledge & Kegan Paul Ltd
Broadway House, 68–74 Carter Lane,
London EC4V 5EL and
9 Park Street,
Boston, Mass. 02108, U.S.A.
Printed in Great Britain by
Cox & Wyman Ltd, London, Fakenham and Reading
© Roy E. Gridley 1972
No part of this book may be reproduced in
any form without permission from the
publisher, except for the quotation of brief
passages in criticism

ISBN 0 7100 7368 2 (c)
ISBN 0 7100 7369 0 (p)

821·8
GRI

General Editor's Preface

Nowadays there is a growing awareness that the specialist areas have much to offer and much to learn from one another. The student of history, for example, is becoming increasingly aware of the value that literature can have in the understanding of the past; equally, the student of literature is turning more and more to the historians for illumination of his area of special interest, and of course philosophy, political science, sociology, and other disciplines have much to give him.

What we are trying to do in the *Author Guides Series* is to offer this illumination and communication by providing for non-specialist readers, whether students or the interested general public, a clear and systematic account of the life and times and works of the major writers and thinkers across a wide range of disciplines. Where the *Author Guides Series* may be seen to differ from other, apparently similar, series, is in its historical emphasis, which will be particularly evident in the treatment of the great literary writers, where we are trying to establish, in so far as this can be done, the social and historical context of the writer's life and times, and the cultural and intellectual tradition in which he stands, always remembering that critical and interpretative principles are implicit to any sound historical approach.

BCS

This book is for Marilyn

Contents

Note on the Text

The quotations from Browning which I give in my text are taken from *The Works of Robert Browning* (Centenary Edition) edited by F. Kenyon, 10 vols (1912), unless otherwise stated in the notes at the end of the book.

I

A Context for Browning's Early Life: 1812-32

When Napoleon began his disastrous invasion of Russia in June 1812, Robert Browning was one month old. Three years later the Battle of Waterloo brought to a close twenty-five years of revolutionary and imperial ferment. Browning had, Chesterton claims, a 'memory like the British Museum Library'. Among the few things Browning said he could not remember, however, was that great battle. The 'mighty ferment in the heads of statesmen and poets, kings and people', as William Hazlitt characterized the years between 1789 and 1815, was never a part of Browning's personal, directly felt experience as it had been for men like Wordsworth, Coleridge and Southey who came of age during the first years of the French Revolution. Wordsworth, walking through France in the summer of 1790, found

... Europe at that time was thrilled with joy,
France standing on the top of golden hours,
And human nature seeming born again.

Southey and Coleridge plotted, in the summer of 1794, to enact in their own lives the democratic ideals of the Revolution by founding a utopian community in America. By the time Browning was born, all three men had recoiled from the violence and injustice of the successive revolutionary governments and Napoleon's empire; each had sought stability in political and religious orthodoxy, and each had to look backward to see his greatest poetical achievement.

Younger men like Byron and Shelley, who came into manhood while Napoleon was being defeated, held more passionately to the revolutionary hopes; still, they drew much of their creative force from their disillusionment at the defeat of those hopes by the reactionary forces restored to power by the Congress of Vienna in 1815. Nearly thirty years after Wordsworth had sensed a joyous birth of human

I

liberty, Shelley could scornfully describe England (and by extension all of Europe) as still ruled by

> An old, mad, blind, despised, and dying king –
> Princes, the dregs of their dull race, who flow
> Through public scorn – mud from a muddy spring;
> Rulers who neither see, nor feel, nor know,
> But leechlike to their fainting country cling,
> Till they drop, blind in blood, without a blow. . . .

Shelley was nearly twenty years older than Browning; he died shortly after Browning's tenth birthday. More than any other writer it was Shelley who passed on to Browning the excitement, energy and idealism of that earlier generation; but, for Browning, it was a vicarious and literary experience. By the time he was twenty, in his first published poem, Browning could already record the passing of those extravagant hopes for human perfection, freedom and love that had been a creative impetus to the older writers. In adolescence, so an anecdote goes, Browning imagined two nightingales in his garden to be the spirits of Keats and Shelley; in maturity he wrote poetry markedly different from that of any of the romantic poets. In his *Essay on Shelley* (1852), written when he was forty years old, Browning briefly speculates upon the relation between literary generations. After the appearance of a great poet, Browning suggests, a 'tribe of successors' grows up to

> dwell on his discoveries and reinforce his doctrine; till, at
> unawares, the world is found to be subsisting wholly on the
> shadow of a reality, on sentiments diluted from passions, on the
> tradition of a fact, the convention of a moral, the straw of last
> year's harvest. Then is the imperative call for another kind of poet,
> who shall at once replace this intellectual rumination of food
> swallowed long ago, by a supply of the fresh and living swathe. . . .

Clearly, Browning is 'another kind of poet' than are the great English poets of the opening decades of the nineteenth century. Browning broke earlier and more completely with romantic modes of expression than any other poet of the century. The cultural forces that shaped the generations of Wordsworth and Shelley were, by the time Browning grew to manhood in the 1830s, quickly becoming the 'shadow of a reality' rather than the reality that Browning and the other long-lived Victorians would explore during the rest of the century.

For the first thirty-four years of his life Browning lived in suburban London. Except for a short time at boarding school in near-by Peckham and an even shorter period in lodgings while attending the new University of London, Browning's entire childhood and youth were passed in Camberwell, from which his father commuted to his minor clerk's job in the Bank of England. Camberwell, as much as Manchester, was a product of Britain's rapidly increasing population, urbanization and industrialization, although the transformation of villages like Camberwell into ever more populous suburban communities was less dramatic and threatening than the growth of the great new industrial towns. During the poet's childhood, Camberwell doubtless retained some of the character of the rural village which Maisie Ward evokes in her recent biography of Browning: Camberwell 'was then surrounded by open fields. Pleasant walks led to Dulwich, to London itself or, farther afield, through woods and country lanes'.[1] It was less so every year. Across the three miles of open fields and other growing villages was the most populous city in the western world. London: 1801, 865,000; 1831, 1,474,000. In those thirty years the number of people living in the Parish of Camberwell quadrupled, and by 1837 the population was about 35,000. Between 1819 and 1821, the Vicar of Camberwell even leased out most of the ancient glebe land to building contractors. The fields were soon filled in. In a letter written in the spring of 1841, Browning describes with obvious delight how as a boy he would run from Camberwell to Bond Street; he ends the letter by mentioning that he has moved yet farther away from the city into another suburban house with 'a garden, and trees, and little green hills of a sort to go out on'. In 1869 William Morris supplied poetic definition to the limits of London when he asked the readers of his *The Earthly Paradise* to

Forget six counties overhung with smoke,
Forget the snorting steam and piston stroke,
Forget the spreading of the hideous town;
Think rather of the pack-horse on the down,
And dream of London, small and white and clean,
The clear Thames bordered by its gardens green. . . .

Morris was addressing Londoners in particular, but at least one whole generation from the English Midlands, the German Ruhr, the factory districts around Lille, Lyons, and Paris would have understood Morris's plea. The smoke, the noise, the spread of the town was a daily and

3

life-long experience for them. It was not simply a background to the life and work of any man of genius living in Western Europe in the nineteenth century. The effects of increased population, of new modes of production, of spreading democracy, of dislocation of traditional values, all were immediate realities. Robert Owen of Lanark was not alone in recognizing in his *Observations on the Effect of the Manufacturing System* (1815) that the 'general diffusion of manufactures throughout a country generates a new character in its inhabitants. . . .' Robert Browning, living in a middle-class suburb, was one of the 'inhabitants' of this new world. A single set of facts about one of the new technologies, railways, may symbolize the scope and pace of change which Browning's generation would witness. When Browning was born in 1812, one of the few continuously operating railways was five miles of track near Leeds over which John Blenkinsop's steam-engine pulled coal cars; by the time Browning died in 1889, there were over 300,000 miles of track in the world, and electric locomotives were being installed in London's underground railway system.

Browning's father maintained the home in Camberwell on a modest salary of some £200 to £300 per year from his clerk's job at the Bank of England, then the largest and most powerful financial institution in the world. The grandfather, too, had been in the Bank of England, with an apparently much more lucrative position. He had come up out of Dorset towards the end of the eighteenth century, married a woman with land-holdings in the West Indies, became a prosperous supporter of the Church of England, and a 'substantial resident of Peckham'. Perhaps Browning was thinking of his grandfather when, in *Red Cotton Night-Cap Country*, he begins his description of the 'rise and progress' of a nineteenth-century bourgeois family:

First comes the bustling man of enterprise,
The fortune-founding father, rightly rough,
As who must grub and grab, play pioneer. . . .

Thomas Mann, in *Buddenbrooks* (1901), attributes the decline and extinction of a nineteenth-century bourgeois family to a gradual infection, over the generations, of an artistic temperament. The Browning family, which arose near the beginning of the century with the 'fortune-founding grandfather' and ran out with the death of the poet's childless son in 1912, roughly follows Mann's pattern. The poet's father, in contrast to the enterprising grandfather, was a gentle, passive man. He collected books and prints, wrote comic verses and retained even into old age a considerable cartoonist's talent: 'an extraordinarily learned and able man', Browning wrote upon his father's death; '[he] might have been a great man had he cared a bit about it. . . .' In the early part of the century the West Indies were Britain's most important source of overseas income. The grandfather certainly profited from that phenomenon, as did the Barretts of Wimpole Street, a family which must have been further enriched by the enormous indemnity (£20,000,000) the government paid slave-holders after the abolition of slavery in 1833. Browning's father, sent out to oversee one of the family's slave plantations, soon refused that kind of work and was promptly disinherited. His refusal may have stemmed from conscious humanitarian ideals fuelled by the revolutionary fervour and the anti-slavery agitation of the period; perhaps it was his kind and quiet temperament which led him to accept disinheritance and thirty years as a routine bank clerk. Whatever the reason, he retained into old age vivid memories of the horrors of his experiences among the slave labourers in the West Indies. On his small income he kept a comfortable house and indulged his bibliomania, a delight in curious learning and his son, whom he encouraged to be a poet. Browning, himself, never seriously sought any other work than poetry. As Betty Miller in her biography rather disapprovingly puts it: 'In his thirty-fourth year – a young man who had "been 'spoiled' in this world" – he was still dependent for every necessity of life upon his father. . . .'[2] After that he was dependent upon Elizabeth's income and a legacy left jointly to him and Elizabeth by John Kenyon in 1856. Only when he was past fifty years old did his poetry sell in sufficient quantity to constitute 'income', and by that time his rather dilettantish son Pen was extravagantly dependent upon him.

'For the great central and solid fact', writes Chesterton with characteristic and engaging exaggeration while discussing Browning's social and family origins, 'is that Browning was a thoroughly typical Englishman of the middle class'. The father held a steady and respectable job, the income from which supported a modest but comfortable home in a quiet suburb. The wider family – the Silverthornes, the Masons, the aunts who ran a day-school at Blackheath – were a part of the growing and ever more influential middle class. Mr Browning probably would have been qualified to vote after the Reform of 1832; Browning himself would not have qualified until he took up the lease on a house near Paddington Station in 1862. Browning, his sister and father regularly attended the York Street Congregational Chapel along with the mother, a pious Scotswoman of German descent. Though precociously learned in Latin and Greek, Browning's religious Non-Conformity kept Oxford and Cambridge closed to him. His was the social class that had most at stake in the agitation for repeal of the Test and Corporation Acts; his was the class that read in its newspapers about the Spa Fields riots of 1816 and the 'Peterloo Massacre' of 1819 and heard by word of mouth of riots in London provoked by the Corn Law of 1815. If, by virtue of his religion and class, Browning was shut out from privileges reserved for the higher classes, he was also insulated from the widespread miseries of the lower classes. Charles Dickens was born the same year as Browning and into a lower-middle-class family. But when Dickens's father fell down the social scale into a debtors' prison, Dickens learned from immediate experience things that Browning, at best, could only have heard or read about: the brutality and injustice of the prison system; the disorder, squalor, and disease of the city streets; the spirit-killing drudgery of child-labour in a factory. And Dickens learned those things in London, which according to one historian of the city, 'to a great extent escaped both the torrent of pauperization which deluged the greater part of agricultural England, and the catastrophic fall in wages which occurred in many places' during the years following Wellington's victory at Waterloo.[3] Where there was employment – in the mines, factories and mills – the conditions of work were often cruel and inhuman. Mr Kitson Clark in his *The Making of Victorian England* frequently emphasizes the violence and brutality of both city and country life during the years of Browning's childhood and youth: man-traps to catch poachers, bears and badgers baited for entertainment, the public hangings at Tyburn, where the condemned person might be guilty of anything from petty theft to parricide or any other of 220 offences for which the law prescribed the death penalty. Had Browning gone 'farther afield' (in a wider sense than Maisie Ward intends) he would have found more than 'woods and country lanes'.

Browning's family violates in many ways our notion of the typical nineteenth-century bourgeois family. There were, for example, only two children, Browning and his sister Sarianna. The family was not a unit organized under stern male discipline designed to protect and extend the family's prosperity and social standing, as bourgeois families in the pages of Balzac, Dickens and Trollope often seem to be. Mr Browning's salary and responsibilities at the bank apparently did not increase much during his forty-year tenure, but there is no recorded anxiety about this failure to advance; nor did there seem to be any anxiety about Sarianna's failure to marry. Although both Browning and his sister could, in old age, display a vulgar pride in Robert's connection with fashionable families, the goddess of 'getting-on' was not worshipped in their parents' home. Child discipline was apparently maintained by indulgence and persuasion, as when his mother counselled Browning against the habit of calling grown-ups 'fools'. Childish whims that would have brought a birch-rod into the hands of the stereotypical Victorian parent – refusal to take medicine until his mother had caught him a toad, appearing before guests naked with a devil's tail attached to his backside, his decision at age fourteen to be henceforth an atheist and vegetarian – provoked no severe discipline or parental anger that we know of. It was a cousin who gave to Browning as a boy the works of Shelley; and it was his own pious mother who gave volumes of Keats and Shelley containing ('almost certainly', says Maisie Ward) Shelley's *Queen Mab* which incited the youthful atheism and vegetarianism. Hints of unease within the family over Browning's diffidence at settling into a profession are fully explored by Betty Miller in her biography. Still, first an aunt and then the father met publication costs for Browning's numerous volumes between 1833 and 1850.

Most of Browning's education took place in this informal and tolerant home atmosphere. Although he attended both a day-school and a boarding-school for short periods, it was probably his father who taught him most of his Latin and Greek. A succession of tutors, riding the suburban circuit around London, taught him French, Italian, and music. Many children of Browning's generation must have found the process of learning an oppressive and fearful experience of rote memorization under the stern and sometimes sadistic discipline of either a schoolmaster or a tutor in the home. Robert Owen's experiments at New Lanark were truly revolutionary when he took care that the 'children were trained and educated without punishment or any fear of it, and were while in school by far the happiest human beings I have known. . . .' The delight and wonder in learning which Keats records in *On First Looking into Chapman's Homer* must have been an unusual experience for a schoolboy in the early nineteenth century. Keats, the son of a London hostler, never learned Greek and had to rely upon translations for the ancient myths which he so richly explored in his poetry. John Stuart Mill, six years Browning's senior, learned Greek at an early age under his father's rigorous utilitarian methodology, a system of education to which Mill himself would attribute his severe emotional crisis as a young man. Browning was more fortunate than either. In a poem written when he was an old man, Browning recalls his initiation into Homer's *Iliad*:

My father was a scholar and knew Greek.
When I was five years old, I asked him once
'What do you read about?'
                                    'The siege of Troy.'
'What is a siege and what is Troy?'
                                    Whereat
He piled up chair and tables for a town,
Set me a-top for Priam, called our cat
– Helen, enticed away from home (he said)
By wicked Paris, who couched somewhere close
Under the footstool, being cowardly,
But whom – since she was worth the pains, poor puss–
Towzer and Tray, – our dogs, the Atreidai, – sought
By taking Troy to get possession of
– Always when great Achilles ceased to sulk,
(My pony in the stable) – forth would prance
And put to flight Hector – our page-boy's self.
This taught me who was who and what was what:
So far I rightly understood the case
At five years old: a huge delight it proved
And still proves – thanks to that instructor sage
My Father, who knew better than turn straight
Learning's full flare on weak-eyed ignorance,
Or, worse yet, leave weak eyes to grow sandblind,
Content with darkness and vacuity.

The poem is not a nostalgic reminiscence of childhood, but an argument for education as a form of play adjusted to the age of the child. Later, his father discovered him playing at the siege of Troy and introduced him to Pope's translation of Homer, then to the Greek itself. As a man Browning could enter, with unabated enthusiasm, into a study of Wolf's *Prolegomena to Homer* (1795), one of the seminal books of the century for the new study of historical and religious texts. The love of learning was to remain with Browning throughout his life, and in 1871 he could describe translating Euripides's *Alcestis* as 'the most delightful of May-month amusements'. The sheer exuberance with which he pours learning into his work is a marked feature of his poetry and was to be the source of much of the obscurity the growing Victorian reading public complained of when they came upon that poetry. 'He had no reason', Chesterton suggests, 'to suppose that everyone did not join in so admirable a game.'

Prudish censorship of what a child might read was not a part of Mr Browning's method. Thomas Bowdler's expurgated *Family Shakespeare*, which offered texts 'unmixed with anything that could raise a blush on the cheek of modesty', was published in ten volumes when Browning was five years old, and became a feature of many middle-class libraries. It is doubtful that it was among the thousands of books in Mr Browning's library. Writing in 1834, Charlotte Brontë recommends to a young friend a list of poets:

> Now don't be startled at the names of Shakespeare and Byron. Both these were great men, and their works are like themselves. You will know how to choose the good, and to avoid the evil; the finest passages are always the purest, the bad are invariably revolting; you will never wish to read them over twice. Omit the comedies of Shakespeare and 'Don Juan', perhaps the 'Cain', of Byron, though the latter is a magnificent poem.

Browning was reading Byron when he was twelve and was probably reading Shakespeare in some eighteenth-century edition before that. The opening lines of his first published poem, the one an aunt paid for, are anything but prudish:

> Pauline, mine own, bend o'er me – thy soft breast
> Shall pant to mine – bend o'er me – thy sweet eyes,
> And loosened hair and breathing lips, and arms
> Drawing me to thee. . . .

By twentieth-century standards Browning's poetry may seem 'pure' enough, but his contemporaries sometimes found him to be the champion of illicit sexual fulfilment. And after 'obscurity', Browning's major faults were found to be 'coarseness' and 'vulgarity'. Gerard Manley Hopkins declined to finish *The Ring and the Book* because he had heard that 'further on it was coarser'. When, in a late poem Browning threatens to have his chamber-pot emptied over the heads of his critics, he betrays an affinity to the rough and ready literary world of Pope and Fielding. Scholars have frequently traced Browning's penchant for the ugly, the deformed and the grotesque, back to his father's library.

There, too, he could find the love poems of John Donne and set some of them to music. Books from that library form the basis for his intellectual autobiography *Parleyings with Certain People of Importance in Their Day* (1887). Many were eighteenth-century books: Bernard de Mandeville's anatomy of private vices, *The Fable of the Bees* (1714); the Marquis de Lassay's *Memoirs* (1756); the *Diary* (1784) of George Bubb Doddington, acquaintance of the infamous Lord Rochester and patron to Fielding; the 1778 English version of Gerard de Lairesse's *The Art of Painting*, with its chapter on 'Things Deformed and Broken', which he read with greater delight as a child than any other book. He must also have enjoyed his father's copy of Samuel Johnson's *Dictionary*, a book which Thackeray's budding Regency courtesan Becky indignantly throws from a coach as a gesture of her independence from the boredom and drudgery of her education.

Browning's religious education, under the direction of his mother, was narrower and more sombre than the literary studies he enjoyed under his father. Its main feature was weekly attendance at the York Street Chapel to listen to sermons and sermon-length prayers. G. M. Young's general portrait of the power of the Victorian pulpit would hold true for the Dissenter community in the two decades before Victoria came to the throne:[4]

> A young man brought up in a careful home might have heard, whether delivered or read aloud, a thousand sermons; an active clergyman was a social asset to a rising neighbourhood, his popularity a source of spiritual danger to himself. The form of preachers was canvassed like the form of public entertainers, and the circulation of some Victorian sermons is a thing to fill a modern writer with despair. If we consider the effect, beginning in childhood, of all the preachers on all the congregations, of men loud or unctuous, authoritative or persuasive, speaking out of a body of acknowledged truth to the respectful audience below them, we can see why the homiletic cadence, more briefly Cant, is so persistent in Victorian oratory and literature.

In his poetry Browning would transcend in a most revolutionary way the values of his culture[5] and would challenge the existence of the 'body of acknowledged truth' the preachers spoke out of. Still, the 'homiletic cadence' could come into his poems, and a younger man like Thomas Hardy could ask with a certain exasperation: 'How could smug Christian optimism worthy of a dissenting grocer find a place

inside a man who was so vast a seer and feeler when on neutral ground?'
One answer might lie in those thousand or more sermons he had heard
as a child and young man. Hearing was not necessarily listening. One
preacher at the York Street Chapel, according to an experiment by
some of Browning's young friends, could be heard clearly at a distance
of several hundred yards; at the same time, the young Browning
could be reprimanded from the pulpit in the small room because he
was not listening. He listened well enough to reproduce such services
in humorous detail in *Christmas-Eve* (1850). There was the preacher's
mode of drawing his 'provings and parallels' from the Bible

> As he poured his doctrine forth, full measure,
>> To meet his audience's avidity.
> You needed not the wit of the Sibyl
>> To guess the cause of it all, in a twinkling:
>> No sooner our friend had got an inkling
> Of treasure hid in the Holy Bible . . .
> Than he handled it so, in fine irreverence,
>> As to hug the book of books to pieces:
> And, a patchwork of chapters and texts in severance,
>> Not improved by the private dog's-ears and creases,
> Having clothed his own soul with, he'd fain see equipt yours, –
> So tossed you again your Holy Scriptures.

The congregation of this imaginary chapel is a bit less genteel, perhaps,
than the one Browning observed as a boy, but the types are convincing.
Among them an

> . . . old fat woman purred with pleasure,
>> And thumb round thumb went twirling faster,
> While she, to his periods keeping measure,
>> Maternally devoured the pastor.

In the prayers or announcements from the pulpit the congregation
would hear of things of more than mere doctrinal interest to the
Dissenter community: pleas for God's help and middle-class money to
support the anti-slavery movement, the British and Foreign School
Society, the British and Foreign Bible Society; perhaps announcements
of meetings called to urge repeal of the Test and Corporation Acts or
to discuss the possible emancipation of Roman Catholics in Britain.
Browning's life-long distrust of the Catholic Church began in this
chapel atmosphere; so, too, did his immense Biblical knowledge and

the skill in religious controversy with which he would challenge the threatening scientific scepticism of the Higher Critics of the Bible in many of his best poems.

Religious doubt afflicted many of Browning's generation. The great pendulum swings between faith and doubt, between hope and despair, which mark Tennyson's *In Memoriam*, had been known personally by thousands of the readers who bought and praised that poem in 1850. In *Sartor Resartus* (1833–4) Thomas Carlyle would record the guilt, anxiety, despair and need for a new authority attendant upon the rejection of traditional Christianity. Much of Matthew Arnold's best poetry would be written in a tone of elegiac regret at the irretrievable loss of personal and cultural wholeness which traditional belief had made possible. The less great also suffered. In 1827 Sarah Flowers, a talented young woman of Dissenter stock, wrote to the Reverend W. J. Fox:

> My mind has been wandering a long time, and now it seems to have lost sight of that only invulnerable hold against the assaults of this warring world, a firm belief in the genuineness of the Scriptures. . . . The cloud came over me gradually, and I did not discover the darkness in which my soul was shrouded until, in seeking to give light to others, my own gloomy state became too settled to admit of doubt. It was in answering Robert Browning that my mind refused to bring forward argument, turned recreant and sided with the enemy.

Browning was then fifteen years old. His sceptical questioning came from a tradition peopled by Hume and Voltaire, Thomas Paine, William Godwin and, most importantly, Shelley, whom the young Browning had recently been reading. Shelley's youthful *Queen Mab* was by itself a sufficient catalogue of arguments for atheism and against the spiritual, political and social oppression of traditional and institutional Christianity. Browning would build his first important poem, *Pauline*, around the spiritual turmoil caused by the rejection of the religion of the chapel. The poem ends with an assertion that the poet has recovered from the crisis and once again believes 'in God and truth/ And love'. Miss Flowers, too, recovered to write the popular hymn 'Nearer My God to Thee'.

The crisis recorded in *Pauline* was not only religious and it was not only Browning's: it is representative of the confused questioning of values known to many young talented men who grew up after 1815.

They came to awareness during the Restoration when the revolutionary vision of social renewal and scope for individual heroic action lay in the immediate past. The young poet of *Pauline* could early share that dream and

> . . . was vowed to liberty,
> Men were to be as gods and earth as heaven,
> And I – ah, what a life was mine to prove!

In those lines Browning is already ironically mocking a dream which could not be sustained; and with its loss came a deeper confusion of values:

> First went my hopes of perfecting mankind,
> Next faith in them, and in freedom's self
> And virtue's self, and then my own motives, ends
> And aims and loves, and human love went last.

By the time a man born in 1812 was twenty years old, *revolution* had acquired the adjectives *industrial* and *bourgeois*. 'What was a gifted young man to do after Napoleon?' asks George Steiner in his recent *In Bluebeard's Castle*:[6]

> How could organisms bred from the electric air of revolution and imperial epic breathe under the leaden sky of middle-class rule? How was it possible for a young man to hear his father's tales of the Terror and of Austerlitz and to amble down the gas-lit boulevard to the counting house? The past drove rat's teeth into the gray mass of the present; it exasperated, it sowed wild dreams.

Browning's most ambitious poems of the 1830s were *Paracelsus* and *Sordello*. Both were explorations of the wild dreams and aspirations of exceptional, superior men; both were studies in exasperation.

2

The Eighteen-Thirties

Pauline Paracelsus Sordello

Nay, if we look well to it, what is all Derangement, and necessity
of great Change, in itself such an evil, but the product simply of
increased resources which the *old methods* can no longer administer;
of new wealth which the old coffers will no longer contain? What
is it, for example, that in our day bursts asunder the bonds of
ancient Political Systems, and perplexes all Europe with the fear
of Change, but even this: the increase of social resources, which
the old social methods will no longer sufficiently administer? The
new omnipotence of the Steam-engine is hewing asunder quite
other mountains than the physical. Have not our economical
distresses, those barnyard Conflagrations themselves, the
frightfulest madness of our mad epoch, their rise also in what is a
real increase: increase of Men; of human Force. . . .

Thomas Carlyle, 1831

In 1832, while the English nation was busy reforming its Parliament
and while the French *bourgeoisie* were further enriching themselves
under Louis-Philippe, Robert Browning was twenty and writing
Pauline. Browning and the *bourgeoisie* came of age in the same decade;
and, for the arts as well as for the economic and social institutions, the
'*old methods*' were to prove inadequate to contain the '*increased resources*'. For Browning the decade was to be one of experimentation
with older literary forms: the confessional *Pauline* (1833); the poetic
drama, *Paracelsus* (1835); *Strafford* (1837), 'An Historical Tragedy';
Sordello (1840), essentially an historical romance contorted into a new
and baffling form. All of these were extensive and ambitious works;
not one of them, however, was a successful vehicle for the particular
wealth Browning had to offer poetry. Nor were they the kind of
literary form which the age seemed to demand. Two smaller, but

more successful and promising experiments, *Johannes Agricola in Meditation* and *Porphyria's Lover* (1836) went unnoticed by the public while the poet himself ignored their form for nearly a decade. By 1840 Browning had published nearly 14,000 lines; and he won a reputation with *Paracelsus*, and he then lost it with 'the inscrutable *Sordello*'.

The 1830s was the most barren decade for English poetry in the nineteenth century. Great numbers of books of poetry were, of course, published; but so few poems have proved to have any lasting value that contemporary reviewers might well be forgiven for echoing so often Thomas Peacock's argument of 1820 that great poetry cannot be produced in an 'Age of Iron'. Shelley had passionately defended the role of the poet against Peacock; but among the ascending middle class, utilitarian values were pervasive, and that arch-utilitarian Jeremy Bentham had classed poetry among such other 'amusements' as ornamental gardening and push-pin. 'The day is past, we fear,' said one of the few reviewers of Browning's *Pauline*, 'for either fee or fame in the service of the muse.' Only the two collections of Tennyson's early poetry, *Poems, Chiefly Lyrical* (1830) and *Poems* (1832), and Browning's experiments command any general interest today, and those largely because Tennyson and Browning would go on to write better poetry. Dramatic literature was, if anything, more impoverished than poetry; the novel was more robust, but among its lasting successes one could number only the early works of Dickens, *Pickwick Papers*, *Oliver Twist* and *Nicholas Nickleby*, all published in the second half of the decade.

The poverty of mature literary achievement in England in the 1830s may have been the result of one of those mysterious troughs of history in which the arts as well as other cultural forms find themselves from time to time. A poem by Wordsworth published in 1835 suggests one reason for the scarcity of literary talent. In *Extempore Effusion upon the Death of James Hogg*, Wordsworth laments not only the death of Hogg but also of Scott, Coleridge, Lamb, Crabbe, and Mrs Felicia Hemans, authoress of *The Landing of the Pilgrim Fathers*. Had Wordsworth been willing to extend his poem and his sympathies, he might have added the names of Keats, Shelley, Byron and Blake. The years 1832–6 recorded the deaths of Bentham, Wilberforce, Malthus, Cobbett, James Mill, and Godwin. The dying-off of a race of giants may go a long way towards explaining the apparent vacuum of talent of the 1830s. A more inexplicable but no less important force on literature during the decade is suggested with startling brevity and clarity in one stanza of Wordsworth's poem:

> Our haughty life is crowned with darkness,
> Like London with its own black wreath,
> On which with thee, O Crabbe! forth-looking,
> I gazed from Hampstead's breezy heath.

Wordsworth, who had celebrated the union of the natural universe with the mind of man, and Crabbe, a relatively realistic poet of rural and village life, are standing in what is essentially a part of suburban London. The smoke hanging above the city becomes a fit symbol, a funeral wreath, for the passing of the older generation of English writers. Industrialization and urbanization were concurrent and synonymous; and it was in the cities that the 'increase of men; of Human Force' in technology, politics and science would be most apparent. Out of the city experience much of the new literature would come. 'Motions and Means, on land and sea', Wordsworth wrote in another poem of 1835, *Steamboats, Viaducts, and Railways*, were 'at war/With old poetic feeling'.

Eighteen-thirty saw the publication of Tennyson's *Poems, Chiefly Lyrical*, but also it saw the opening of the Liverpool–Manchester Railway when Robert Stephenson's *Rocket* attained a speed of thirty-six miles per hour taking the reforming MP Huskisson, whom it had run over, to the hospital. *The Rocket* took human beings faster than they had ever travelled; Tennyson would soon be a passenger. Also that year Charles Lyell began to publish his *Principles of Geology*, in time for Darwin to take along on his voyage with *The Beagle*. When, in 1833, Browning's first poem *Pauline* was published, the first reformed British Parliament was sitting, slavery was abolished in the British colonies, and the first of the Factory Acts limited the labour of children to twelve hours per day. In 1835, while English readers could follow the aspirations of Browning's proto-scientist Paracelsus or the nostalgic rambles of Dickens's Pickwickians, the Place de la Concorde received its first covering of asphalt. Only three years separate Browning's choice of Paracelsus, the 'father of pharmacology', as a hero, from the cholera epidemic of 1830 against which civil authorities in Britain could do little more than declare days of prayer, while Russian troops shot anyone leaving infected villages and the entire Austrian border was sealed by troops against the 'invader'. Browning's Sordello finally allies himself with the cause of the suffering masses. His story was written and re-written during seven years of a decade that began with the Bristol riots and continued with the agricultural unrest which Carlyle labelled 'barnyard Conflagrations . . . the frightfulest madness of our mad epoch'. The decade ended with the Chartist agitation and a riot which left more destruction in Birmingham, thought the Duke of Wellington, than in any sacked city he had seen during the Napoleonic Wars.

France changed monarchs in 1830, as did Britain. The death of George IV and the accession of William IV was hardly an important political event for the British, who had been in the process of troubled but certain evolutionary reform during the 1820s. In France the change was more revolutionary. Louis-Philippe's assumption of power in July returned the republican tricolour to the Hotel de Ville and ended the reactionary and repressive Bourbon regime, epitomized by Charles X. The French had a Citizen-King and a constitution; although fewer Frenchmen were now enfranchised than were Englishmen under their unreformed parliament, power had clearly passed to the bourgeoisie. French industrialization and the building of railroads lagged behind the British; but trade and particularly finance prospered while the bourgeoisie began to stamp their values on French life. It was not really Louis-Philippe who ruled, Balzac assured his readers; it was 'the holy, venerable, solid, amiable, gracious, beautiful, noble, young, all-powerful five-franc piece'. Here adjectives previously belonging to the heroes of romantic fiction are deeded over to money. Delacroix's *Liberty Guiding the People*, purchased by Louis-Philippe, celebrates that year's revolution. Liberty herself strikes the eye as an allegorical embodiment of ideals of the Revolution of 1789; but the man on her right, with his drab suit and cylindrical hat, is a man of the hour. In contrast to the poverty of recognized artistic accomplishment in England, France was particularly rich. Berlioz finished his *Symphonie Fantastique*, and Hugo's *Hernani* had its tempestuous first performance. Also in that *annus mirabilis* 1830, Balzac began his *Scènes de la vie privée* with the publication of *Gobseck*, while Stendhal's *Le Rouge et le Noir* began to appear in serial form. Each of these novels represents a successful adaptation of a literary form to new cultural realities. The realistic novel, as perfected by Balzac and Stendhal during the 1830s and 1840s, was to prove the most expressive literary form for the new modes of industrial, commercial, urban life enjoyed by the middle classes and endured by lower classes. In *Gobseck*, as in many other novels during the decade, Balzac creates a convincing illusion as well as a critique of bourgeois society by amassing prosaic details and by describing the intricacy of mundane financial and legal transactions. Stendhal, with his interest in analysis of motive and action and in ironic criticism gives us a classic statement of nineteenth-century youthful ambition in *Le Rouge et le Noir* and cynically reveals many contemporary illusions in *La Chartreuse de Parme* (1836).

Balzac and Stendhal were the master literary artists during the decade that the young Browning was learning his trade. By the end of the 1830s, at the latest, Browning would follow the serial publication of Balzac's fiction in *La Siècle*, 'from Paris two days old'. Balzac was to remain a great favourite of Browning, and the poet's more mature work was to have many similarities to that novelist's art. By the mid-1840s, he found in Elizabeth Barrett a fellow enthusiast for French fiction. 'I entirely agree with you', he wrote to Elizabeth, 'in your estimate of the comparative value of French and English Romance-writers. I bade the completest adieu to the latter on my first introduction to Balzac'. During the early days of the courtship Elizabeth had found *Le Rouge et le Noir* 'so dark and deep . . . very powerful and full of deep significance' that Stendhal's masterwork had ridden her 'like an incubus for several days'. In his mature work Browning seems closer in spirit to Stendhal than he does to, say, the earlier generation of English romantic writers or to his contemporary Tennyson. They share a fondness for irony, for representations of complex psychological states, and for the motivation of action rather than of action itself. Both were for long periods of their lives serious resident students of Italian culture. Each developed a wide knowledge and appreciation of Italian painting, sculpture, and music; each delighted in the colourful life of the Italian towns and countryside; each spent many hours rummaging through old books and manuscripts in Italian libraries in their enthusiasm for renaissance history and in search of documentary material to be used in their realistic art. And both were to see their public reputations at home retarded, in part, by their long sojourns in Italy.

The public acceptance of Browning's poetry is often pictured as unjustly slow. It is true that he was over fifty years old when, in the 1860s, he would receive recognition commensurate to his mature achievement. He would, however, have had little reason to complain of his progress towards public fame in the earliest years of his career. When he published *Pauline*, anonymously and at the expense of his aunt in the spring of 1833, Browning's circle of acquaintance was limited largely to his own family and to a few other middle-class, dissenting London families. Within scarcely three years he would be at the home of one of the age's leading playwrights, Sergeant Talfourd, where he would sit down at table with Landor, Wordsworth, the novelist Miss Mitford, and the busy young reviewer and essayist John Forster; after dinner, Macready, the leading actor and theatre manager of the day, would ask him to write him a play. By the following spring *Strafford* opened at Covent Garden, Macready in the title role. There were only five performances, but *Strafford* received extensive, serious and generally favourable notice in the Press. By that year, 1837, Robert Browning was twenty-five and something of a literary personality in London. Literary intelligence, in the form of the reviewer for *The Athenaeum*, was concerned lest another had anticipated the subject of the long poem on Sordello upon which Browning was known to be working. He would attend plays with the water-colourist and illustrator George Cattermole and the Christmas Pantomime with the already famous Charles Dickens.

Much of Browning's outward, social life at this period partakes of that phenomenon of the 1830s which Carlyle called the 'dandiacal'. His literary life was centred on the theatre, he attended dinners and balls, sometimes arriving back in suburban Camberwell at dawn. He rode, fenced, played the piano, spoke French and Italian. He was 'slim and dark and very handsome', recalled Mrs Bridell-Fox, 'and – may I hint it – just a trifle of a dandy, addicted to lemon-coloured kid-gloves and such things: quite "the glass of fashion and the mould of form".' Baudelaire would claim that the 'dandy appears in transitional epochs, when democracy is not yet all-powerful and aristocracy is only partially tottering and debased'. Perhaps Browning's careful attention to fashion and gentlemanly pursuits reflects his acquaintance with Chevalier George de Benkhausen, the Russian consul with whom he visited St Petersburg in 1834, or with the French royalist Comte Amédée de Ripert-Monclar, to whom he dedicated *Paracelsus* in 1835. These connections were formed while Browning was considering a future vocation, and a career in the foreign service seemed preferable to the law or a clerkship in the Bank of England. At a time when 'the old ideal of Manhood has grown obsolete, and the new is still invisible to us', Carlyle said sarcastically, young men of genius were turning to 'Werterism, Byronism, even Brummelism'. Had those been the only social roles open, Browning might well have chosen the latter.

At the same time, Browning was, by his own admission and by the observation of others, 'full of ambition, eager for success, eager for fame'. Years later, Browning would explain to Forster that his first published poem, *Pauline*, had its inception in a 'foolish plan' to give an unsuspecting public a series of literary works in each of which the author was to assume a different character: 'meanwhile the world was never to guess that "Brown, Smith, Jones & Robinson" (as the spelling books have it) the respective authors of this poem, the other novel, such an opera, such a speech, etc., etc., were no other than one and the same individual'. 'The present abortion', as Browning described *Pauline*, did little to arouse in the public any curiosity as to the identity of the anonymous author. Browning himself did not publicly acknowledge authorship for another thirty-five years, although by then he was generally known to be the author. By 1847, his close friends Joseph Arnould and Alfred Domett knew, and the same year Dante Gabriel Rossetti suspected it and transcribed the poem from the British Museum copy. When it was published in the spring of 1833, one reviewer thought it was surely written by a Whig minister, citing its 'folly, incoherence, and reckless assertion' as evidence. Others found it 'not a little unintelligible' and 'a piece of pure bewilderment'. Although such public reception undoubtedly hurt Browning, he was probably more discouraged and embarrassed by the penetrating criticism made by John Stuart Mill in notes towards a review which was never published but which Browning soon read.

Mill's commentary remains a most useful introduction to *Pauline*: 'With considerable poetic powers, the writer seems to me possessed with a more intense and morbid self-consciousness than I ever knew in any sane human being.' *Pauline* is a poem about the sins of religious doubt. It describes the growth and ramifications of such doubt; it ends by an announcement to Shelley that a victory has been won over the forces of spiritual despair:

> Sun-treader, I believe in God and truth
> And love; and as one just escaped from death
> Would bind himself in bands of friends to feel
> He lives indeed, so, I would lean on thee!

The history of the young poet's doubt, as Mill noted, is more moving and convincing than the assertion to spiritual health and reaffirmation. Still, throughout the poem, the unreality of Pauline (to whom the poet is supposedly speaking), the stridency of tone, and the self-consciousness, force one to partially agree with G. K. Chesterton that the writer is taking too seriously doubts and sins common to adolescence. Even those interested enough in the poem to translate the Latin quotation from Agrippa prefixed to it will not be convinced that 'the gate of hell is in this book'. A reader will more willingly assent to Agrippa's concluding plea: 'forgive my youth; I wrote this work when I was less than a youth'. We remain interested in *Pauline* because it was Robert Browning's first serious experiment in poetry. He had thought to write a novel, an opera, 'a speech, etc., etc.', but *Pauline* was the 'work of the Poet of the batch, who would have been more legitimately *myself* than most of the others. . . .' Browning's first literary expression was not only in the form of poetry, but of a particular kind of poetry: he writes in the mode of the personal lyric, in which he takes his own doubts, sins, aspirations, and hopes as his subject. It may not be 'thoroughly autobiographical', as one fine Browning scholar asserts,[1] but this first poem is in marked contrast to his later poetry which he described as 'dramatic in principle, and so many utterances of so many imaginary persons, not mine'.

The lyrical, confessional form of *Pauline* looks back to the dominant mode of the romantic poets rather than forward to Browning's mid-Victorian achievement. One of the great triumphs of romantic poetry had been the articulation of the private vision, the personal experience, the interior life of the mind and emotions. Coleridge's *Frost at Midnight* and *Dejection*, Byron's *Childe Harold*, the lyrics of Shelley and the odes of Keats express personal and often subjective experiences rather than mirror the objective world common to most men. Wordsworth, writing about *The Prelude*, knew that his poem was 'a thing unprecedented in literary history that a man should talk so much about himself'. The introspection and consciousness of one's self which had so enriched English poetry during the first quarter of the nineteenth century was, by the early 1830s, beginning to be thought of as a debilitating disease. It is not surprising that Mill emphasized the 'morbid self-consciousness' of *Pauline*: already in his essay *The Spirit of the Age* (1831) he had noted that excessive introspection was an unhealthy part of the intellectual and emotional climate of England. In the same year, Carlyle diagnosed self-consciousness as the major sickness afflicting not only young men of genius – the Byrons, the Shelleys, the Schlegels, the Hazlitts – but also all social institutions: 'Thus does Literature also, like a sick thing, superabundantly "listen to itself".' The young Tennyson was warned against confessional poetry by his friend Richard Trench:

> After one or two revolutions in thought and opinion, all our
> boasted poetry, all or nearly all, of Keats and Shelley and
> Wordsworth and Byron, will become unintelligible. When
> except in our times, did men seek to build up their poetry on
> their own individual experiences instead of some objective
> foundations common to all men?

Nevertheless the young Browning took as his model the subjective
poetry of the dead Shelley.

Browning affixed to *Pauline* a subtitle: *A Fragment of a Confession*. The
phrase is a precise description of the poem's form as well as an anticipation of reaction of many readers who have found the poet's closing
assertion that he has regained his faith less convincing than his re-
counting of the doubts. As Mill put it: 'the psychological history of
himself is powerful and truthful – *truth-like* certainly, all but the last
stage'. The poem ends, one might say, rather than concludes. It may be
the fate of all autobiographical literature to be fragmentary: accounts
of an author's life come to an end while he moves towards further
experience. English romantic poetry is particularly rich in poetic
fragments. *The Prelude* traced the growth of Wordsworth's mind up to
his thirty-fifth year; it was to remain unpublished in his lifetime while
Wordsworth continued to think of it as a 'preparatory poem' to a more
objective but unfinished philosophical poem. Keats's two ambitious
attempts to write a poem about Apollo succeeding Hyperion both
break off when the problems of Keats and his young hero begin to
merge. Coleridge was interrupted by the Man from Porlock while he
transcribed his opium dream, so *Kubla Khan* too gets the subtitle, 'A
Fragment'. The deaths of Byron and Shelley brought an end to *Don
Juan* and *The Triumph of Life*. But Byron knew that his ironic commentary on the follies of mankind could well be endless, and he spoke of
writing fifty cantos, though the poem breaks off in the sixteenth canto.
Shelley's poem stops, much as do Keats's Hyperion poems, just as the
poet is about to receive an answer to his question, 'what is life?'
Browning began the final and least successful section of his poem with
a similar question:

> O God, where do they tend – these struggling aims?
> What would I have? What is this 'sleep' which seems
> To bound all? can there be a 'waking' point
> Of Crowning life?

Browning's greatest poems are named after the persons who speak the poems (e.g. Fra Lippo Lippi, Andrea del Sarto, Pompilia), whereas Pauline is the supposed listener. She is the conventional lady to whom the lyric poet addresses his utterance. Her shadowy unreality adds to the 'somewhat mystical' quality of the poem which one reviewer noted. The opening lines begin with a sensuous Keatsian exhortation:

> Pauline, mine own, bend o'er me – thy soft breast
> Shall pant to mine – bend o'er me – thy sweet eyes,
> And loosened hair and breathing lips, and arms
> Drawing me to thee – these build up a screen
> To shut me in with thee. . . .

But, despite this promising opening, Pauline remains a distant, unsubstantial figure not unlike that remote, exotic, 'romantic' landscape to which the poet later invites her:

> Night, and one single ridge of narrow path
> Between the sullen river and the woods
> Waving and muttering, for the moonless night
> Has shaped them into images of life,
> Like the uprising of the giant-ghosts. . . .

Here the objects of the natural world are charged with human emotion: trees bend over the water in the same attitude as 'wild men watch a sleeping girl'; the water itself sleeps and dreams. In a bit of gothic grotesquerie, a huge cloud moves through a blue sky 'like a dead whale that white birds pick. . . .'

The landscape has become an emblem for the poet's own interior life, his emotions, feelings, and thoughts. In the poem, Pauline as a listener becomes an excuse for the poet to talk with himself about 'the dim orb of self'. In particular he wants to 'tell the past', the history of his religious doubt which he now calls 'a sad sick dream'. Like Wordsworth in *Tintern Abbey*, Browning hopes to trace the 'elements' in his experience which have brought him to his present state of consciousness, though he will not provide the Wordsworthian emphasis upon infancy:

> I strip my mind bare, whose first elements
> I shall unveil – not as they struggled forth
> In infancy, nor as they now exist,
> When I am grown above them and can rule –

> But in that middle stage when they were full
> Yet ere I had disposed them to my will;
> And then I shall show how these elements
> Produced my present state, and what it is.

He describes his early awareness of the presence of God even though he would later doubt His existence. 'A need, a trust, a yearning after God' had been constant. He gives an account of his delight in the 'wisest ancient books', then hints at deeds which spotted him with 'cunning, envy, falsehood'. He moves on to his early attempts at verse and his dedication to human liberty by which 'men were to be as gods and earth as heaven'. But his dreams were but delusions. At the end of this collapse of moral values, the poet thinks of his soul as a temple where

> . . . incense rolls
> Around the altar, only God is gone
> And some dark spirit sitteth in his seat.

The dark spirit is eventually exorcized by the renewal of human love for Pauline and the recognition that his 'hunger' for God is evidence of God's existence.

Pauline is a romantic poem, but it also betrays elements that we have come to think of as Victorian. One such element is the terribly earnest anxiety that the poet feels when he begins to doubt traditional Christianity. Biographers of Browning often find in the poem a remorse for the poet's having betrayed his mother's rather narrow Protestantism. Read in this way, *Pauline* reveals its kinship with early Tennyson poems like *The Two Voices*, a debate between doubt and faith, or *Supposed Confessions of a Second-Rate Sensitive Mind Not in Unity with Itself*. There Tennyson regrets that he cannot share his mother's simple faith. For many men and women of Tennyson's and Browning's generation, as for the young Frederick Robertson, it was 'an awful hour when this life has lost its meaning and seems shrivelled into a span; when the grave appears to be the end of all, human goodness nothing but a name, and the sky above this universe a dead expanse, black with the void from which God himself has disappeared'. The disappearance of God becomes a major theme in the literature of the nineteenth century.[2] Dostoievski would build his great tragedy in *The Brothers Karamazov* (1880) on the terrifying proposition that when belief in God and immortality is gone, all is permissible.

Browning recovered his faith in God and was to hold on to it, some-times rather boisterously, until the end of his life. At the same time, while writing *Pauline* he was quite aware that he had within himself an almost god-like energy and power. Indeed, he analysed at some length the phenomenon that the vacuum created by the absence of God was filled by 'selfishness'. Mill might accuse him of an 'intense and morbid self-consciousness', but Browning had already come to that know-ledge; and although 'selfishness' might be sinful, the sense of oneself as a distinct creative human being was not. The poet gives with evident pride this description and definition of himself:

I am made up of an intensest life,
Of a most clear idea of consciousness
Of self, distinct from all its qualities,
From all affections, passions, feelings, powers;
And thus far it exists, if tracked, in all:
But linked, in me, to self-supremacy,
Existing as a centre to all things,
Most potent to create and rule and call
Upon all things to minister to it;
And to a principle of restlessness
Which would be all, have, see, know, taste, feel, all –
This is myself. . . .

In *Pauline*, the 'author is in the confessional', noted one reviewer. Browning had published the poem anonymously, but he clearly felt that he made a mistake in revealing too much of himself. His next poem would be about a man possessed of a similar 'principle of rest-lessness' to know all experience. But this man, Paracelsus, would be drawn from the history books not from the intense inner life of Robert Browning.

Paracelsus, the great Renaissance physician, was suggested to Brown-ing as a poetic subject by Comte Amédée de Ripert-Monclar. Brown-ing had begun a close acquaintance with Ripert-Monclar soon after his return from a journey to St Petersburg in the spring of 1834. Browning was thinking about a career in the diplomatic service, and it is probable that the journey to Russia in the entourage of the Russian Consul George de Benkhausen as well as the friendship with the young Bourbon agent Ripert-Monclar were associated with Browning's thoughts about such a career. The young poet did not apparently seek a position in the foreign service with any great enthusiasm. In a letter

c

written about this time he is relieved that another, not he, has received an appointment to Bagdad, where, even in October, the temperature is '127 Fahrenheit in the shade'. Ripert-Monclar also had some association, as did Browning's uncles Reuben and William, with Rothschilds' bank in Paris, but Browning seems never to have seriously considered following his uncles and his father into banking. Instead, he wrote the poem which Ripert-Monclar suggested, and poetry became his only profession. He would not make a living from poetry for another thirty years, but *Paracelsus* gave him a position among the most promising poets of the day. John Forster wrote: 'we may safely predict for him a brilliant career, if he continues true to the present promise of his genius.' Walter Savage Landor then replied to Forster: 'When you told us that the author of Paracelsus would be a great poet, you came rather too late in the exercise of prophecy – he was one already, and will be among the greatest.' A few months later, in another essay, Forster announced: 'Without the slightest hesitation we name Mr. Robert Browning at once with Shelley, Coleridge, Wordsworth. He has entitled himself to a place among the acknowledged poets of the age.'

Paracelsus, who took that name to indicate his equality with the great physician Celsus, was not an altogether appropriate figure to embody many of the romantic themes that Browning had expressed in *Pauline*. In an extended note which he appended to his poem, Browning provides an outline of the man's career:

Paracelsus (Philippus Aureolus Theophrastus Bombastus ab Hohenheim) was born in 1493 at Einsiedeln, a little town in the canton of Schwyz, some leagues distant from Zurich . . . he spent part of his youth in pursuing the life common to the travelling *literati* of the age; that is to say, in wandering from country to country, predicting the future by astrology and cheiromancy, evoking apparitions, and practising the different operations of magic and alchemy . . . Paracelsus travelled . . . to be initiated in the mysteries of the oriental adepts, and to observe the secrets of nature and the famous mountain of loadstone . . . at about the age of thirty-three, many astonishing cures which he wrought on eminent personages procured him such celebrity, that he was called in 1526 . . . to fill a chair of physic and surgery at the University of Basle. There Paracelsus began by burning publicly in the amphitheatre the works of Avicenna and Galen, assuring his auditors that the latchets of his shoes were more instructed than those two physicians; that all universities, all writers put together, were less gifted than the hair of his beard and of the crown of his head.

In his knowledge of the occult, his miraculous cures, his exotic wanderings, and his gigantic egotism, Paracelsus is a romantic, Faust-like character. Browning was to mould these aspects of the half-historical, half-legendary Paracelsus into his own hero who aspired to know the absolute, who sought TRUTH. The young Browning made little use, however, of the more unsavoury but potentially humorous activities of Philippus Aureolus Theophrastus Bombastus ab Hohenheim, a name in which an older Browning would have delighted:

at Basle it was speedily perceived that the new Professor was no better than an egregious quack. Scarcely a year elapsed before his lectures had fairly driven away an audience incapable of comprehending their emphatic jargon . . . Paracelsus scarcely ever ascended the lecture-desk unless half drunk, and only dictated to his secretaries when in a state of intoxication: if summoned to attend the sick, he rarely proceeded thither without previously drenching himself with wine. He was accustomed to retire to bed without changing his clothes; sometimes he spent the night in pot-houses with peasants, and in the morning he no longer knew what he was about. . . .

Paracelsus was dismissed from his post at Basle and once again took up has wanderings. His death at Salzburg in 1541 provides the setting of the fifth and final section of Browning's poem.

Browning claims in his note that he has taken only 'very trifling' liberties with his subject but they were many. In his later years, in *Fra Lippo Lippi*, in *Andrea del Sarto*, and supremely in *The Ring and the Book*, Browning worked towards a scrupulous fidelity to historical details of the subjects he chose for his poems. The life of Paracelsus, however, was for him a vehicle to explore that desire to know all experience which he had voiced in *Pauline*. In the opening scene the young Paracelsus debates with his friend Festus. Paracelsus is filled with zeal and 'fierce energy' to exercise his godlike potential 'to KNOW' the secrets of the universe, the absolute:

. . . to comprehend the works of God,
And God himself, and all God's intercourse
With the human mind. . . .

Quietly, the young friend Festus expresses his fear that such a high aim, such a dangerous quest may not succeed by means of the mind, of the intellect, alone: he begs Paracelsus not to cut himself off from human love. In the second scene Paracelsus reviews the progress he has made towards Knowledge during the past nine years. He is prematurely aged, 'left with gray hair, faded hands/And a furrowed brow'; and he despairs of fulfilling his youthful aspiration. He meets the poet Aprile, who has sought God only by Love to the exclusion of Knowledge; Paracelsus learns that Aprile also has failed in the quest, and he recognizes himself and Aprile as 'halves of one disserved world'. Aprile dies, but Paracelsus has 'attained' the realization that the paths of Love and of Knowledge are, separately, inadequate. Paracelsus's experience has taught him that pursuit of knowledge leads to despair; Aprile has told him that love of beauty and desire to create beauty lead to selfishness and away from God.

Five years pass, and in the third scene Paracelsus, now a famous professor at Basle, talks once again with Festus. Paracelsus confesses that Aprile had led him to dedicate himself to serve his fellow man; he is now, however, bitterly contemptuous of the stupidity of those he would help with his learning. He acknowledges that the emotions – 'Love, hope, fear, faith' – are an essential mark of one's humanity, perhaps more important than the reason and the intellect. But he has lost those feelings. God has not disappeared from his view, but His ways have become inscrutable. Two years later, Paracelsus, driven from his post in Basle and now in Alsatia, talks again with Festus, revealing his bitterness at the ignorant fools who could not appreciate his learning. In his exile and anger he has determined to snatch at every 'meanest earthliest sensualist delight'; thus, he has transmuted the great 'joy' of which Aprile sang into mere animal enjoyment. He sings a song of sorrowful resignation; and, then, to Festus's plea that he return with him to their childhood home, Paracelsus replies:

No way, no way! it would not turn to good.
A spotless child sleeps on the flowering moss –
'T is well for him; but when a sinful man,
Envying such slumber, may desire to put
His guilt away, shall he return at once
To rest by lying there? Our sires knew well
(Spite of the grave discoveries of their sons)
The fitting course for such: dark cells, dim lamps,

A stone floor one may writhe on like a worm:
No mossy pillow blue with violets!

It is in such a dark cell that the final scene takes place. Paracelsus is
dying, while Festus listens to his delirious review of his life. Distressed
at his failure, he finds some consolation that in death at least he shall be
human. When he regains consciousness, he tries to 'Impart the meagre
knowledge' he has gained. His greatest happiness had come when he
had vowed himself to help other men; he recognizes the limits of man's
knowledge of God, but he envisions man's ultimate perfection. All
lower orders of life tend towards man, he asserts; and in man there is a
'tendency to God'. He dies with a faith not only in God and in man's
future perfection, but also in personal immortality.

Such is the 'story' or 'plot' of *Paracelsus*; but as the synopsis shows,
there are few outward actions to make up the narrative line of the poem.
Each scene is essentially a debate which provokes Paracelsus to express
his thoughts, feelings, and gradual understanding. The hero's aspirations and attainments are cast in an ostensibly dramatic form. The
dramatic poem was a common genre of the period. John Forster
named several, among them Browning's *Paracelsus* and John Taylor's
now forgotten *Philip Van Artevelde: A Dramatic Romance, in Two
Parts*, as 'Evidences for a New Genius for Dramatic Poetry' in an essay
in 1836. 'It is strange,' says the narrator of Dostoievski's *The Devils*,
'but in those days, that is in the thirties, people often wrote that kind of
poetic drama. I am rather at a loss to tell you what it is all about because,
to be frank, I can't make head or tail of it. It is some sort of allegory in
lyrical and dramatic form, recalling the second act of *Faust*.' Given the
character and career of Paracelsus Browning might well have modelled
his dramatic poem upon *Faust*; given the theme of Paracelsus's gradual
realization of the power of Love and the perfection of mankind, he
might have been tempted to imitate Shelley's allegorical 'lyrical
drama', *Prometheus Unbound*; or he might have attempted a stage play
of the kind he wrote the following year in *Strafford* and continued
writing during the late 1830s and early 1840s. Instead, Browning
experimented with dramatic form. In a preface to the poem he describes the experiment:

> it is an attempt, probably more novel than happy, to reverse the
> method usually adopted by writers whose aim it is to set forth any
> phenomena of the mind or the passions, by the operation of
> persons and events; and that, instead of having recourse to an

external machinery of incidents to create and evolve the crisis I
desire to produce, I have ventured to display somewhat minutely
the mood itself in its rise and progress. . . .

Anxious to anticipate and thus allay criticism of this the first poem to
which he had put his name, Browning ends the preface asking the
reader

for his indulgence towards a poem which had not been imagined
six months ago; and that even should he think slightingly of the
present (an experiment I am in no case likely to repeat) he will
not be prejudiced against other productions which may follow in
a more popular, and perhaps less difficult form.

The poem was well received; indeed some reviewers took their cue
from Browning's preface and forgave him certain faults in the construction on the grounds that he was experimenting. Harsher criticism
was embodied in words and phrases that would be used against
Browning for the rest of his life: 'dreamy and obscure', 'an air of
mystical or dreamy vagueness'. His old friend W. J. Fox thought some
passages 'would bear condensation'; Leigh Hunt, an old friend of
Keats, Shelley and Byron, defended 'his long and often somewhat
intricately involved sentences' but not the 'harsh, awkward' diction
and versification. The praise of his new-found friend John Forster must
have pleased Browning most. *Pauline* had been criticized, most
importantly by Mill, as a revelation of the 'morbid self-consciousness'
of Browning himself. In *Paracelsus* he abandoned the confessional mode,
and cast many of the same thoughts and feeling of *Pauline* into dramatic
form. And, by Forster's witness, he had been successful: 'Mr. Browning
has the power of a great dramatic poet; we never think of Mr. Browning while we read his poem; we are not identified with him, but with
the persons into whom he has flung his genius.'

In the terms Forster gives, *Paracelsus* was a personal as well as an
artistic success for Browning. Henceforth his poetry would be 'dramatic in principle'; and, although he would write occasional personal
lyrics, he would continue to insist upon the total separation between
a man's poetry and his inner, personal life. In the 1870s when many
were reading Shakespeare's sonnets as intimate autobiography and
after Dante Gabriel Rossetti had published his personal sonnet sequence
The House of Life, Browning wrote a poem called *House*. He imagines
the public searching through a man's poems as they might gaze into

his house after an earthquake has torn away the outside walls. He
lectures the curious crowd:

> Outside should suffice for evidence:
>   And whoso desires to penetrate
> Deeper, must dive by the spirit-sense –
>   No optics like yours, at any rate.

> 'Hoit-toity! A street to explore,
>   Your house the exception! "With this same key
> Shakespeare unlocked his heart," once more!'
>   Did Shakespeare? If so, the less Shakespeare he.

In the 1870s and 1880s people were often puzzled to discover that
the too ebullient, talkative man whom one often saw at dinner parties
dressed like a banker was Robert Browning, the famous philosophical
and dramatic poet. The keen eyes of Henry James were as puzzled as
the more innocent eyes of visiting American bluestockings. Already in
the 1830s there was apparently a discrepancy between the intense,
somewhat mystical poet and the young, dandified man-about-town.
Biographers of Browning, particularly Mrs Betty Miller, read *Paracelsus* as thinly veiled autobiography; his contemporary Forster, however, praised him for not allowing his own personality to intrude into
the poem. Two small poems that Browning published soon after, in
January of 1836, are still more impersonal, more fully dramatic. The
two poems, *Johannes Agricola in Meditation* and *Porphyria's Lover*, are
objective studies in morbid psychology. In the first, Agricola speaks
out his fanatical certainty that he is among the Elect of God; in the
other, the lover describes in horrifying detail how he came to murder
Porphyria. Here Browning 'has flung his genius' into persons wholly
unlike himself, and has allowed the characters to reveal the intricate
movements of their minds directly to the reader. Browning had
proudly affixed his name to *Paracelsus*; but these two soliloquies, such
promising prototypes of his later monologues, were published in an
obscure magazine and signed only by the initial 'Z'.

Browning was soon exercising his talent for dramatic forms by
writing a stage play. Among the readers who found *Paracelsus* 'of
great merit' was the actor and theatre manager W. C. Macready. The
young poet and the established actor became friends; and, when
Macready jokingly invited Browning to write him a play and thus
save him from emigrating to America, Browning promised to have a

tragedy ready in six months. He chose for his subject Lord Strafford, the general and statesman who had defended Charles I against Parliament and who was executed in 1641. *Strafford: An Historical Tragedy* was completed on time, and after several months of hesitation by Macready it opened at Covent Garden, 1 May 1837. It ran only four nights, but reviewers were generous and saw great promise towards Browning's ability to write plays. The reviews were, of course, sprinkled with words already familiar to criticism of Browning's work: there was much that was 'obscure', 'unintelligible', and 'diffuse'. Others complained of the minutiae of historical detail, of the numerous 'broken sentences', and that Browning had 'rudely discarded the grace of diction'. Few modern readers would be so kind. The dialogue is stilted, Strafford's motivation is vague and his conflict with Pym lacks meaningful tension. Browning himself did not think highly of the play, and he left it out of his collected works in 1849. Students of Browning remain interested in *Strafford* because of its association with Macready and Helen Faucit, who played Lady Carlisle, and because it is Browning's first full-scale attempt to write dramatic, realistic dialogue. One also finds in it a characteristic Browning preference for historical subjects and a fondness for minute historical detail. Further, in a preface Browning reasserts and clarifies the experimental intentions he had announced in the preface to *Paracelsus*. Browning knew early in his career what he was trying to do; in the preface he describes the play as 'one of Action in Character, rather than Character in Action'. The phrase remains the most concise and accurate description of the unique gift Browning gave to poetry in his great dramatic monologues.

'Sordello, in Six Books' was advertised as 'nearly ready' in the printed version of *Strafford* of April 1837, but it would be another three years before that ambitious and ill-fated poem would be given to an expectant but unappreciative and disappointed public. Browning had begun this poem about the thirteenth-century troubadour soon after he had published *Pauline* in 1833. He had laid it aside to write *Paracelsus*, then again to write the play for Macready. Browning scholars have generally assumed that early versions of the poem apparently dealt with Sordello's youth in the small Italian village of Goito, his aspirations towards poetry, his growing love for Palma and his gradual awareness that he should lead a life of action as a warrior. Before Browning could complete his poem in 1837, a Mrs Busk published a six-book poem describing Sordello's feats of love and war. Browning then began to infuse into his story the historical milieu in which

Sordello's life was acted out. The list of books Browning read in preparation is long and the volumes ponderous: after Dante, there was the *Biographie Universelle*, then Cerutti's *De Simboli Trasportati al Morale*, Platina's *Historia Urbis Mantuae*, Muratori's *Rerum Italicarum Scriptores*, Verci's three-volume *Storia degli Ecelini*. These tomes and more, as well as a journey in 1838 to northern Italy, went to build up Browning's knowledge of thirteenth-century Italy and the great struggle between the Guelphs and the Ghibellines. An example of how Browning poured his erudition into his poem while at the same time wryly suggesting that such learning is open to his reader comes in a passage early in the first book:

> Six hundred years ago!
> Such the time's aspect and peculiar woe
> (Yourselves may spell it yet in chronicles,
> Albeit the worm, our busy brother, drills
> His sprawling path through letters anciently
> Made fine and large to suit some abbot's eye)
> When the new Hohenstauffen dropped the mask,
> Flung John of Brienne's favor from his casque,
> Forswore crusading, had no mind to leave
> Saint Peter's proxy leisure to retrieve
> Losses to Otho and to Barbaross,
> Or make the Alps less easy to recross;
> And, thus confirming Pope Honorius's fear,
> Was excommunicate that very year.

Much of Browning's obscurity throughout his career, but supremely in *Sordello*, derives from his assumption that readers may be as intelligent and learned as he himself was. They were not. A notice in a society journal *Belle Assemblée* complained: '*Sordello* is full of hard names, and nonsense.' Less frivolous readers were just as baffled and dismayed by the fragmented narrative, the allusive diction, the unusual often elliptical syntax. The poem opens with this line: 'Who will, may hear Sordello's story told'; and nearly six thousand lines later it ends with: 'Who would has heard Sordello's story told.' Tennyson claimed these were the only lines he had understood and that both were lies. Macready found it '*not* readable'. Charles Kingsley, in his novel *Alton Locke* (1850), makes the poem into a kind of bridge between otherwise estranged social classes. The low-born tailor-poet Alton has a conversation with the loved but high-born and therefore unattainable Lillian:

> She talked about poetry, Tennyson and Wordsworth; asked me if
> I understood Browning's *Sordello*; and then comforted me, after
> my stammering confession that I did not, by telling me she was
> delighted to hear that; for she did not understand it either, and it
> was so pleasant to have a companion in ignorance.

Later, James Russell Lowell would offer his copy of *Sordello* to anyone
who would 'put his hand upon his heart and say he understands it'.

Sordello's *story*, if by that one means the outward events of his life,
is not exceptionally difficult. In Browning's version, Sordello is the son
of the great Ghibelline warrior Salinguerra, who believes his son was
slaughtered at birth during a seige in Vincenza. Sordello is brought up
at Goito, near Mantua, by Queen Adelaide. Sordello is unaware of his
origin, and he spends a quiet and peaceful youth at Goito. Then, he
reveals his unsuspected (even to himself) gift for poetry in a contest
with Eglamor, the court poet to Adelaide and her daughter Palma. He
wins the singing prize at the Mantuan court, is entranced by Palma's
beauty, and dreams of a great future. He learns, mistakenly, that he is
the son of a base-born soldier Elcorte; temporarily discouraged, he
aspires to superiority over other men by his gift of poetry. He becomes
a successful troubadour at Adelaide's court, but is frustrated in his
attempts to express in traditional poetic modes his more profound
perceptions. He retires to Goito and contemplates his love for the
unattainable Palma. Then, Palma's weak father betroths her to an
enemy Guelph leader Boniface, whom the fierce old Ghibelline Salinguerra immediately imprisons in Ferrara. Palma sends for Sordello,
acknowledges her love for him, and urges him to join Salinguerra. In
seige-torn Ferrara, Palma and Sordello meet Salinguerra, and Palma
reveals that they are father and son. Sordello is offered the power he
can inherit from Salinguerra and marriage to his beloved Palma. But
Sordello has come to believe that the Guelph cause, rather than the
Ghibelline, is the cause of the people. He retires into another room to
choose between his new-found faith in humanity and the offer of
power and love. He dies in the struggle to decide.

This tale of a gifted young man of uncertain parentage who aspires
to passionate love and political idealism may be intricate but it is not
bafflingly obscure. But Browning was not interested in displaying an
orderly sequence of incidents. His interest, as he said in a preface added
many years later, lay 'on the incidents in the development of a soul'.
To exhibit such a 'development' Browning found it necessary to

wrench and contort the traditional form of a narrative poem into a complex and startlingly new form. He boldly created a kind of compendium or anatomy, large and free enough to accommodate not only the history of Sordello and his historical milieu, but commodious enough to include disquisitions on the sources of poetic inspiration, on the adequacy of language to express truth, on the relation between body and soul, between the individual and the mass, between the individual and God. Further, he found room to display Sordello's vaguest but profoundest perception, to describe the peaceful or violent Italian landscape and the war-torn bodies and cities; there was room, too, to indulge in humour and to even bring himself, Robert Browning, into the poem so he could talk to his readers about the poem they were reading. The result was 'so rich and rare a chaos' that an overwhelmed Victorian audience ridiculed the poem while later generations have generally steered clear of this, in Professor Lounsbury's words, 'colossal derelict upon the sea of literature, inflicting damage on the strongest intellects that graze it even slightly, and hopelessly wrecking the frailer mental craft that come into full collision with it'.[3]

The style of *Sordello*, as well as its odd construction, was an obstacle to its early readers and has remained an obstacle. Throughout the poem we can discover many passages that would now be labelled *Browningesque*, though one reviewer dubbed them 'exercises for asthmatics' while another confidently asserted that 'like any system of short-hand, the author's scheme of syntax may, with some trouble, be acquired'. Here is a passage in which Browning mockingly warns against unlocking the Pandora's box of history which contains the story of Sordello. In it he mixes harsh, grotesque diction with allusions to history and myth. The syntax is elliptical and the pace hurried while he declares his intention to get on with Sordello's story.

> Woe, then, worth
> Any officious babble letting forth
> The leprosy confirmed and ruinous
> To spirit lodged in a contracted house!
> Go back to the beginning rather; blend
> It gently with Sordello's life; the end
> Is piteous, you may see, but much between
> Pleasant enough. Meantime, some pyx to screen
> The grown-pest, some lid to shut upon
> The goblin! So they found at Babylon,

(Colleagues, mad Lucius and sage Antonine)
Sacking the city, by Apollo's shrine,
In rummaging among the rarities,
A certain coffer; he who made the prize
Opened it greedily; and out there curled
Just such another plague, for half the world
Was stung. Crawl in then, hag, and couch asquat,
Keeping that blotchy bosom thick in spot
Until your time is ripe! The coffer-lid
Is fastened, and the coffer safely hid
Under the Loxian's choicest gifts of gold.
   Who will may hear Sordello's story told. . . .

Still, *Sordello* has always had sturdy readers. Dante Gabriel Rossetti read it aloud to the Pre-Raphaelite Brotherhood; Swinburne may have memorized it; Ezra Pound, in his *Cantos*, envies Browning's achievement and in *The ABC of Reading* scorns the 'Victorian half-wits' who found the poem obscure. Scholars continue to find it a rich storehouse in their study of Browning's mind and art, while one highly respected critic has recently called it the 'key' poem of the Victorian period.[4] It contains many characteristically Victorian themes: the hunger after God, anxiety about the state of the individual soul, the growing awareness of the multiplicity of experience coupled with a desire to know wholeness, the alienation of the artist from his society. Sordello scornfully cuts himself off from mankind in his decision to prove his superiority through the medium of poetry:

        . . . never again
Sordello could in his sight remain
One of the many, one with hopes and cares
And interests nowise distinct from theirs. . . .
Never again for him and for the crowd
A common law. . . . The divorce
Is clear: why needs Sordello square his course
By any known example?

Sordello separates himself not only from the common ways of men but from artistic tradition. This action allows Browning to dramatize his conceptions of the poetic process. Eglamore, whom Sordello had defeated in the singing contest, is the traditional poet. He is a perfect craftsman who, by means of accepted poetic modes, sings of the world known to men. Sordello soon masters this art, but is as quickly dissatisfied. Out of his intense self-consciousness he has had visionary apprehensions of the infinite, of the essential unity of the universe rather than the parts of which the lesser poet Eglamore must sing. Soon Sordello learns that

> ... perceptions whole, like that he sought
> To clothe, reject so pure a work of thought
> As language. ...

He struggles and fails to create a new 'Language, – welding words into the crude/Mass from the new speech around him'. Not only is he out of unity with mankind, Sordello also suffers a division within himself: 'The Poet thwarting hopelessly the Man.'

Many a romantic saw in the poet the highest type of man. In Sordello, however, the Poet-as-Hero is frustrated, evidence perhaps of a shift towards a more Victorian sensibility. Two months after the publication of *Sordello* Browning would attend Carlyle's lecture on the Hero as Poet. Carlyle's examples of the poet as the mediator between God and Man, between the infinite and the finite, were Dante and Shakespeare. The day had passed, he argued, for poets to act as heroes for their culture; Carlyle looked to the 'Steam-engine Captains of Industry' to fill that role. A similar shift in roles had occurred in Browning's poem. In the third book of the poem, Palma urges Sordello to a life of action in the Ghibelline cause. The scene breaks off, and Browning himself appears sitting in Venice in 1838. He sees in a poor prostitute the emblem of suffering humanity. As he contemplates her, the ideal of the perfectibility of man (so fully expressed in the closing scene of *Paracelsus*) is transformed into a deep sympathy for suffering humanity. This sympathy is transferred to Sordello in the final three books of the poem. He comes gradually to believe that the unification of Italy and the Guelph cause is the cause of the people and that 'Collective man/Outstrips the individual'. But faced with the temptation of power from Salinguerra and love from Palma, Sordello is unable to enact his new-found faith. Sordello was no political and social reformer, but he might have signed the People's Charter of 1839, or he might cautiously have mounted the barricades in 1848.

Browning wrote and re-wrote *Sordello* intermittently during the seven years after the publication of *Pauline* in 1833. In the meantime, *Paracelsus* and *Strafford* had been accepted by influential readers as works of

great promise. Nearly every reviewer of 1840 voiced his disappointment at Browning's failure to fulfil that promise in *Sordello*. It seemed
to most that he had wilfully exaggerated the sins of obscurity which
they had warned against but had tolerated in the earlier poems. In 1835
English readers were ready to grant him 'a place among the acknowledged poets of the age'; by 1840 their patience had run out, and they
chose to 'leave him to the peaceable enjoyment of that obscurity which
he has courted'. A perceptive few, like Carlyle, recognized the 'rare
spiritual gift, poetical, pictorial, intellectual' that Browning had
brought to English poetry. But after a decade of experimentation he
had not found a form to contain that gift.

3

The Eighteen-Forties

Bells and Pomegranites

But we will complain no more: though, indeed, our complaints
are really compliments; for had we not felt certain that Mr.
Browning was worthy of better things, we should have left the
matter to clear itself, as all poems do pretty accurately in 'the
righteous sieve of Time'. But there are fine ballads in the second
volume, healthy and English, clear of all that Italianesque pedantry,
that *crambe repetita* of olives and lizards, artists and monks, with
which the English public, for its sins, has been spoon-fed for the
last half-century, ever since Childe Harold, in a luckless hour,
thought a warmer climate might make him a better man. . . .

How can Mr. Browning help England? By leaving henceforth
'the dead to bury their dead', in effete and enervating Italy, and
casting all his rugged genial force into the questions and the
struggles of that mother-country to whom, and not to Italy at all,
he owes all his most valuable characteristics.

Charles Kingsley, 1851

The eighteen-forties was a decade of unrest, agitation, and revolution;
for Browning it was a decade of withdrawal from the social and literary
life he had known briefly in London. The great literary document of the
decade was *The Communist Manifesto*, commissioned by the London
Communist League. Browning's plays and poems, published in a
series of eight cheap pamphlets, rarely directly confront 'the questions
and struggles' to which Kingsley hoped Browning would eventually
address himself and which Marx had so brilliantly summarized. The
vast expansion of manufacture and its concentration in urban centres
had created a new class of industrial poor whose sufferings under the
new system of industrial capitalism were now highly visible. In England
Parliamentary committees and government inspectors observed and

published the brutalizing horrors of working conditions in factories and sweat-shops and of sanitary conditions in the crowded slums. In Chartism the new poor and the dispossessed artisans found a vehicle to articulate their grievances and to organize their strength sufficiently to arouse hopes as well as fears of revolution. The proletariat of Belgium, France, Germany, and Italy found agitators if not spokesmen in analytical communists like Marx and Engels, in Socialists like Proudhon, or in terrorists like Weitling and Bakunin. The forties were filled with schemes aimed at reforming economic, social, political, even personal relationships. Henry David Thoreau tried out a new form of 'economy' in solitude in his hut on Walden Pond; European utopians tried out communal experiments in New York and Indiana, Kentucky and Texas. In *The Communist Manifesto* Marx suggests the variety of reformist ferment in England, although he scorned the English horror of violence and lack of revolutionary theory: there were 'economists, philanthropists, humanitarian improvers of the conditions of the working class, organizers of charity, members of societies for the prevention of cruelty to animals, temperance fanatics, hole-in-the-corner reformers of every imaginable kind'. There were romantic Tories like Disraeli and his Young England movement; there must have been thousands of matrons like Dickens's Mrs Jellyby who collected funds and clothes for the natives of Borrioboola-Gha while her family and house went to rack and ruin.

The 'troubles' of the 1840s coincided in England with a more generous supply of literary talent than was present in the previous decade. Dickens produced five major novels, opening the decade with *The Old Curiosity Shop* and closing it with *David Copperfield*. In 1847 Thackeray published *Vanity Fair*, while the Brontës contributed *Jane Eyre*, *Wuthering Heights*, and *The Tenant of Wildfell Hall*. Disraeli turned from the 'silver-fork' novels about high society he had written in the 1830s to an examination of the 'Condition of England' in a trilogy whose second volume, *Sybil* (1845), bore the subtitle 'The Two Nations' to indicate the great gulf that had opened between the rich and the poor. In *Past and Present* (1843) Carlyle lashed out angrily at the new system of free competition which had replaced traditional and more 'natural' relations between master and worker with a simple 'Cash-Nexus': 'Truly they are strange results to which this of leaving all to "Cash"; of quietly shutting up the God's Temple, and gradually opening wide-open the Mammon's Temple, with "Laissez-faire, and

Every man for himself'', – have led us in these days!' In *Sybil*, the young Chartist Stephen Morley describes the estrangement among individuals and between classes in an England that has become an 'aggregation' rather than a 'community':

> in cities that condition is aggravated. A density of population
> implies a severer struggle for existence, and a consequent repulsion
> of elements brought into too close contact. In great cities men
> are brought together by the desire of gain. They are not in a state
> of cooperation, but of isolation, as to the making of fortunes; and
> for all the rest they are careless of neighbours. Christianity teaches
> us to love our neighbour as ourself; modern society acknowledges
> no neighbour.

Kingsley in *Yeast* (1848) and *Alton Locke* (1850) and Mrs Gaskell in *Mary Barton* (1848) further explored and sympathized with the labouring poor.

The poetry of the 1840s was less lively and of less permanent value than the prose. Again, as in the 1830s, only the poems of Tennyson and Browning still attract general readers in the twentieth century, although the early poems of Arnold and Rossetti appeared in 1849 and 1850 respectively. Tennyson's poems reflect the contemporary unrest much more obviously than do Browning's. The artist's responsibility to speak out on the problems of his own time is a major theme in the life and poetry of Tennyson. His *Morte D'Arthur*, written during the 1830s but published in 1842, suggests something of the tension within a poet attracted to the beauty of the legendary past but sensing the need to speak to his own time. The central section of that poem is a re-telling in heroic style of Malory's legend of Arthur's death; this section, however, is framed by opening and closing passages set in the present. The situation is a Christmas gathering of former university friends of the poet Everard. They play games, and they discuss contemporary problems in witty, conversational language. Then, they ask Everard about the epic in twelve books which he had intended, as an undergraduate, to write. One explains that he has burnt the poem because

> He thought that nothing new was said, or else
> Something so said 'twas nothing – that a truth
> Looks freshest in the fashion of the day. . . .

Everard replies that he burnt it because an heroic poem on Arthur is anachronistic and obsolete:[1]

Why take the style of those heroic times?
For nature brings not back the mastodon,
Nor we those times; and why should any man
Remodel models? these twelve books of mine
Were faint Homeric echoes, nothing worth,
Mere chaff and draff, much better burnt.

But the *Morte D'Arthur* had been saved, and the poet reads it. The response of the small group suggests the reaction Tennyson must have anticipated from his contemporary readers. The parson, who had been arguing about the decay of faith in the modern world, has fallen asleep. The other friends like the poem because they are his friends or, perhaps, because he read aloud so well, 'mouthing out his hollow o's and a's'; and

Perhaps some modern touches here and there
Redeemed it from the charge of nothingness. . . .

There are many more 'modern touches' in another Tennyson poem of 1842, *Locksley Hall*. In that poem, the disappointed lover manages in just under two hundred lines to mention nearly every important public issue of the day: the increased importance of money and social position, the progress of science and popular education, the commercial competition among nations, opportunity in an expanding British empire, 'a hungry people' at home where London lights up the night sky 'like a dreary dawn'. Lesser poets, too, turned to social issues. Hood sang the plight of the sweated garment workers in *Song of the Shirt*, while in *The Cry of the Children* Elizabeth Barrett voiced the suffering which Ashley's Act of 1842 regulating the working conditions of women and children in mines was designed to alleviate. In *Casa Guidi Windows* (1849/1851) she celebrated the aims and aspirations of the Risorgimento.

Browning was neither ignorant of, nor indifferent to, the great unrest of the 1840s. He, too, read the newspapers and perhaps even the 'Blue Books', in which government commissions reported on working and living conditions. The new friend and warm admirer of his poetry (including *Sordello*), R. H. Horne, was chairman of one such commission. Another new and close friend, Alfred Domett, was one of the thousands who emigrated from England during the financial depression of the early forties. In 1842, Browning wrote morosely to his absent friend, 'Here everything goes flatly on, except the fierce political reality (as it begins to be). Our poems, etc., are poor child's play.' Five of the six plays he published between 1842 and 1846 take as their central theme political struggles between liberal and repressive forces, though all are set in the past. Some of the shorter poems also mirror or indirectly reflect the 'fierce political reality'. The romantic nationalism which swelled the revolutions of 1848 is memorably voiced, in *The Italian in England*, by an exiled patriot as he recounts his escape from the Austrian 'blood-hounds' and expresses his desire to

> . . . grasp Metternich until
> I felt his red wet throat distil
> In blood through these two hands.

A companion poem is *The Englishman in Italy*. It was written during the wet summer of 1845 which had ruined the English grain crop and had begun the Irish potato blight, events that greatly increased the agitation for repeal of the taxes on grain imposed by the Corn Laws. The poem describes the harmony and joy with which the Italian peasants gather their harvest before the oncoming winds of the sirocco. The poem ends:

> . . . in England at home,
>   Men meet gravely to-day
> And debate, if abolishing Corn-Laws
>   Be righteous and wise
> – If 't were proper, Scirocco should vanish
>   In black from the skies.

But, in comparison to the popular propaganda of *Corn-Law Rhymes*, Browning's commentary upon this particular contemporary issue is indirect indeed. Mr Hood's and Miss Barrett's poems are straightforward pleas for sympathy for public problems. Tennyson, too, in a poem like *Locksley Hall*, manages to be quite direct, and scarcely any historian of nineteenth-century England can avoid at least one quotation from that poem. David Thompson, in his list of 'Suggested Books' in his *England and the Nineteenth Century*, rightly ends with this injunction: 'The poems of Lord Tennyson are indispensable.' In histories of the period, Browning, if he is quoted at all, is usually represented by the lines from *Pippa Passes* which declare

> God's in his heaven —
> All's right with the world!

Pippa Passes, published in 1841 (a year after *Sordello*), is a good example of Browning's indirect, oblique commentary upon the cultural crises of his time and place. Two stanzas from Elizabeth's *The Cry of the Children* may supply a contrast to *Pippa* as well as suggest why Miss Barrett was a popular poet while Browning's father had to continue to pay publication costs for Robert's poems:

'For oh,' say the children, 'we are weary,
    And we cannot run or leap;
If we cared for any meadows, it were merely
    To drop down in them and sleep.
Our knees tremble sorely in the stooping,
    We fall upon our faces, trying to go;
And, underneath our heavy eyelids drooping,
    The reddest flower would look as pale as snow.
For, all day, we drag our burden tiring
    Through the coal-dark, underground;
Or, all day, we drive the wheels of iron
    In the factories, round and round.

'For, all day, the wheels are droning, turning;
    Their wind comes in our faces,
Till our hearts turn, our heads with pulses burning,
    And the walls turn in their places:
Turns the sky in the high window blank and reeling,
    Turns the long light that drops down the wall,
Turn the black flies that crawl along the ceiling,
    All are turning, all the day, and we with all.
And all day, the iron wheels are droning,
    And sometimes we could pray,
"O ye wheels," (breaking out in a mad moaning)
    "Stop! be silent for to-day."'

Pippa, too, is a child-labourer: she works three hundred and sixty-four days a year in a Po Valley silk-mill. But Browning presents her on her yearly day of freedom from the monotonous and stupefying drudgery described in *The Cry of the Children*.

Pippa expects to return to the factory on the morrow, but she greets this one day of leisure with eager and joyful anticipation:

Day!
Faster and more fast,
O'er night's brim, day boils at last:

Boils, pure gold, o'er the cloud-cup's brim
Where spurting and suppressed it lay,
For not a froth-flake touched the rim
Of yonder gap in solid gray
Of the eastern cloud, an hour away;
But forth one wavelet, then another, curled,
Till the whole sunrise, not to be suppressed,
Rose, reddened, and its seething breast
Flickered in bounds, grew gold, then overflowed the world.
– My Day, if I squander such labour or leisure,
Then shame fall on Asolo, mischief on me!

A good deal of shame does fall on the little town of Asolo that day, and a good deal of dark mischief hovers around the unaware little factory girl as she passes through the town singing her various songs. In the shuttered house of the mill-owner, the owner's wife Ottima and her lover Sebald reveal that they have killed the husband and now they re-live in words their erotic love-making. Pippa's passing song moves them to repentance; and, at Ottima's bidding, Sebald kills her then himself in remorse. Pippa's unconscious song has certainly worked the good of repentance; but the shuttered house now enfolds three corpses where before there was but one. By noon she passes the house of Jules, the young painter, who has just married. He has just learned that he has been tricked into marrying the low-born Phene. Jules is ready to coldly reject Phene until Pippa's song about Kate the Queen brings him to affirm his love while promising to take her with him to an impossible 'unsuspected isle in far-off seas'. Evening finds Pippa outside a turret in which Luigi's mother pleads with her rather weak-minded son not to undertake a mission to assassinate (in the Carbonari cause) the Austrian king. Luigi's faltering patriotism is rekindled by Pippa's song of a just and generous king, and Luigi sets out on his mission under the close and scowling observation of the Austrian police. The night scene reveals the Monsignor, arrived in Asolo, to claim an inheritance from a dead brother; but the Monsignor learns that a niece, presumed dead, is no other than Pippa. He is tempted by another dead brother's steward to assent to a plot to have Pippa raped and then sold into prostitution in Rome, a place where 'courtesans perish off every three years'. This time (by a timely song), Pippa saves herself. Or at least readers have always assumed she is saved and that she will be acknowledged as the lost heiress in the morning. All the reader really knows is that the Monsignor has the tempter, if not the temptation, quickly removed from the room. The scene closes with the Monsignor's shout:

> My people – one and all – all – within there! Gag this villain –
> tie him hand and foot! He dares . . . I know not half he dares –
> but remove him – quick! *Miserere mei, Domine!* Quick, I say!

The poem ends by Pippa's misreading the little she has seen of the day's events in which she has played an unconscious but decisive role. The world has been revealed as much darker and more sinister than Pippa's opening paean to the dawn would imply. Pippa seems to realize subconsciously what has happened as she sits in her bare room preparing to sleep:

> . . . morning's rule has moved away,
> Dispensed with, *never more to be allowed*!
> Day's turn is over, now arrives the night's.
> Oh lark, be day's apostle
> To mavis, merle and throstle
> Bid them their betters jostle
> From day and its delights!
> But at night, brother owlet, over the woods,
> Toll the world to thy chantry;
> Sing to the bats' sleek sisterhoods
> Full complines with gallantry:
> Then, owls and bats,
> Cowls and twats,
> Monks and nuns, in a cloister's moods,
> Adjourn to the oak-stump pantry!

God may be in his heaven, but very little is right in the world represented by the village of Asolo. The shuttered windows of the murdered mill-owner's house are a fit symbol of this world. Hidden to Pippa's eyes, but not to the reader, are deception and cynical intrigue. The police, ready to follow without question their orders to arrest Luigi on any 'pretence', notice but are indifferent to the shuttered windows. They are also officially ignorant of Bluphocks's plot to sell Pippa into prostitution. The sinister Englishman Bluphocks passes himself off as an inspector of working conditions in the factory, in order to further his scheme; and the vulgar village girls help him. There is mirrored here not only moral evil but the social evil of a town which, in Disraeli's Chartist hero's words, has become an 'aggregation' rather than a 'community', and which 'acknowledges no neighbour'. Pippa is not so much protected by her innocence as she is isolated by her obliviousness. At the beginning of the poem the lonely Pippa imagines and envies the passionate love of Ottima and Sebald, the love Luigi's mother has for her son, the love of the engaged Jules and Phene, the Monsignor's love of God. But passionate love turns carnal, then murderous and finally suicidal. Browning deliberately characterizes Luigi as a simple-minded tool of revolutionaries whose ideas he cannot understand; and a mother's love is unavailing against misguided political idealism. Jules's and Phene's marriage is founded on a cruel hoax though Jules hopes to sustain the love with a vague romantic ideal, which the Monsignor gently mocks. Only the ascetic and humble Monsignor's love of God remains uncompromised as he persists in his plan to redeem the 'century after century' of wickedness by his family by giving his wealth to the church. But, then, the wealth really belongs to Pippa, though the reader cannot be certain that she will receive it.

Pippa passes through this world and her presence changes it, but that is not to say that she unequivocally improves it. Browning's good friend Mrs Sutherland Orr gives this account of the inspiration for *Pippa Passes*:

> Mr. Browning was walking alone, in a wood near Dulwich, when the image flashed upon him of some one walking thus alone through life; one apparently too obscure to leave a trace of his or her passage, yet exercising a lasting though unconscious influence at every step of it. . . .

Pippa's most 'lasting' influence has, of course, been felt by the dead Ottima and Sebald. On every character she has produced dramatic and obvious change. It is less clear that she has been an agent for good. She may be the unconscious agent of God's inscrutable will; then, again, she may be an agent of chance. And the possibility that chance governed the world was as horrifying a spectre to the Victorian as was the one Marx proclaimed to be hovering over Europe. Marx called it communism; Victorian scientists, economists, historians, and social philosophers and other ideologists diligently had sought 'laws' to rule out chance.

In *Pippa* Browning developed a nearly perfect form to display that mixture of good and evil, of the beautiful and the ugly, which so marks

his vision of life. The too-contrived plot and the occasionally heightened speech verge towards that favoured Victorian form, the melodrama. But the purpose and effect of melodrama is to simplify moral
issues by presenting to an audience clear-cut villains, heroes and
heroines whom they can instantly hiss or applaud. Browning compli-
cates rather than simplifies the reader's judgment of characters and
actions. He rigorously excludes his own judgments, and there is no
'spokesman' to relay to the reader the author's commentary on the
scene he is exposing. Browning leaves the plot unresolved so that the
reader himself must determine from the whole poem whether Pippa
will return to the silk-mill or whether she will awaken to find herself
an heiress. All the while the reader must contend with a variety of
irony, beginning with the fact that the little play begins a New Year
and ending with Pippa's thought that the silk she winds tomorrow may
bind 'Ottima's cloak's hem;' the reader knows that any silk Pippa may
wind would go to bind Ottima's shroud.

Pippa Passes was the first pamphlet in a series which Browning called
Bells and Pomegranates. None of his earlier poems had sold well: only
one hundred and fifty-seven copies of *Sordello* at six shillings and sixpence
had been sold by his publisher Moxon. Browning's father continued
to pay publication costs, so the inexpensive pamphlet series was
decided upon. *Pippa* cost only sixpence, but no new edition was ever
called for. Browning, inexplicably, hoped that he would attract a
wider public, 'a sort of Pit-audience', by this cheap mode of publication. It was the poetry, however, rather than the price, that limited his
audience. The title of the series is an example of Browning's apparent
blindness to the gulf which lay between himself and the British reading
public. As the series progressed from 1841 to 1846, reviewers continued
to query the 'whimsical title'; they saw in it evidence of Browning's
persisting in 'wayward perverseness' and obscurity. After their
courtship began, Elizabeth Barrett expressed her puzzlement at
the title though it was not until shortly before their marriage that
Browning, in the eighth and final pamphlet, explained the title to his
readers:

> I only meant by that title to indicate an endeavour towards
> something like an alternation, or mixture, of music with
> discoursing, sound with sense, poetry with thought; which looks
> too ambitious, thus expressed, so the symbol was preferred. It is
> little to the purpose, that such is actually one of the most familiar

of the many Rabbinical (and Patristic) acceptations of the phrase; because I confess that, letting authority alone, I suppose the bare words, in such juxtaposition, would sufficiently convey the desired meaning.

Few readers were up to the difficult demands Browning made upon them. '"Rabbinical, indeed! We want English, not Hebrew, sir!"' replies a 'testy old gentleman' in George Henry Lewes's otherwise favourable review of that last pamphlet.

Five of the eight pamphlets were devoted to plays written as continuing experiments in the vein of Browning's first play, *Strafford*. *Pippa Passes*, although subtitled 'A Drama', is clearly meant for reading rather than for the stage. *King Victor and King Charles*, published in 1842 as the second volume of *Bells and Pomegranates*, was designed for the stage, but it was rejected by Macready. It is an historical play of political intrigue in the Sardinian court in the 1730s. In a preface to the play Browning recognizes that he cannot expect his readers 'to be versed, nor desirous of becoming so, in all the detail of the memoirs, correspondence, and relations of the time'. Still, the historical allusions are no more obscure than is the action which brings the cynical old King Victor to recognize in the final death scene the nobility of character embodied in his son Charles. Macready had also rejected *The Return of the Druses* (1843); however, a month after its publication he allowed *A Blot on the 'Scutcheon* to open for a three-day run in his Drury Lane theatre. This was the 'spick and span new Tragedy' which Browning had buoyantly promised Macready; and he assured the temperamental actor that there 'is *action* in it, drabbing, stabbing, et autres gentilesses. . . .' The setting is an eighteenth-century English country house. The heroine's inexplicable refusal to admit that her secret lover (and her quite acceptable fiancé) are the same person causes the deaths of both the lovers and of the heroine's honour-conscious brother. Though that central motivating action is vague, the play is not encumbered by Browning's usual fondness for historical detail. Dickens was deeply moved when he read the play in manuscript, and the play was popular enough with the public to be revived twice for short runs later in the decade. Browning offered his next dramatic work, *Colombe's Birthday* (1844), to Macready's rival, Charles Kean; but Kean procrastinated, so Browning printed it as Number VI of his pamphlet series. Browning gave what seems a rather curious reason for his decision to print the play: 'I *must* print, or risk the hold, such as it is, I have at present on *my* public.' John Forster's cool review reduced Browning's public and, briefly, his circle of friends by one. In the 1850s *Colombe's Birthday* was to have relatively successful runs in London, Manchester, and Boston; but while he was re-working his last two plays (*Luria* and *A Soul's Tragedy*, 1846) he confessed to Elizabeth Barrett: 'I have lost, of late, interest in dramatic writing, as you know, and, perhaps, occasion.'

When his first play, *Strafford*, had appeared in 1837 Browning declared in the preface that he had written a play about 'Action in Character, rather than Character in Action'. For nearly a decade following, in six plays, Browning tried to fit that formula into fairly traditional forms of stage plays. His attempts to display inward psychological or spiritual action by means of acts, scenes and dialogue among the characters failed. Often the failure was most obvious at those points in the plays when a profound spiritual recognition must issue in some outward and visible action – such as death. Often the result is neither clear nor convincing. The three deaths in *A Blot on the 'Scutcheon* are of this kind; so are the surprising conversions of the old king and his cynical prime minister D'Ormea in the final scene of *King Victor*. The suicide of Luria is another. The death of Anael in *The Return of the Druses* provides a further, and more extreme, example. Anael loves Djabal, who, to further his plans to free his people from a tyrannical Prefect, pretends to be the reincarnation of Hakeem, a dead leader and god to the enslaved Druses. Anael doubts that her human love is worthy of Djabal-Hakeem's godliness; so, she assassinates the Prefect to prove her worthiness. When Djabal reveals that he is merely human, Anael shouts 'Hakeem!' and falls dead. 'Why, or by what instrument, she dies, is in no way explained', complained one reviewer. The modern reader would echo his complaint. She seems to die of that abstraction, *recognition*; a recognition that but for deception she might have known Djabal's human love. Anael's death is a variant upon Sordello's earlier death by indecision.

No one has ever regretted Browning's decision to leave off the writing of plays, and only the most devoted of Browningites would claim any artistic merit for them. The plays were laboratories in which he explored and developed his gift for a poetry 'dramatic in principle', and in which he elaborated themes which would occupy him throughout his life. A favourite theme, spiritual growth through inner struggle, proved fatal to the plays themselves, as did his penchant for obscure historical detail. In part the plays belong to the genre of Victorian

Historical Plays, of which Bulwer-Lytton's popular and still readable *Richelieu* was an example. But Bulwer chose a famous name from history, a man whose life and times were relatively familiar to his audience. Browning chose a King Victor of Sardinia or a Strafford, or he invented exotic ones like Djabal and the Othello-like Moor, Luria. It is understandable that his most popular play, *A Blot on the 'Scutcheon*, is peopled by nearly contemporary English lords and ladies. That was also the only play that did not take as its central action a political struggle between repressive and liberal factions. The tempestuous politics of the 1840s certainly left their mark upon his plays, but by 1846 Browning was disillusioned with politics. In the final play, *A Soul's Tragedy*, he dramatizes the moral decline of a good and successful liberal leader who assumes *autocratic* rule under the familiar guise of its being 'for the good of the people'. It may be significant that this final play is also the only comedy among the plays. Equally significant is the easy, witty, colloquial speech that ends the play: it is the closest Browning comes in his plays to the short soliloquies and monologues he was publishing throughout the 1840s and perfected in following decades.

In 1842 and in 1845 Browning gathered together his shorter, less ambitious poems under the titles *Dramatic Lyrics* and *Dramatic Romances and Lyrics*. They were published as the third and seventh pamphlets of the *Bells and Pomegranates* series. There were thirty-seven poems; but, printed as they were in small, double-columned type, they took up only forty pages. Reviewers noticed them even less than they did his plays, and there is no evidence that Browning himself had any great expectations for them. These poems were usually written quickly when an idea or occasion suggested itself at moments when he was not about the serious business of writing a stage play. In them Browning's rich imagination found expression in a great variety of subject, form, meter and tone. Walter Savage Landor, to the delight of Browning and especially of his father, paid tribute to this rich abundance in a poem in *The Morning Chronicle* in November 1845:

Browning! Since Chaucer was alive and hale,
No man hath walkt along our road with step
So active, so inquiring eye, or tongue
So varied in discourse.

Within the varied discourse are many of the stylistic elements that we now associate particularly with Browning. In *The Pied Piper of*

Hamelin his fondness for grotesque images blended with his jocular high spirits in his retelling of the old legend:

> Rats!
> They fought the dogs and killed the cats,
>   And bit the babies in the cradles,
> And ate the cheeses out of the vats,
>   And licked the soup from the cooks' own ladles,
> Split open the kegs of salted sprats,
> Made nests inside men's Sunday hats,
> And even spoiled the women's chats
>   By drowning their speaking
>   With shrieking and squeaking
> In fifty different sharps and flats.

In *Johannes Agricola*, reprinted in 1842 as *Madhouse Cells II*, the grotesque is infected and heightened by the speaker's fanatical belief that he is among the elect of God. Secure in his bliss, Agricola looks down with sneering malice on those who sought to please God by good works alone:

> I gaze below on hell's fierce bed,
>   And those its waves of flame oppress,
>   Swarming in ghastly wretchedness;
> Whose life on earth aspired to be
>   One altar-smoke, so pure! – to win
> If not love like God's for me,
>   At least to keep his anger in;
>   And all their striving turned to sin.
> Priest, doctor, hermit, monk grown white
>   With prayer, the broken-hearted nun,
> The martyr, the wan acolyte,
>   The incense-swinging child, – undone
> Before God fashioned star and sun!

The utterance of the sensual, senile churchman in *The Bishop Orders His Tomb* reveals a startling fusion between the spiritual and the physical as the bishop longs

> ... to hear the blessed mutter of the mass
> And see God made and eaten all day long. ...

or describes the size and colour of a piece of stone as

Big as a Jew's head cut off at the nape,
Blue as a vein o'er the Madonna's breast. . . .

In contrast to the often confused, stream-of-consciousness language of
the Bishop is the confident and skilful speech of the Duke in *My Last
Duchess* or the solemn lyric cadences of *Parting at Morning*:

Round the cape of a sudden came the sea,
And the sun looked over the mountain's rim:
And straight was a path of gold for him,
And the need of a world of men for me.

Among these poems of the 1840s there is a marked absence of one of
the persistent moods in much romantic and Victorian poetry – the
mood of sad resignation, of gentle melancholy, the 'drowsy numbness'
of Keats or the 'mild-minded melancholy 'of Tennyson's *The Lotus-
Eaters*. Many of Browning's contemporaries expressed this mood as an
alternative to what Matthew Arnold called 'this strange disease of
modern life, With its sick hurry, its divided aims. . . .' Swinburne,
Rossetti, and Meredith thought Edward Fitzgerald had given consum-
mate expression to that mood in his version of *The Rubáiyát*, the most
famous stanza of which is

A Book of Verses underneath the Bough,
A Jug of Wine, a Loaf of Bread – and Thou
   Beside me singing in the Wilderness –
Oh, Wilderness were Paradise enow!

Here is Browning, after he has maliciously left a pedantic book to
moulder in his garden:

Then I went indoors, brought out a loaf,
   Half a cheese, and a bottle of Chablis;
Lay on the grass and forgot the oaf
   Over a jolly chapter of Rabelais.

Of course Browning's is a poem of 1842 whereas *The Rubáiyát* was
published in 1859 along with the unnerving *Origin of the Species*.
Moods became darker and more disillusioned in the 1850s and 1860s.
But Browning never lost the robust energy he exhibits here: in the
1860s Rossetti would compare his exuberance to a man drunk of
'7-Dials gin' and reviewers would begin to compare him to Balzac. In
the 1840s Landor saw Chaucer as the proper comparison: Chaucer,

the father and master of the vulgar, colloquial tradition in English poetry.

Another master of the colloquial tradition was John Donne, a poet little read and little appreciated throughout the nineteenth century. Coleridge, usually flawless in his literary judgments, wrote this short piece which describes rather well but does not praise Donne's poetry:

> With Donne, whose muse on dromedary trots,
> Wreathe iron pokers into true-love knots;
> Rhyme's sturdy cripple, fancy's maze and clue,
> Wit's forge and fire-blast, meaning's press and screw.

Perhaps one advantage Browning gained by his lack of regular schooling and a university education was that he read and admired John Donne's poetry and was able to quote much of it from memory. As a boy he set to music the poem *Go and catch a falling star*, and he would even recite much of Donne's verse in deliriums during an illness in the 1840s. Donne's poetry and the short poems Browning was writing share many similarities. There are the rough, irregular cadences and the startling images in which the spiritual and its assumed opposite, the physical, are yoked. Also, there are the abrupt opening lines:

> My heart sank with our Claret-flask. . . .
> Now that I, tying thy glass mask tightly. . . .
> Plague take all you pedants, say I!
> Gr-r-r – there, go, my heart's abhorrence. . . .

Most important, many of Donne's poems were dramatic monologues in which a single speaker addresses his words to an implied listener. Browning had studied Shakespeare, without any great success, as a model for his plays. In Donne's poems and perhaps in Shakespeare's dramatic soliloquies, Browning found a native tradition on which he could build and within which he could experiment.[2]

The essence and advantage of the dramatic monologue, as Browning came to practise it, was that the words of a single speaker (who was clearly not the poet) could convey to the reader a setting, a present action, and a sense of who was listening to the speaker. The act of speech itself, then, reveals to the reader the speaker's character. For many reasons this form better fits Browning's preoccupations than did the conventional stage drama. It allowed him to be fully 'dramatic in principle' while at the same time he was able to stress 'Action in Character, rather than Character in Action', a preoccupation that had been the source of so much obscurity in his plays. The 'action' in a dramatic monologue is mental, psychological, and verbal. Although Browning would become adept at indicating physical action and gesture, the important action is the act of speaking – of arguing, pleading, informing, reminiscing, of meditating aloud or of justifying oneself. The form also allowed him to indulge his fondness for eccentric or often morally reprehensible characters[3] and opinions while, at the same time, it freed him of the responsibility of bringing his villain to justice in the fifth act. Browning's penchant for historical subjects is also well served by the dramatic monologue form. Of the treacherously intricate historical detail of *Sordello* Browning said: 'The historical decoration was purposely of no more importance than a background requires. . . .' Still, a keen reader like Mrs Carlyle claimed that she could not tell whether Sordello was a book, or a man, or a city. The 'historical decoration' doubtless contributed to her confusion. In the monologues, historical detail is rigorously selected to become a part of the living experience of the character who is speaking. For these, and many more reasons, Browning's particular genius found its fullest expression in the dramatic monologue.

Three poems, written over a space of ten years (1834–45), illustrate Browning's experiments with the kind of poem that has become one of the dominant poetic forms of the past one hundred years. They are *Porphyria's Lover, My Last Duchess*, and *The Bishop Orders His Tomb at St. Praxed's Church*. All are favourite anthology pieces and each has been admirably and admiringly explicated by dozens of Browning scholars. These poems went virtually unnoticed by the reviewers of the 1840s, although in 1851 Kingsley picked out *Porphyria's Lover* and *The Bishop Orders His Tomb* for particular scorn. The former poem had been published, along with *Johannes Agricola*, in the Unitarian magazine *The Monthly Repository* in 1836. It may have been written during Browning's visit to St Petersburg, and DeVane suggests that perhaps 'some of the atmosphere of Russia still lingers in the poem'.[4] Certainly the lover of Porphyria exists in a world of obsession and nightmare not unlike the one Dostoievski, whose first novel appeared in 1846, so frequently describes; on the other hand, the lover's obsessive madness is a good deal more total and more sinister than the mental distortion caused by obsession in Gogol's *Dead Souls* (1842), or by an *idée fixe* in Balzac's *Pere Goriot* (1834) or *Cousin Pons* (1848). In these novels, the author's commentary or other characters provide a standard or 'norm' against which mental aberration can be measured. The lover in Browning's poem is as removed from the normal world as were those isolated madmen whom Gericault studied and painted in the 1820s.

The restriction of the world to a single point of view, to the words of the character who is speaking, is the source of much of the richness and power of the dramatic monologue as Browning developed it. The reader of *Porphyria's Lover* will soon deduce, even without the 1842 title of *Madhouse Cells II*, that the speaker is insane. Midway through his recitation, the 'lover' tells us that he 'found a thing to do' once he has realized that Porphyria loves him:

> . . . all her hair
> In one long yellow string I wound
> Three times her little throat around
> And strangled her.

He compounds his strange act by planting a 'burning kiss' upon the dead woman's blushing cheek, and then propping her head against his shoulder. The poem ends:

> And thus we sit together now,
> And all night long we have not stirred,
> And yet God has not said a word!

The poem is not a simple illustration of Oscar Wilde's dictum that all men kill the thing they love. The speaker has revealed himself successively as a murderer, a necrophiliac, and finally as a man so filled with twisted pride that he believes God's silence indicates that God condones his act. Or is the reader able to detect a tone of dreadful anxiety in that final line, so that the emphasis falls on the fact that God has not *yet* spoken but the speaker fearfully awaits God's judgment on his sins? By giving the reader only the lover's version of events, Browning has created a poem that is fundamentally and richly ambiguous. Any reader's quick judgment of this murderer and necrophiliac is complicated nearly to the point of paralysis. To begin, the man's madness extenuates his crime. Still, we have only a madman's word that there *was* a crime and that it was committed in such a way. He may, in his insanity, merely imagine what he would do were a woman, who has previously ignored him, to come to him in the night. The speaker recites the events as though they had just occurred but the title, *Madhouse Cells*, suggests that the action had taken place much earlier. If that be the case, then the lover's mind must be trapped within the memory of that night in the same way he hoped to stop time and pre-serve for ever the moment of love Porphyria showed him. Once a reader's imagination is engaged by these ambiguities, every line in the poem becomes an index into the complex human mind Browning has portrayed. The opening lines, for example, do not so much describe a setting for the macabre events to be related, as they provide a map of the speaker's mind:

> The rain set early in to-night,
>   The sullen wind was soon awake,
> It tore the elm-tops down for spite,
>   And did its worst to vex the lake.

It is the man, not the wind, that is sullen, spiteful and vexatious.

Porphyria's Lover is technically a soliloquy rather than a dramatic monologue, for there is present no listener or audience to hear the lover's utterance. In Browning's later and more typical monologues a listener is usually clearly indicated so that the poem becomes 'one end of a conversation' which the reader is permitted to overhear. In this early poem the absence of a listener amplifies the isolation of the speaker, but it also raises the question of why, dramatically, does the man speak. It is likely that he does not speak *aloud* at all. Many years later Browning added to the title of the companion poem, *Johannes Agricola*, the phrase 'in Meditation', suggesting that he thought of that poem as an internal, unspoken stream of thought. If the lover speaks aloud, he speaks to himself or to the silent God, retelling the events of that night as a penitent tells his beads. Albeit, he does not seem particu-larly repentant.

My Last Duchess (1842) represents a definite advance towards dramatic monologues which convey a clearer and more convincing illusion of objective reality. The setting is more precise, the Duke's motive for speaking is more definite, the language is more natural, and the person to whom the Duke speaks is more openly and dramatically indicated. The device of including someone within the poem, someone to listen to the utterance, perhaps more than any other single element, accounts for the greater sense of reality. The speech of Porphyria's lover has its own mad logic, but when one speaks to oneself or to God, the logic need not be too clear. In contrast, the Duke uses his speech as a keen instrument of policy: he wishes to relay certain information to a particular man whom he confidently hopes to manipulate. He is a man talking to another man. The heightened language, the regular cadences, and insistent rhyme of *Porphyria's Lover* give way to a less artificial, more conversational style:

> That's my last Duchess painted on the wall,
> Looking as if she were alive. I call
> That piece a wonder now: Fra Pandolf's hands
> Worked busily a day, and there she stands.

The listener is asked to 'sit and look at her', while the Duke describes the painting and the character of the Duchess. As the poem closes the listener will be asked politely to rise from the chair and walk side-by-side with the Duke down the stairs, pausing for a moment to notice a bronze statue. In a few brief but vivid phrases Browning has described the physical action of the poem and suggested both the floor plan and the furnishings of the Duke's palace. He has also displayed the Duke's confident superiority over the man to whom he is speaking.

The listener is an envoy from the Count, whose daughter will be the next Duchess; so, the Duke carefully tailors his speech to lay down a code of behaviour for the new Duchess by describing the flaws in the character of the previous one. His speech is filled with calculated pauses and even with a mock-humility about his powers as a rhetorician:

> She thanked me, – good! but thanked
> Somehow – I know not how – as if she ranked
> My gift of a nine-hundred-years-old name
> With anybody's gift. Who'd stoop to blame
> This sort of trifling? Even had you skill
> In speech – (which I have not) – to make your will
> Quite clear to such, and say. . . .

As so often in Browning's monologues, here the Duke can carry on a kind of dialogue with his listener by anticipating the questions or responses of the listener: 'Who'd stoop to blame this sort of trifling?' It is a concise and economical device for gaining the advantage of dialogue while retaining the advantages of a single speaker. Gesture and setting exhibit a similar economy. The bronze statue of Neptune taming a sea-horse, which the envoy is asked to notice, supplies a detail of stage-setting, acts as reminder that the Duke intends to 'tame' the new Duchess, and underscores the Duke's pride in possession. In the course of his short utterance, the Duke has revealed himself to the envoy and to the reader: his pride in station and possession has led him to treat people as possessions, objects, things. The last Duchess has become a mere art-object and the envoy a tool to be used. At the same time, by sketching out the Duchess' warm and almost democratic sentiments, the Duke has created for the reader a standard, a foil, against which his own character can be judged. The fact that he is an aristocrat of the Italian Renaissance, accustomed to autocratic power, may mitigate the harshness of the reader's judgment. But the Duke is also a representative of the dehumanizing forces at work in the 1840s; *My Last Duchess* is an oblique version of Emerson's more open complaint of 1847: 'Things are in the saddle/And ride mankind.'

The Flight of the Duchess (1846) has interesting similarities, and equally interesting dissimilarities, to *My Last Duchess*. It is more obviously contemporary in subject and setting, but the poem is also less 'modern' in its form. The Duke supplements his income by turning part of his estate into

> ... one vast red drear burnt-up plain,
> Branched through and through with many a vein
> Whence iron's dug, and copper's dealt;
> Look right, look left, look straight before, –
> Beneath they mine, above they smelt,
> Copper-ore and iron-ore,
> And forge and furnace mould and melt,
> And so on, more and ever more. ...

On the basis of this new industrial wealth the Duke 'revived all usages thoroughly worn-out'; then, he re-created at his manor a medieval court, complete with an earthy and angry old huntsman clad unwillingly in medieval garb. Into this world of pretence and fakery is brought the new Duchess, filled with a spontaneous 'life and gladness' which causes her to suffer under the anachronistic and artificial code of the Duke. She successfully flees with a band of gypsies, among whose free and natural life she can fulfil her innate capacities for joy. The poem is, in part, a satiric attack upon the cult of medievalism which had been growing since the late eighteenth century. This cult found expression in the poems of Coleridge and Keats, as well as in Scott's novels, poems and his house, Abbotsford. In his *La Confessions d'un Enfant du Siècle* (1835) Alfred Musset would complain that 'Eclectilism is our badge ... we live on wrecks, as if the end of the world was at hand'. Certainly by the eighteen-forties, the dominant strain in Victorian eclecticism was neo-Gothic, neo-medieval. The order and shared prosperity of a medieval monastery contrasts completely with the chaos and injustice of modern capitalism in Carlyle's *Past and Present* (1843). Medievalism informed the politics of Disraeli's Young England Movement and supported the drift towards a more ritualistic High Church. It found expression in the new Houses of Parliament, the fake castles on the Rhine, the codes of German student societies and the jousting tournaments held on American slave plantations. Browning's *The Flight of the Duchess* might be read, along with Twain's belated *A Connecticut Yankee in King Arthur's Court* (1889), as a commentary upon this cult, although the American humorist's hero defeats the medieval knights by his technological ingenuity; Browning relies on the gypsies.

The form of *The Flight of the Duchess* is less experimental than that of *My Last Duchess*. Browning called the former a 'dramatic romance' and the latter a 'dramatic lyric'. The reader's interest in *The Flight of the Duchess* is commanded more by the story, the sequence of events as they are told, than by the character of the teller. True, the old huntsman who relates the events is an admirable dramatic creation, but the focus of attention is on what happens to the Duke and to his Duchess, rather than the telling itself as in *My Last Duchess*. Emily Brontë's *Wuthering Heights* (1847) makes use of a similar story-telling technique: the old servant Nellie Deans tells the story, but the novel is really *about* Heathcliff and Catherine, not Nellie Deans. The old huntsman's story moves at a much more leisurely pace than the concise, economical utterance of *My Last Duchess* (926 lines versus 56 lines). At the same time, the characters in *The Flight of the Duchess* tend more towards types, towards caricature: there is the Sancho-like huntsman, the Quixotic duke, the sensitive young wife, the hateful mother-in-law, the wily old gypsy woman. Both poems have become favourites with twentieth-century readers, but *My Last Duchess* more clearly foreshadows twentieth-century poetry.

The Bishop Orders His Tomb at St. Praxed's Church (1845) brought the dramatic monologue to full and mature expression. Also, in Browning's mind at least, the poem was a commentary upon a particular aspect of the medievalism he had satirized in *The Flight of the Duchess*. When he sent the poem to the editor of *Hood's Magazine* he described it as 'just the thing for the time – what with the Oxford business. . . .' The 'Oxford business' was the Oxford or Tractarian Movement, an effort by various Anglican divines to re-establish within the Church of England beliefs and rituals of the church prior to the Reformation. A high point within the movement was the publication of Tract XC, which argued that there was little difference in belief between the Anglican and the Roman Catholic faiths. Tract XC appeared in 1841; in 1845, the year of Browning's poem, its author, John Henry Newman, became a Roman Catholic. Newman's conversion to Catholicism was momentous if not unexpected. Browning was by birth, training and temperament a Nonconformist Protestant who always distrusted the 'raree-show' of Catholic ritual, and he distrusted as well the Roman church's dogmatic restrictions on human thought. In 1842 he had portrayed the petty spite of a ritualist monk (*Soliloquy of the Spanish Cloister*) and a priest's violation of the secrecy of Confession to betray a Spanish revolutionary (*The Confessional*). In *The Bishop Orders His Tomb*, the dying sixteenth-century Roman Bishop ordering his tomb continues Browning's commentary upon the reactionary forces of the 1840s.

The Bishop's world is, of course, not the medieval world. He belongs to the decadent late Renaissance; and he embodies, in John Ruskin's famous words, that period's 'worldliness, inconsistency, pride, hypocrisy, ignorance of itself, love of art, of luxury, and of good Latin'. The basic flaw of the Renaissance churchman is that he has confounded the physical with the spiritual. He is the heir of centuries of ritualism. Because of the period in which he lives and because of his own senility he is not able to distinguish between 'outward and visible symbols' and inward and spiritual reality. To him the dome of the church has become the dome of heaven 'where live the Angels'; God really is 'made and eaten' during the Eucharist; he really can, through intercession with St Praxed, get horses, rare books, and mistresses for his sons. As his monologue progresses he becomes an object of humour and then of sympathy. Often it is his fusion of the physical and the spiritual which makes him laughable; sometimes it is his mixture of the sacred and the profane, as evidenced in his description of a bas-relief he wants for his tomb:

> The Saviour at his sermon on the mount,
> Saint Praxed in a glory, and one Pan
> Ready to twitch the Nymph's last garment off,
> And Moses with the tables. . . .

He becomes pathetic as his senile confusion deepens and as he begins to sense that his sons will not grant his wish for a magnificent tomb of marble. They will probably bury him in a tomb of sandstone of

> Clammy squares which sweat
> As if the corpse they keep were oozing through. . . .

The satiric edge of this poem is somewhat dulled by Browning's success in creating a convincingly real human personality. Satire requires *type* or flat characters at whose obvious follies or weaknesses the reader is invited to laugh. By the time his monologue has ended, the Bishop is no longer *typical* of anything; he is not representative of The Corrupt Renaissance Churchman. He has become, so to speak, himself – unique and individual. Sensual and unconsciously vain, the Bishop is appreciative of beauty, whether it be found in stone or language or women. To assure himself of the tomb that he so desperately desires, he cajoles, commands, bribes, threatens, and plays upon any sympathy or vestigial filial piety his sons may have. Because they obstinately withhold their promise, the Bishop even proposes a compromise on the quality of stone. Then, through his confused mind, drift scraps of Latin, pious homilies, and the sinister eyes of their mother. Once he has realized that all strategies have failed, he is capable of sudden anger:

> There, leave me, there!
> For ye have stabbed me with ingratitude
> To death – ye wish it – God, ye wish it! Stone –
> Gritstone, a-crumble!

Just as suddenly, he relapses into peaceful acceptance that his plea has failed; and he takes gloating satisfaction in remembering that it was he, not his rival Gandolf, who had the love of a beautiful woman.

E. M. Forster has said that a 'round' character, as opposed to a type or 'flat' character, has the capacity to surprise the reader. Such a character is sufficiently complex so that his behaviour is not predictable. Forster was proposing a test for characters in realistic novels, but Browning's Bishop would certainly pass that test. With this poem, Browning brought into English poetry qualities which had previously been reserved to the realistic novel. To the eyes of Charles Kingsley this poem might be just so much 'Italianesque pedantry', but the next generation of readers recognized Browning's kinship with the novelists. Oscar Wilde would call him 'the most supreme writer of fiction', and offer this comparison with the novelist George Meredith: 'Meredith is a prose-Browning, and so is Browning.' Gerard Manley Hopkins and Robert Louis Stevenson noted the resemblance of Browning to Balzac, but both preferred the French novelist. To Swinburne, however, a Browning monologue was a 'model of intense and punctilious realism . . . so triumphant a thing that on its own ground it can be matched by no poet; to match it we must look back to Balzac'. Hopkins and Swin-burne were talking about *The Ring and the Book* (1868–9); Stevenson about *The Inn Album* (1875). But by the middle of the 1840s, in *The Bishop Orders His Tomb*, Browning had fully displayed his genius for 'intense and punctilious realism'. That poem was the culmination of ten years of experiments which began with *Porphyria's Lover* and *Johannes Agricola* in 1836. It would be another full decade before, in 1855, he would publish his full gallery of realistic portraits, *Men and Women*.

There is a great variety among the poems and plays published in the eight issues of *Bells and Pomegranates*. When they were collected into a single volume in 1849, Matthew Arnold would complain of 'a confused multitudinousness'. Browning's sources of inspiration were equally various. Many were drawn from reading he had done for his plays or for *Sordello*; others grew out of his second journey to Italy, made in 1844. A surprising number are the result of contemporary occasions or issues. *Cavalier Tunes*, 'healthy and English', Kingsley said, celebrate the bicentennial of the English Civil War; *Cristina* comments on the abdication in 1840 of Queen Cristina of Spain; *Incident in a French Camp* is a timely anecdote about Napoleon, whose body was returned and buried in Paris in 1841. Few modern readers would suspect that behind the exotic title and elaborate rhyme scheme (*ride* rhymes sixty-five times in forty lines) of *Through the Metidja to Abd-el-Kadr* is a poem memorializing the Algerian struggle for independence from French colonial power. Browning's poems of the 1840s also begin to reveal that his vision was more broadly 'European' or cosmopolitan than that of most English Victorian authors. Among the settings or subjects in the thirty-six poems and six plays are Spain, France, Italy, Switzerland, Bavaria, Holstein, Provence, Belgium, Greece, Sardinia, Hungary, and, for good measure, references to Moscow and Transylvania. The 1840s was a period of intense seeking after national identities. Browning, sometimes playfully and sometimes seriously, joins that mood. In *Nationality in Drinks* he finds the essence of France in Claret, Hungary in Tokay, but England in Nelson and 'British Beer'. The original titles of several of his poems suggest that he often thought of the poems as illustrations of essential national characteristics: thus, *My Last Duchess* was originally *Italy* and the *Italian in England* was *Italy in England*. The change of titles for the collected edition of 1849 suggests that Browning realized that his characters were too individual and too particular to be mere national types. The change of *The Bishop Orders His Tomb at*

Saint Praxed's Church (*Rome, 15 –*) from the earlier *The Tomb at St. Praxed's* further illustrates Browning's penchant for the particular; the change also draws the reader's attention away from the tomb itself and focuses attention on the important action of *ordering* the tomb.

The changes in titles Browning made for the collected edition of 1849 raise a question of how conscious he was of the form and the direction which his experiments were taking during the decade. Numerous other changes were made in most poems; they were not made, as he promised his publishers, 'by cutting them up and reconstructing them, but by affording just the proper revision they ought to have had before they were printed at all'. *Pauline, Strafford*, and *Sordello* were left out. Often the changes bear the influence of Elizabeth Barrett Browning. Long before their famous correspondence and courtship began in 1845, they had admired each other's poetry. He was chivalrously un-critical, as typified by the opening words of his first letter to her: 'I love your verses with all my heart, dear Miss Barrett. . . .' Her craftsman's eyes were more open, especially to the difficulty of his language. A few months after Browning's first letter she wrote to another correspondent: 'He cuts his language into bits – and one has to join them together, as young children do their dissected maps.' Many of the changes made in 1849 after Robert and Elizabeth had been married three years were attempts at clarity. It was Elizabeth who convinced him to explain publicly his title *Bells and Pomegranates*; she also hoped he would supply more helpful titles to individual poems or 'some word of introduction as others do, you know. . . .' She chided him for his 'Sordelloisms' and the 'Sphynxine' nature of his poems. Yet, there is little in their letters to suggest that either Browning or Miss Barrett recognized, as later generations have, that his particular talent was for the 'dramatic lyric' or monologue. One letter, however, expresses more intimately than his many prefaces, his commitment to, indeed deep need for, a mode of poetry that is 'dramatic in principle': 'My poetry is far from "the completest expression of my being" – I hate to refer to it, or could I tell you why, wherefore. . . . You speak out, *you*, – I only make men and women speak – give you the truth broken into prismatic hues, and fear the pure white light. . . .'

Ten years later he would dedicate his two volumes of *Men and Women* to Elizabeth. Those two volumes testify not only to Browning's varied and mature talent; they also mark an important cultural shift. Taken collectively, the poems in those volumes tell us that truth, 'the white light', is conditioned and broken by human individuality; that the best we can do is record versions or 'perspectives' towards reality. In America, Herman Melville was exploring this 'maddening ambiguity of the universe' in *Moby-Dick* (1851) and *Pierre; or The Ambiguities* (1853); Nathaniel Hawthorne was exploiting the shadow realm of romantic fantasy for much the same reason, while Walt Whitman confidently embraced the infinite variety of the universe in *Leaves of Grass*, published the same year as *Men and Women*. In France, Flaubert's *Madame Bovary* (1856) analysed the tragic effects of romantic idealism and shocked the French public with his own version of reality, a version as publicly unacceptable as the more sordid ones offered by Baudelaire in *Les Fleurs du mal* (1857), from which objective reality had nearly disappeared completely. Manet's canvasses would soon insist that art should portray how we look at the world rather than what we think the world is. Browning's dramatic monologues were an excellent form to embody this new uncertainty. The form, in Robert Langbaum's words, 'imitates not life, but a particular perspective towards life, somebody's experience of it'.[3] During the 1840s Browning developed and mastered a way of rendering the 'prismatic hues' of human experience. At the beginning of the 1840s, in *Sordello*, Browning still allowed himself to enter the poem. 'We take leave of Mr Browning at the end of *Sordello*,' wrote James Russell Lowell in the *North American Review* in 1848, 'and, except in some shorter lyrics, see no more of him. His men and women *are* men and women, and not Mr Browning masquerading in different-coloured dominos.'

4

The Eighteen-Fifties

Men and Women

Robert Browning is a name which will serve the future
historian of English literature of the nineteenth century to point
the moral of genius unfaithful to its trust. . . . He commits the
crime of a man who, entrusted with the germ of a great scientific
discovery, and endowed with the faculties to work it out to a
clear result, refuses to undergo the labour necessary for this
purpose. We believe that Mr. Browning might, had he chosen,
have become the interpreter of our modern life to us. . . .

Review in *Fraser's*, 1855

I am rather surprised that Browning's conversation should be so
clear, and so much to the purpose at the moment, since his poetry
can seldom proceed far without running into the high grass of
latent meanings and obscure illusions.

Nathaniel Hawthorne, 1858

By the time the revolutions of 1848 came and passed, Robert and
Elizabeth Browning were installed in their Casa Guidi apartments in
Florence. There they would live until Mrs Browning's death in 1861.
England and America became places of refuge for many continental
political exiles after 1848. It was rather characteristic of Browning to
go in the opposite direction a couple of years ahead of time. The
Brownings were not, of course, conscious ex-patriots in the way
Byron and Shelley had been and so many twentieth-century artists
were to be. They went to Italy immediately after their marriage in
1846 in the hope that the milder climate would restore Elizabeth's
health and in the certainty that her £300 a year from an inheritance
would go further there. They also went there because it was the
foreign country Browning knew and loved best from his earlier

journeys and his studies: 'Italy', he said, had been his 'university'. They remained because it did prove healthier and cheaper, because their son was born there, because Casa Guidi (filled with cheaply purchased antique furniture and works of art) became their home, where 'people fall in for coffee and talk'. An extended visit to London and Paris in 1851-2 confirmed their decision to continue to live in Florence. Elizabeth learned painfully that any reconciliation with her father, almost psychotically estranged by her marriage, was impossible. Browning's English home, too, was gone. His mother had died in 1849. In 1852 his father lost a breach-of-promise suit brought by a Mrs Von Muller. To avoid paying her an £800 judgment, Browning hurriedly removed his father and sister to Paris, where they lived until the father's death in 1866.

The Brownings made that first journey back to London via Paris, taking advantage of the cheap railway rates designed to encourage visitors to the Crystal Palace Exhibition of 1851. In Paris they talked with Tennyson, who, in his new position as Poet Laureate, had celebrated the exhibition of The Industry of All Nations:

> ... shapes and hues of Art divine!
> All of beauty, all of use,
> That one fair planet can produce.

In private he told the Brownings that England was 'the greatest nation in the world and the most vulgar'. No student of economic statistics could deny the first assertion; no student of industrial and domestic design could deny the latter. The Great Exhibition was a fit symbol of the new industrial society Britain had become. It also inaugurated twenty years of increasing prosperity and general domestic and international peace following the turmoil of the 1840s. The exhibits of the other nations showed that they shared Britain's taste for excessive and eclectic decoration if not her industrial might. The 1850s and 1860s were to be the high point of that Victorian culture which later generations were to find so distasteful for its overstuffed furniture and its equally stuffy morality, its sentimentality, hypocrisy, inhibition and prudery. It was a time when, in G. M. Young's masterful phrase, 'old lords have to guard their words for fear of shocking young lords'. When William Morris married his Jane in 1858, he found nothing in the London shops with which a man of taste could furnish his home; he decided to found a firm to make his own furniture and fabrics. That decision would lead him to a critique of industrial modes of production, and finally into

Marxism and into the streets in protest. But that would be in the 1880s; there was little protest in the 1850s.

Even the irascible Carlyle, whom the Brownings saw often on their visit to London in 1851, moderated in the 1850s the angry sense of apocalypse he had expressed during the previous decade. He accompanied the Brownings on their return to Paris in September, venting his anger more at railway timetables and porters than at the system which had brought them into being. The Brownings stayed on in Paris through the winter and spring. There they witnessed more evidence of the new stability which was coming to Europe. On December 2, from their hotel window, they watched Louis-Napoleon parade down the Champs-Elysée after he had applied a *coup de grace* to the republic established after the 1848 revolution. Palmerston, who like Queen Victoria thought Louis-Napoleon 'safe', approved the act. Elizabeth thoroughly admired this man who 'rode in the name of the people', but Browning was 'not as *one*' with her. A decade later Elizabeth died mourning Cavour but still trusting that Louis-Napoleon would unify Italy; Browning would wait until after the surrender of Louis-Napoleon to the Prussians at Sedan in 1870 before he would publish his version of what excuses the man 'was likely to make for himself, if inclined to try':

> A conservator, call me, if you please,
> Not a creator nor destroyer: one
> Who keeps the world safe.

Such is the defence Prince Hohenstiel-Schwangau, alias Napoleon III, gives for himself in Browning's poem of 1871. Browning's distrust of and disdain for the man had been continuous since 1851, but he waited twenty years to bring the man into his poetry and when he did he, typically, allowed Louis-Napoleon to plead a good case for himself. Marx's reaction to Louis-Napoleon's assumption of power was immediate and direct: Louis-Napoleon brought political stability to France and Europe by exchanging 'Liberty, Equality, Fraternity' for 'Infantry, Cavalry, Artillery'.

The two dominant features in G. M. Young's portrait of Victorian England are 'the transition from oligarchic to democratic representation' and 'the dethronement of ancient faith by natural science and historical criticism'.[1] In the 1850s the political and economic unrest of the previous decade was temporarily calmed and, to a large extent, was replaced by religious and scientific issues. The 'ancient faith' had been steadily eroded by rationalism since the Renaissance, but by the middle of the nineteenth century the problem of belief in traditional religion had become acute throughout western culture. Kierkegaard might argue in the 1840s that the agony of belief was a-historical, that each individual must go through it; but many individual Victorians, with a strong sense of history, expressed their awareness that theirs was a time of unprecedented religious crisis. Many would assent to Arnold's famous formulation that they were 'Wandering between two worlds, one dead, The other powerless to be born'. Those lines were published in 1855, the same year as Browning's *Bishop Blougram's Apology*. Browning's Roman Catholic Bishop believes, but he admits that believing and being a bishop of a traditional church was a bit awkward in the middle of the nineteenth century:

It's through my coming in the tail of time,
Nicking the minute with a happy tact.
Had I been born three hundred years ago
They'd say, 'What's strange? Blougram of course believes';
And, seventy years since, 'disbelieves of course'.
But now, 'He may believe; and yet, and yet
How can he?'

In *Christmas-Eve and Easter-Day*, Browning's first poem of the new decade, he asks that question at some length. The closing words of that 142-page poem were to be: 'who can say?'

Christmas-Eve and Easter-Day was written quickly during the winter of 1849–50 and was published in time for the Easter trade in April 1850. Though greatly overshadowed by two other personal testaments of nineteenth-century doubt and faith published later in the year (Tennyson's *In Memoriam* and Wordsworth's *The Prelude*) Browning's poem remains an interesting personal as well as cultural document. The *Christmas-Eve* section dramatizes reactions to three modes of Christian worship: English Nonconformity as revealed during a service in a Dissenter chapel in a London slum; Roman Catholicism (and by implication, High Anglicanism) as expressed in the rich pageantry of Mass in St Peter's in Rome; finally, we see a group of German rationalists in a Gottingen lecture hall trying to derive some sustenance from the husks of Christianity left to them after David Strauss's Hegelian analysis of the Myth of Christ had been perpetrated in 1835. The *Easter-Day* section is a debate on 'How very hard it is to be/A Christian' in the year 1850. The narrator examines the new philosophical, historical, geological and paleontological evidences until he spins 'dervish-like . . . through circling sciences,/Philosophies, and histories!' Then, in a visionary trance, he affirms and submits to belief in a resurrected Christ. For Browning, the affirmation of a divine Jesus is primarily an affirmation of God's love. Man's faculties can discover in nature God's power, but only by His incarnation in Christ is Divine Love made evident to man. This was an idea which Browning would hold and elaborate throughout his life.[2]

Still, it is not completely clear just what Browning did believe when he wrote this poem; again, it is the dramatic form into which he casts these thoughts that causes the trouble. Those other two poems of 1850, *In Memoriam* and *The Prelude*, are openly confessional poems. The sentiments expressed there by Tennyson and Wordsworth are, within the limits of art, the sentiments held by the authors themselves at the time the lines were written. Both of those poems end with affirmations of divine love and order in the universe: Wordsworth by his description of the visionary experience atop Mount Snowdon; Tennyson with his powerful assertion of faith in

> That God, which ever lives and loves,
>> One God, one law, one element.
>> And one far-off divine event,
> To which the whole creation moves.

The man who attends the various religious services and the one who experiences the visionary trance in Browning's poem are not, ostensibly at least, Robert Browning. They have many striking similarities to the Robert Browning who grew up listening to a thousand sermons in the York Street Chapel, who disliked the 'raree-show' of Catholic and High Anglican ritual, who doubtless had read George Eliot's 1846 translation of Strauss's *Leben Jesu*. Also, Browning had been nearly prostrated by the recent death of his pious mother, and he was married to a woman who frequently urged him to write 'in the directest and most impressive way, the mask thrown off [in] your own voice speaking of yourself'. But still the mask remained, however transparent.

The mask is that of a man who has come up on the train from Manchester and has sought shelter from the rain in the Zion Chapel. Caught, he remains for the service and sermon, 'words and tones,/(So many texts in so many groans). . . .' Among the congregation are the fat old woman twirling her thumbs and maternally devouring the preacher; a man with a handkerchief tied around his jaw bandaging a 'horrible wen'; a shoemaker's apprentice trying discreetly and chokingly to stifle his coughs. The man flings himself from the church in exasperation and near the gas street-lamp meets a spirit who conducts him – Scrooge-like – on a Christmas Eve visit to St Peter's and then to a lecture hall in Germany. The Mass at St Peter's, with its music and incense, is in complete contrast to the austere and sparsely attended Zion Chapel. In Rome

> The whole Basilica alive!
> Men in the Chancel, body and nave,
> Men on the pillars' architrave,
> Men on statues, men on the tombs
> With popes and kings in their porphyry wombs,
> All famishing in expectation
> Of the main altar's consummation.

When the man from Manchester complains that so much beauty clouds the intellect, the spirit deposits him in the Gottingen lecture hall where the audience 'Ranged decent and symmetrical' await their Straussian lecture

> . . . while ascends
> By the creaking rail to the lecture-desk,
> Step by step deliberate
> Because of his cranium's over-freight,
> Three parts sublime to one grotesque,
> If I had proved an accurate guesser,
> The hawk-nosed, high-cheekboned Professor.

The lecture over, the narrator sums up his impressions of the various services by describing what they do to the air from which he should like to breathe a healthy Christianity. The Dissenter poisons the air 'by his daily fare's vulgarity,/Its gust of broken meat and garlic'; the Catholic and High Anglican by the 'frankincense's fuming'. But the rationalist Higher Critic

> . . . leaves no air to poison;
> Pumps out with ruthless ingenuity
> Atom by atom, and leaves you – vacuity.

The man awakens with a start back in Zion Chapel, the woman next to him shifting contemptuously away. He must have dozed off and dreamt his visits. Yet he had been alert enough to hear the sermon, for he asks ingenuously:

Unless I heard it, could I have judged it?
Could I report as I do at the close,
First, the preacher speaks through his nose:
Second, his gesture is too emphatic:
Thirdly, to waive what's pedagogic,
The subject-matter itself lacks logic:
Fourthly, the English is ungrammatic.

Nevertheless, he prefers this service to what he has seen at St Peter's and in the German lecture hall. So, without further apology, he joins in

The last five verses of the third section
Of the seventeenth hymn of Whitefield's Collection,
To conclude with the doxology.

His choice of Nonconformity among the Christian forms is something less than enthusiastic; and the satiric, humorous tone consistently undercuts serious religious meditation into which the man from Manchester occasionally lapses. In his old age a cult grew up around Browning, 'the religious and philosophical teacher'; but that was after he had written more gravely argumentative poems. Many of the same religious ideas would be expressed in his later poems, but in this poem of 1850 the ideas are imbedded in high-spirited colloquial humour and what Donald Smalley has called the 'stark realism' of portraiture and setting.[3] Reviewers, who accepted and often insisted upon realism in novels, would seldom tolerate it in poetry, particularly poetry that dealt with Christian belief: 'Realism in Art,' one warned solemnly, 'has Truth as an Aim, Ugliness as a pitfall.' Another objected to 'the mysteries of faith, doubt, and eternity' being expressed in 'strange and offensive oddities of versification'. The levity is less insistent in the *Easter-Day* section. A new narrator, a man who reads Fourier and studies the latest geological and paleontological findings, sardonically hopes that someone will discover a 'mummy-scrap' to prove that Moses lived or find a cavity the size and form of Jonah's whale. But it was his vision of the Day of Judgment that brought him to belief. Since that experience he has been addicted to watching the Easter dawn over the 'chimney-stacks and roofs' of London. He is not sure that the vision was authentic:

Was this a vision? False or true?
Since then, three varied years are spent,
And commonly my mind is bent

To think it was a dream – be sure
A mere dream and distemperature. . . .

The former certainty of belief almost returns as the poem ends:

> But Easter-Day breaks! But
> Christ rises! Mercy every way
> Is infinite, – and who can say?

The irresolution and indecisiveness of this poem is typical of many mid-Victorian poems. It reflects a condition of mind which Tennyson called that 'damned vacillating state'. Few poets could sustain the mystical certitude Emily Brontë expressed just before she died in 1848:

> No coward soul is mine,
> No trembler in the world's storm-troubled sphere;
> I see Heaven's glories shine,
> And faith shines equal, arming me from fear.

Hers was a personal and intuitive assurance; the new sciences and the historical examinations of biblical texts destroyed rather than bolstered such assurances. Ruskin complained that he could hear the clink of geologists' hammers 'at the end of every cadence' of the Bible verses. The careful philological study of ancient religious texts causes Browning's Bishop Blougram to comment that 'Greek endings' have become 'each a little passing-bell that signifies some faith's about to die'. Fossils of extinct species suggested to Tennyson that God and Nature were at war rather than in unity as earlier romantic poets, particularly Wordsworth, had taught. His *In Memoriam*, in which so many Victorian intellectuals and scientists recognized their own private spiritual crises, is essentially a poem which counterpoints or alternates between moods of doubt and faith, despair and hope. The mid-century poems of Arthur Hugh Clough, with whom Browning had talked in Florence in 1849, exhibit a similar vacillation between a powerful will to believe and the inability to do so. Doubt among the intellectuals was paralleled by indifference to or ignorance of Christian worship among the masses. During the Easter season of 1851, a religious census revealed that only forty per cent of the nearly 18,000,000 people in England and Wales attended any service at all. A slight majority of those who did attended Dissenter services. If Browning chose Zion Chapel in his poem, he had voted with the majority. The Roman Catholic population consisted largely of impoverished Irish immigrants living in urban slums where there were few churches in which to hold services and few priests to officiate. The English fears of a 'Papal Invasion' when Pius the Ninth re-established the Catholic hierarchy in England in 1850 must reflect insecurity rather than reality.

Browning wrote a number of other religious poems during the early 1850s and published them in his *Men and Women* of 1855. Among them, there are four major ones which address themselves rather specifically to contemporary spiritual unease: *Saul, An Epistle Containing the Strange Medical Experience of Karshish, Cleon,* and *Bishop Blougram's Apology.* The first three confront, from different historical directions, the issue of the divinity of Jesus. The fourth is an ingenious and elaborate defence of traditional Christian belief in the contemporary world. All are dramatic in form: *Saul* is spoken by David, *An Epistle* by an Arab physician, *Cleon* by a Greek philosopher, and *Bishop Blougram* by a man closely resembling Cardinal Wiseman, who in 1850 became Catholic Archbishop of Westminster. Taken together these poems exhibit much of the 'depth, intensity, irony, paradox, wit, whimsy and humor'[4] which mark Browning's mature achievement, while at the same time they illustrate a variety of Browning's characteristic religious attitudes.

Saul is the earliest of these poems, having been published as a fragment in 1845, then completed probably soon after his return to Florence from the 1851-2 journey to London and Paris. It is also more lyrical than the other three poems: the language more heightened and formal than the colloquial, conversational style of the later poems. Further, *Saul* is less a dramatic monologue: David relates his experience with the despairing Saul not to any particular listener but much as he does in the *Psalms,* to mankind and to God. William Morris, then an undergraduate at Oxford, referred to it in his enthusiastic review of 1856 as an 'ecstasy of prayer and love', a phrase that well describes the dominant tone. David comes to the tent of King Saul to try his singing to unburden Saul's dark despair. David's description of Saul prefigures a crucified Christ and at the same time reveals Browning's awareness that the Higher Critics associated the Christ-figure with fertility cults:

> He stood as erect as the tent-prop, both arms
> stretched out wide
> On the great cross-support in the centre,
> that goes to each side;

He relaxed not a muscle, but hung there as,
    caught in his pangs
And waiting his change, the king-serpent all
    heavily hangs,
Far away from his kind, in the pine, till
    deliverance come
With the spring-time, – so agonized Saul, drear
    and stark, blind and dumb.

David's song, listing in traditional Old Testament manner the glories of God's power, fails to rouse Saul. Then David, caught up in a mystical rapture, becomes a vehicle of God's revelation: the imperfections of man's world are evidence of the perfection of God, and David's human love for Saul is evidence of God's perfect love for man, a love which will become incarnate in Christ. Saul is restored by the song; and David, exhausted and dazed, moves off towards his home through a landscape filled with 'wonder and dread'.

Absent from *Saul* is the vacillation and debate which create the mood of uncertainty in *Christmas-Eve and Easter-Day*. David's ecstatic song asserts, rather than argues for, the authenticity of divine revelation and of divine incarnation. The fact that the revelation comes to David while he is in a state of divine madness does not cast doubt on the authenticity of the revelation; on the contrary, it is only through David's enraptured, mystical song that God's truth can be apprehended. David is a successful Poet-as-Hero in a way that Sordello, for example, had not been. David is like Shelley, about whom Browning wrote a long essay during the autumn of 1851 while in Paris: David's song gives him 'simultaneous perception of Power and Love in the absolute. . . .' Implicit in *Saul* is Browning's trust of intuitive knowledge and distrust of reason. He values song over speech, art over argument. This emphasis upon personal, intuitive apprehension of truth creates a paradox for students of Browning: the tough-minded and learned poet, so skilled at putting ingenious rational arguments into the mouths of his characters, often allies himself to the strong anti-intellectual current which runs through the nineteenth century and into the twentieth. His heroes and heroines are those who apprehend and act upon truths not open to intellectual inquiry. Although Browning's mind was always quick to trace the possible pessimistic implications of the new scientific and rationalist thought, his own faith in a loving God was never seriously shaken. Indeed, even while so frequently writing poems about grotesque evil, he maintained a kind of bumptious optimism while many of his contemporaries moved towards despair. Browning's acknowledged optimism was intuitive, almost visceral. This element in Browning's life and work is similar to the stance of D. H. Lawrence, who could dismiss the Darwinian hypothesis by thumping his guts and declaring that he did not feel the theory's truth there. Browning's position simply – too simply – was this: the imperfections of this world implied God's perfection, but divine perfection was unknowable to man except in moments of mystical rapture or intuitive apprehension; further, such apprehensions are ineffable and cannot be translated to others through the distorting media of reason and human speech. However, 'song' (and by extension all great art) can lead the artist to such perception and can at the same time approximate it for others. Browning worked out his ideas about the function of the artist in some detail in that essay on Shelley he wrote not long before he finished *Saul* by adding the sections which depict David in the act of inspired, revelatory song. Though Browning's own greatest contributions are those poems in which he depicts in a rugged and realistic conversational style human beings caught up in what one of his characters calls 'the filthy rags of speech', Browning consistently looked upon 'song' and music as the highest of the arts; and at the end of his masterwork, *The Ring and the Book*, he rather boastfully expressed to his reader the hope that the poem would 'note by note, bring music from your mind,/Deeper than ever e'en Beethoven dived. . . .' That a great realistic poet should rank music above his own medium is, perhaps, a bit surprising; but Browning had a deep love and experience with music, and he seems to have shared the widespread nineteenth-century notion that music could more successfully embody ineffable truth than could other arts. That notion has less currency in the twentieth century. The notion that there was any absolute truth to be known has become almost bankrupt in our century, thanks largely to the success of nineteenth-century scientific rationalism against which David's song was a protest.

In *An Epistle* and *Cleon* Browning's gift for writing realistic monologues came into the service of religious controversy. *Saul* had been written in imitation of the 'mad' eighteenth-century poet Christopher Smart's *Song of David*, itself an imitation of the *Psalms*. The two new poems took their form from the experiments Browning had made in dramatic monologues in *Bells and Pomegranates* and, in part, from the nature of the contemporary controversy itself. The Higher Critics had based their destructive analyses of the Christ Myth upon careful scrutiny of biblical texts and other contemporary documents. *An Epistle* and *Cleon* purport to be such documents: both are manuscript letters or 'epistles' written by men living soon after the death of Jesus. Browning was to use this device of creating an 'historical document' with greater elaboration in *A Death in the Desert* in 1864. His knowledge of the physical sciences was not profound, although in *Easter-Day*, for example, he could turn the image of a fossil being uncovered by a geologist's hammer into an elaborate simile. But his knowledge of what we would now call scientific historiography was deeper. There he met Strauss, and later Renan, on a common ground. Since *Paracelsus*, Browning's poetic imagination had been consistently historical – and *historical* as opposed to just a general interest in the past. Many of his poems and plays are informed by, and sometimes marred by, his careful and extensive research into historical documents. Browning, more than any other poet of his time, reflects what Morse Peckham has called 'the historicization of European culture'.[5] It was a force which made itself felt in the romantic novels of Scott, Cooper, and Hugo as well as in the analytic methods of Marx or Cuvier and the great 'time sciences' of the nineteenth century – geology, biology, and archeology. Historians, most notably the German school headed by Niebhur and Leopold von Ranke, had developed methods of historical inquiry imitated by the Higher Critics. Browning had developed a strikingly similar perspective towards historical materials; particularly similar, as Morse Peckham has convincingly argued, to Ranke's emphasis upon documentary evidence and evaluation of 'the sources of the documents by seizing the personality of the writer of the primary document and evaluating what he says in terms of what he is'.[6] Peckham is essentially concerned with *The Ring and the Book* (1868–9), which was based on actual historical documents; but his description of Browning's method could well be applied to the imaginary historical characters Browning created in *An Epistle* and *Cleon*.

An Epistle is a letter written by an Arab physician Karshish to his master Abib. His quest for new scientific and medical knowledge has brought him, in the year A.D. 66, to the Palestinian town of Bethany. The town, he informs his correspondent in macabre medical-student humour, is near Jerusalem, lying 'scarce the distance thence/A man with plague-sores at the third degree/Runs till he drops down dead'. He begins to relay to his master his new-found knowledge of herbs, cures for sleeping sickness, odd behaviour in spiders; but he breaks off, fearful that the Syrian who will carry the letter might steal the secrets.

So he turns to an account of a man called Lazarus who suffers from a 'case of mania – subinduced/By epilepsy, at the turning-point/Of trance prolonged unduly some three days'. The case is common and insignificant enough that it will not matter if the Syrian steals the letter. Or so he writes to his master before whom he is reluctant to reveal how disturbing his meeting with Lazarus has been. His rationalist attitude and scientific training have not prepared him for the sense of religious awe he feels while learning Lazarus's story. His first meeting with Lazarus suggests something of the same 'wonder and dread' David felt after his visionary experience while singing to Saul: 'I met him thus', he tells Abib:

> I crossed a ridge of short sharp broken hills
> Like an old lion's cheek teeth. Out there came
> A moon made like a face with certain spots
> Multiform, manifold, and menacing:
> Then a wind rose behind me. So we met
> In this old sleepy town at unaware,
> The man and I.

Lazarus, who was raised from the dead by a 'learned leech' from Nazareth, is as menacing to Karshish's orderly, reasonable view of the world as was the landscape in which they met. He vacillates between possible belief and scientific scepticism as he describes Lazarus's history and present state of child-like gentleness and love. If Lazarus's version of his experience is true then here is evidence of God's love as well as His power. But Karshish, inhibited by his training and by Abib to whom he writes, while at the same time deeply moved by what he has seen and heard, can neither accept nor reject the implication that God's love has been revealed and made flesh in the wizard from Nazareth who perished during a rebellion several years ago:

> The very God! think, Abib; dost thou think?
> So, the All-Great, were the All-Loving too –
> So, through the thunder comes a human voice
> Saying, 'O heart I made, a heart beats here!
> Face, my hands fashioned, see it in myself!
> Thou hast no power nor mayst conceive of mine,
> But love I gave thee, with myself to love,
> And thou must love me who have died for thee!'
> The madman saith He said so: it is strange.

The power of *An Epistle* lies in its persuasive portraiture of a man receptive to new experience; his rational curiosity and his emotions are engaged by phenomena inexplicable by reason alone. Karshish, like the kings who visit the infant Jesus in T. S. Eliot's *Journey of the Magi*, can be 'no longer at ease' with his former version of the world. The document, i.e., the poem, in which Karshish records his experience is hesitant and indecisive, partly because he has no terms to articulate this 'strange medical experience' and partly because he does not wish to appear a fool in the eyes of his master Abib. Still, the document exists because Karshish cannot ignore the implications of what he has seen:

> I half resolve to tell thee, yet I blush,
> What set me off a-writing first of all.
> An itch, a sting to write, a tang!
> For, be it this town's barrenness – or else
> The Man had something in the look of him –
> His case has struck me far more than 't is worth.

The aged first-century Greek philosopher Cleon is less open to the Christian revelation than was Karshish. Cleon ends his letter by arrogantly assuring his correspondent King Protus that he should not be curious about the new doctrine being preached by the Apostle Paul:

> ... one called Paulus; we have heard his fame
> Indeed, if Christus be not one with him –
> I know not, nor am troubled much to know.
> Thou canst not think a mere barbarian Jew,
> As Paulus proves to be, one circumcised,
> Hath access to a secret shut from us?

Karshish reflects much of nineteenth-century scientific spirit that Browning would have admired: its eager curiosity and healthy but not destructive scepticism. Cleon reflects a less admirable current of nineteenth-century thought: the frequently expressed smug assumption that the nineteenth century had 'progressed' dramatically beyond all previous civilizations. At its most banal this spirit could lead Macaulay to measure human progress in terms of miles of railway track or yards of cheap cotton cloth. Or it would lead Kingsley's hero in *Yeast* (1848) into a diatribe against Roman Catholicism:

> When your party compare sneeringly Romish Sanctity, and
> English Civilization, I say, 'Take you the Sanctity, and give me
> the Civilization!' ... Give me the political economist, the sanitary

reformer, the engineer; and take your saints and virgins, relics and miracles. The spinning-jenny and the railroad, Cunard's liners and the electric telegraph, are to me, if not to you, signs that we are, on some points at least, in harmony with the universe. . . .

At the same time, Henry David Thoreau, trying to march to a different drummer and avoid a life of 'quiet desperation', could remark wryly from his hut on Walden Pond: 'We are in great haste to construct a magnetic telegraph from Maine to Texas; but Maine and Texas, it may be, have nothing important to communicate.' Browning's Cleon combines, philosophically and without the technological imagery, these moods. He believes that men have reached the pinnacle of human progress with his culture in his time, i.e., Greece, circa A.D. 50; nevertheless, he senses the inadequacy of the accomplishments, and soberly agrees that 'Most progress is most failure'. He is something of a first-century Hegelian who has, as it were, misplaced his 'synthesis'. Cleon, with xenophobic blindness, views his own culture as the ultimate achievement of historic progress and 'In such a synthesis the labour ends'. Cleon is deeply dissatisfied, however; and at times he dares imagine 'Some future state revealed to us by Zeus,/Unlimited in capability/For joy. . . .' Yet he cannot open his eyes to Paul's message, a doctrine which 'could be held by no sane man'.

Cleon is nothing if not sane and reasonable. He carefully answers questions posed by Protus, drawing illustrations from geometric figures, the weight of air in a sphere, the selective improvement of grapes, plums, and flowers. He has himself successfully imitated all the arts of the past:

> That epos on thy hundred plates of gold
> Is mine, – and also the little chant,
> So sure to rise from every fishing-bark
> When, lights at prow, the seamen haul their net.
> The image of the sun-god on the phare,
> Men turn from the sun's self to see, is mine;
> The Poecile, o'er-storied its whole length,
> As thou didst hear, with painting, is mine too.
> I know the true proportions of a man
> And woman also, not observed before;
> And I have written three books on the soul,
> Proving absurd all written hitherto,
> And putting us to ignorance again.

He accounts for his achievement by enunciating a theory of the evolution of human consciousness beyond 'life's mechanics', the mere physical perfection man shares with animals. Gradually, as he elaborates this theory, Cleon's calm and reasonable tone gives way to a tone of personal, emotional involvement in the consequences of this human development:

> We struggle, fain to enlarge
> Our bounded physical recipiency,
> Increase our power, supply fresh oil to life,
> Repair the waste of age and sickness: no,
> It skills not!

He wonders whether it is Zeus's malice or carelessness that has given man the faculty to perceive unbounded possibility for joy while at the same time allowing that faculty, the 'soul', to perish with the body. Protus had suggested that Cleon should be consoled because his 'living works' of art will give him immortality. The thought only deepens Cleon's despair:

> Say rather that my fate is deadlier still,
> In this, that every day my sense of joy
> Grows more acute, my soul (intensified
> By power and insight) more enlarged, more keen. . . .

Cleon's horror that he, 'the feeling, thinking, acting man', must die becomes so intense that he imagines 'Some future state revealed to us by Zeus' in which his 'joy-hunger' can be satisfied. Cleon's terrible emotional desperation has brought him to a vision similar to that in which Christ was revealed to David; but Cleon stops short. He breaks off the letter by his arrogant dismissal of Paul as a 'mere barbarian Jew'.

Irony and convincingly realistic characterization are the key techniques used by Browning in these poems which pretend to be documents surviving from the first century of the Christian era. The ideal reader for these poems would be a mid-nineteenth-century Higher Critic whose method of studying documents is to seize 'the personality of the writer of the primary document' and to evaluate 'what he says in terms of what he is'. Cleon's knowledge of Paul's doctrine is only hearsay knowledge, 'gathered from a bystander', and he even suspects Paul and Christ to be one and the same man. He scorns Paul's teaching; but, then, he is a proud and accomplished man conditioned by the circumstance that he lives in what John Stuart Mill and followers of the French philosopher Saint-Simon called 'the critical or sceptical period of the Greek philosophers'. Matthew Arnold had depicted a similar man in his *Empedocles on Etna* (1852), a poem which Browning greatly admired. Ironically, though, Cleon's thought combined with his deep emotional needs has forced him to 'imagine' just such a doctrine as Paul preached on the Areopagus in Athens. Karshish's indecisive testimony is also conditioned by what Karshish, himself, is. An apprentice scientist, he examines one of the more famous 'miracles' from which, in the words of the Straussian lecturer in *Christmas-Eve*,

> This Myth of Christ is derivable;
> Demanding from the evidence,
> (Since plainly no such life was livable)
> How these phenomena should class?

Karshish's diagnosis of Lazarus's condition as 'mania – sub-induced/By epilepsy' satisfies Karshish no more than it satisfies the reader. His designation of the man who worked the cure as either a 'learned leech' or a 'wizard' is similarly unsatisfactory; he makes such a diagnosis and so classes Christ because (1) he has no other terms to explain the phenomenon, and (2) he wishes to appear tough-minded to his master. The overriding irony is that a man so inhibited both by historic and personal circumstance could arrive at the tentative conclusion that in Christ God revealed himself as 'the All-Great' and 'the All-Loving, too. . . .'

Bishop Blougram's Apology is the longest and most complex poem in Browning's *Men and Women*. It is also the most thoroughly contemporary in mood and topical allusion. Reading this poem it is easy to understand why the reviewer in *Fraser's* believed that Browning might 'have become the interpreter of our modern life'. The Bishop is modelled on a clearly recognizable public figure, Cardinal Wiseman, head of the newly established Catholic hierarchy in England. His conversation is saturated with details of European life at mid-century: the conversation takes place in a building recently (the stucco decorations still smell of the lime-kiln) designed by 'brother Pugin', and into the conversation drift the opinions of Newman, Strauss and Fichte as do references to the Crimean War, processes for making steel from iron at high temperatures, the power of *The Times* newspaper to humiliate a man by public exposure, the new Catholic dogma of the immaculate Conception and the impending one of Papal infallibility, the publication of all of Balzac's novels in a 'new edition fifty volumes long'. Reinforcing the topicality of the poem is Blougram's awareness that public opinion or judgment by one's peers is replacing traditional religiously-based codes of behaviour, his awareness of the function of 'role-playing' by public figures, his frequent recourse to the language of trade and commerce for his metaphors as in his rather bourgeois version of Pascal's wager. Here Blougram sarcastically refuses to join the reforming and sceptical tradition of Luther and Strauss because it would neither pay nor be a good gamble:

> State the facts,
> Read the right text, emancipate the world –
> The emancipated world enjoys itself
> With scarce a thank-you: Blougram told it first
> It could not *owe* a *farthing*, – not to him
> More than Saint Paul! 't would press its *pay*, you think?
> Then *add* there's still that plaguy hundredth *chance*
> Strauss may be wrong. And so a *risk* is run –
> For what *gain*?

The italics are mine, but the words are spoken (Browning steps in at the end to inform us) in conversation by

> Sylvester Blougram, styled *in partibus*
> *Episcopus, nec non* – (the deuce knows what
> It's changed to by our novel hierarchy)
> With Gigadibs the literary man. . . .

Gigadibs is the most fully drawn listener Browning had yet created in his dramatic monologues. He is the liberated Victorian intellectual who has, with self-conscious candour and honesty albeit unacknowledged naïveté, accepted the new science and Higher Criticism and has given up any pretensions to religious faith. He is no match for the intelligent, witty, sensitive, learned and worldly Bishop. Here is the devastating description Blougram gives Gigadibs to his face:

> You, Gigadibs, who, thirty years of age,
> Write stately for Blackwood's Magazine,
> Believe you see two points in Hamlet's soul
> Unseized by the Germans yet – which view you'll print –
> Meantime the best you have to show being still
> That lively lightsome article we took
> Almost for the true Dickens, – what's its name?

'The Slum and Cellar, or Whitechapel life
Limned after dark!' it made me laugh, I know,
And pleased a month, and brought you in ten pounds.

Gigadibs despises Blougram for either a hypocrite or a fool because
the Bishop continues at this late date in history to embrace the traditional Catholic faith. On Corpus Christi day over their after-dinner
wine, Blougram justifies himself with skilful casuistry and carefully
deflates Gigadibs' pretensions with obvious relish and urbane humour.
For the sake of argument, Blougram accepts Gigadibs' premise that an
intelligent and reasonable man can no longer believe in divine revelation; nevertheless, the Bishop goes on to prove that a life of faith is not
only possible but brings him the rewards of this world ('*Status, entourage*, worldly circumstance') and offers an insurance against the
uncertainties of the next world. Blougram's 'apologia' proceeds by
Blougram stating Gigadibs' assumptions and by anticipating his objec-
tions to the Bishop's logic. Gigadibs himself remains silent: he

... played with spoons, explored his plate's design,
And ranged the olive-stones about its edge. ...

Within a week of the conversation, Gigadibs has given up his life of a
free-thinking London intellectual and taken ship to become a farmer
in Australia.

Blougram's fertile imagination and his quick and lively intelligence
are too much for a third-rate journalist like Gigadibs. The wily Bishop
knows, for example, why the journalist and the English public find
him so fascinating: they are intrigued by the spectacle of so intelligent
and learned a man still holding to the ancient faith. He is engaged in a
public balancing act, and public curiosity focuses on his apparently
paradoxical personality just as it buys newspapers and novels to read
about

The honest thief, the tender murderer,
The superstitious atheist, demirep
That loves and saves her soul in new French books. ...

His wit is supple enough to turn the act of offering snuff to his guest
into a demonstration that doubt is good because it exercises and
strengthens faith just as a pinch of snuff excites and overcomes 'the
torpor of the inside-nose'. He can be eloquently persuasive as in his
assertion that it is impossible to guard total unbelief against occasional
incursions of belief: just when a man seems safest in his scepticism

... there's a sunset-touch,
A fancy from a flower-bell, some one's death,
A chorus-ending from Euripides, –
And that's enough for fifty hopes and fears
As old and new at once as nature's self,
To rap and knock and enter in our soul,
Take hands and dance there, a fantastic ring,
Round the ancient idol, on his base again, –
The grand *Perhaps*!

Blougram can also turn his casual reading to quick account. A French ethnologist whom he had recently read had argued that the custom of having sexual intercourse in private rather than in public originated because it was dangerous for primitive man to throw down his club and 'prosecute his loves' in the open field: some 'brother savage, club in hand' might knock the undefended lover on the head. If Gigadibs believes the ethnologist rather than the priest, why doesn't he – now that there are no 'brother savages' to knock him on the head – make love in public? act out his beliefs? or is he as 'conscious [a] coward and hypocrite' as he thinks Blougram to be?

Put natural religion to the test
You've just demolished the revealed with – quick,
Down to the root of all that checks your will,
All prohibition to lie, kill, and thieve,
Or even be an atheistic priest!

Blougram has pushed Gigadibs to the same conclusion that so horrified Dostoievski in *The Devils* and *The Brothers Karamazov*: take away the support of revealed religion and 'all is permissible'.

These few examples do not do justice to the variety and depth of Blougram's personality that Browning created in this 'remarkable poem of what we may call the dramatic-psychological kind. . . .' The praise came from George Eliot in her enthusiastic review of 1856; she, too, protested that 'the poem is too strictly consecutive for any fragments of it to be a fair specimen'. This tribute to the organic unity of his poem must have pleased Browning. Another review, one Browning believed to be by Cardinal Wiseman himself, must have puzzled and amused him: that reviewer complained that 'It is scandalous in Mr Browning *first* to show so plainly *whom* he means . . . *then* to go on sketching a fancy portrait which is abominably untrue. . . .'; the reviewer ends, however, maintaining that '*we should never feel surprise at his* [Browning's] *conversion*'. Browning could only feel pain and anger at reviewers who, for example, described the style of *Bishop Blougram's Apology* as 'a tissue of violent contrast and provoking incongruities – fine irony and coarse abuse, subtle reasoning and halting twaddle, the lofty and the low, the refined and the vulgar, earnestness and levity, outpoured pell-mell by the blustering yet "pawky" bishop over his wine'. The description is really quite accurate of Browning's revolutionary style, but the reviewer did not mean it as praise. There is a 'fine sense of discrimination which I never cease to meditate upon and admire in the public', Browning wrote to his publisher a few months later; 'they cry out for new things and when you furnish them with what they cried for, "it's *so* new", they grunt'.

Fifty-one poems made up the two volumes of *Men and Women*. They range from the lengthy and complex *Bishop Blougram's Apology* to the simple lyrical eloquence of *A Woman's Last Word*:

> Let's contend no more Love,
>   Strive nor weep:
> All be as before, Love,
>   – Only sleep!

There is the gentle humour of the 'Italian Person of Quality' who longs to live among the colour and vitality of town life but fears the expense:

> ... bless you, it's dear – it's dear! fowls,
>   wine, at double the rate.
> They have clapped a new tax upon salt, and
>   what oil pays passing the gate
> It's a horror to think of. And so, the villa for
>   me, not the city!

Browning's admiration for Keats and his anger that Keats was neglected found contorted expression in *Popularity*; he uses the figure of the murex, source of a royal blue dye, to comment caustically on the latter-day imitators of Keats:

> Hobbs hints blue, – straight he turtle eats:
>   Nobbs prints blue, – claret crowns his cup:
> Nokes outdares Stokes in azure feats, –
>   Both gorge. Who fished the murex up?
> What porridge had John Keats?

Dante Gabriel Rossetti, himself a superior imitator of Keats, was an early and enthusiastic reader of Browning and, by 1855, a friend. Browning sent a copy of *Men and Women* to Rossetti, whose admiration now knew no bounds. Rossetti's method of reading the poems can still be imitated with profit:

> heard them read by William; since then read them on the journey again, and some a third time at intervals; but they'll bear lots of squeezing yet. My prime favourites (without the book by me) are 'Childe Roland', 'Bishop Blougram', 'Karshish', 'The Contemporary', 'Lippo Lippi', 'Cleon', and 'Popularity'; about the other lyrical ones I can't quite speak yet, and their names don't stick in my head. . . .

Substitute *Andrea del Sarto* for 'The Contemporary' and 'Popularity' and Rossetti's list of favourites, compiled only one week after publication, becomes almost identical with the list worked out by generations of anthologists and scholars who have found that these poems 'bear lots of squeezing'.

No poem of Browning's has been squeezed for meaning more often than the one that heads Rossetti's list – the enigmatic *Childe Roland to the Dark Tower Came*. The reviewer in *Fraser's* complained that the poem stuck to him like an uncomfortable burr: 'from beginning to end we can discover no hint as to what the allegory means, and find only description preparatory to some adventure which is to disclose the symbol of the "dark tower" and its terrible neighbourhood – but the adventure never comes off in the poem. . . .' The 'terrible neighbourhood' over which Childe Roland moves is detailed in lurid, nightmarish clarity: the grass 'scant as hair in leprosy'; the 'One stiff blind horse'; the harrow with 'its rusty teeth of steel' perhaps designed 'to reel/Men's bodies out like silk'; finally, 'The round squat turret, blind as the fool's heart'. But the significance of Roland reaching the tower and there announcing his arrival by a blast on his horn is less clear, and perhaps the action is fundamentally ambiguous. In Browning's old age, the society formed in his honour was fond of studying the puzzle; once he rather half-heartedly agreed that the 'moral' might be 'He that endureth to the end shall be saved'. Roland's own testimony, however, insists that he seeks not salvation but only an 'end' to his quest and to his life. Passive despair rather than heroic perseverance is the dominant tone of the poem.

Childe Roland was written in Paris in 1852, about a month after the

Brownings watched Louis-Napoleon's *coup d'état*. It was written quickly after 'a kind of dream'; commentators have generally assumed that because of the rapidity of composition and because of its origin in a dream, the poem reveals deeper levels of Browning's unconscious mind than do his more dramatic poems. His most recent biographer, Maisie Ward, suggests that Browning's worry over his father's affair with Mrs Von Muller contributes something to the pervasive anxiety of the poem; an earlier biographer, Betty Miller, attributes the anxiety to Browning's feeling of guilt for having failed to fully express his great poetic gifts. Like Coleridge's *Kubla Khan, Childe Roland's* dreamlike logic can accommodate a bewildering array of images drawn from Browning's reading – from *Jack and the Beanstalk* to Dante to the brutal industrial landscape lying behind Elizabeth's *The Cry of the Children*. In religious poems of the 1850s Browning allays anxiety about the loss of a loving God by humorous realism and skilful casuistry; the twenty-fifth stanza of this poem suggests that this world has been created by a 'fool' who has whimsically blighted and abandoned his creation. *Childe Roland* shares a terrible *angst* with contemporary documents like Kierkegaard's *Fear and Trembling* and Carlyle's *Sartor Resartus*. In the words of Carlyle's hero Teufelsdrockh, 'the Universe was all void of Life, of Purpose, of Volition, even of Hostility: it was one huge, dead, immeasurable Steam-engine, rolling on, in its dead indifference, to grind me limb from limb'. Teufelsdrockh's response to this meaningless, negative universe was defiance: 'Indignation and grim fire-eyed Defiance'. Albert Camus would call it 'rebellion'. Roland's closing words after his trek across a wasteland filled with meaningless malice and suicidal despair are:

> And yet
> Dauntless the slug-horn to my lips I set,
> And blew. '*Childe Roland to the Dark Tower came.*'

So ends this 'gloomy hieroglyphic'poem whose suggestive symbolic style is in almost complete contrast to the psychological realism of Browning's dramatic monologues; it is closer in manner and mood to the allusive and symbolic '*souvenirs a demi-rêves*' in Gerard de Nerval's *Les Chimères* (1853):

> Je suis le ténébreux, – le veuf, – l'inconsolé,
> Le prince d'Acquitaine à la tour abolie:
> Ma seule *étoile* est morte, – et mon luth constellé
> Porte le *soleil* noir de la *Mélancolie*.

Childe Roland is Browning's contribution to an evolving portrait of a spiritual wasteland which found expression in Tennyson's *The Holy Grail* (1869), in Thomson's *The City of Dreadful Night* (1874), in Hardy's *The Darkling Thrush* (1900), and which culminated in Eliot's *The Waste Land* (1922).

While the Brownings were in Paris during the winter of 1851–2, Robert began his life-long friendship with the French art and literary critic Joseph Milsand. During the previous summer, Milsand had published a twenty-eight-page essay, praising Browning's poetry, in the *Revue des Deux Mondes*, the journal which, incidentally, published many of Nerval's poems. About the time Browning was writing *Childe Roland* (January 1852) Milsand published a similar essay on Elizabeth's poetry; in 1855 he undertook to translate several poems from *Men and Women* for the *Revue des Deux Mondes* and to provide a review. When the Brownings were in Paris again in the autumn and winter of 1855–6, Milsand was a constant companion, and he spent a ten-day holiday with them at Le Havre in 1858. After Elizabeth's death Browning and Milsand often saw each other in Paris and on holidays in Normandy and Brittany. Milsand provided a link to French literary and artistic life which Browning never entered despite his meetings in 1852 with Dumas and George Sand and his continued enthusiasm for Balzac followed by his great admiration for Flaubert's *Madame Bovary*, which came out in serial form while Browning was in Paris in 1856. Certainly the temper of the artistic milieu in Paris in the 1850s was more in keeping with Browning's literary realism than was the Anglo-American society he knew in Florence or the expectations of reviewers in the London literary journals. In Paris '*le réalisme*' was a public issue, complete with a journal by that name, manifestos, and, by 1855, Courbet's *Pavillon du Réalisme*.

If Browning's dramatic monologues have analogies in painting, Courbet and Corot furnish those analogies more adequately than does Turner, to whom English reviewers often turned for comparison because Turner's brush like Browning's pen was 'fitful and obscure'. One complained of Browning's literal 'daguerreotyping': 'art's realism is surely not to be confounded with literalness, the artist's business is not to make people speak and look exactly as they would speak and look, with all the accidents of human weakness about them'. Another, turning to the 'sister art of painting', found 'an almost perfect analogy in the pictures of a certain modern school. Our author resembles the pre-Raffaelites both in choice of subject and in style of treatment. He has the same vivid and realizing touch, and the same love of exquisite detail.' Browning certainly shared with Rossetti and other members of the Pre-Raphaelite Brotherhood a preference for the more naturalistic Christian painting which preceded Raphael; and, as Rossetti testified after a tour of the Louvre with Browning in 1856, 'his knowledge of early Italian art [was] beyond that of anyone I ever met, – encyclopaedically beyond that of Ruskin himself'. Nevertheless, Browning's monologues are not like Rossetti's paintings. The 'exquisite detail' of a Pre-Raphaelite painting generally exists as a symbol to create a moral narrative or allegory; detail in a Browning monologue goes to build up a convincing and complex illusion of a human personality. Like the canvases of Courbet and Corot, Browning's monologues are almost devoid of symbolic meaning, the great and brilliant *Childe Roland* excepted.

Andrea del Sarto is a good example of Browning's use of imagery as an index to character rather than as a symbol of a larger, indefinite meaning as is the tower in *Childe Roland*. Andrea is a 'Faultless Painter', but he is trapped, imprisoned in his very perfection of technique in painting. He talks with his restless, sensual wife Lucrezia, who is anxiously awaiting the arrival of her lover. Andrea speaks in part to justify himself to her and to himself, and in a rather half-hearted attempt to rekindle the love they once shared. His marriage, like his art, is emotionally sterile. The setting is appropriate to his psychological state: it is evening; it is autumn; he sits within the confines of the four walls of the room where he paints. His mind runs habitually to images which suggest confinement and decline of vital and energetic powers. Outside the window is all the vigorous life of Renaissance Florence, but Andrea shuns that life as does

> . . . a weak-eyed bat no sun should tempt
> Out of the grange whose four walls make his world.

When he looks out of the window, Andrea sees not the passionate life Lucrezia is determined to enjoy; his eyes fix on the autumn twilight descending on the little hill town of Fiesole, a scene which he knows to be a reflection of his own inner condition:

> My youth, my hope, my art, being all toned down
> To yonder sober pleasant Fiesole.
> There's the bell clinking from the chapel-top;
> That length of convent-wall across the way

Holds the trees safer, huddled more inside;
The last monk leaves the garden; days decrease,
And autumn grows, autumn in everything.
Eh? the whole seems to fall into shape
As if I saw alike my work and self
And all that I was born to be and do,
A twilight-piece. Love, we are in God's hand,
How strange now looks the life he makes us lead;
So free we seem, so fettered fast we are!

Hands, like walls, are to Andrea objects which encurl, protect, restrain.
When he speaks the oft-quoted lines –

Ah, but a man's reach should exceed his grasp,
Or what's a heaven for?

he does so in full and pathetic knowledge that he himself cannot and
will not strive after some unattainable ideal. And when he imagines
heaven, heaven becomes only a more glorious version of his studio
room:

In heaven, perhaps, new chances, one more chance –
Four great walls in the New Jerusalem,
Meted on each side by the angel's reed,
For Leonard, Rafael, Agnolo and me
To cover. . . .

Roland's dark tower symbolizes, 'stands for', something beyond itself,
perhaps the terrible enigma of evil in this world; Andrea's 'four
great walls' provide the reader with a measure of Andrea's mind rather
than a symbol of paradise.

Painting, after religion and history, is the great theme and subject
of Browning's poetry. In *Fra Lippo Lippi* he fused painting, history and
religion into a demonstration of, and argument for, realism in art. The
young George Eliot was grateful for the poem: 'we would rather have
"Fra Lippo Lippi" than any essay on Realism in Art', she said in her
review of 1856. Three years later, she would publish her first realistic
novel, *Adam Bede*, and consciously invoke within that novel the tradition of realism in painting. In yet another three years (1862–3), George
Eliot would publish *Romola*, set, like *Fra Lippo Lippi*, in the Florence of
the Medici. Browning didn't read it as it came out in *Cornhill*, and he
had some trouble getting it from Mudie's lending library. (Tennyson,

who was either a more favoured customer of Mudie's or else had his own copy, was reading it in bed when Browning visited him in July 1863.) Yet, by November Browning had read all four volumes and made a complaint which might seem odd to a modern reader of *Romola* exhausted by the minute historical detail of the first two volumes: he regretted that in the last two volumes Eliot paid more attention to her hero and his story and less to the historical background. Browning had really done much the same thing in *Fra Lippo Lippi*. The licentious painter-monk is firmly set in Florentine life of the early fifteenth century, but he is not imbedded or buried in historical detail as Sordello had been; the focus is on the man's life and attitudes, shaped by personal and historical circumstance. Fra Lippo's robust and vital individuality chafes against a variety of circumstances by which he is caught: a childhood of poverty, the hypocritical asceticism of the church, a sterile and stylized tradition in painting, the burgher patronage of the Medici. But Brother Lippo's energy and humanity, like that of the Renaissance in which he lives, are finally irrepressible.

As the poem opens Fra Lippo has been quite literally caught, by the police, past midnight 'at an alley's end/Where sportive ladies leave their doors ajar'. He quickly extricates himself from this embarrassing circumstance by calculated indignation and, by-the-by, dropping the name of his patron, Cosimo of the Medici. Sending the underling police off to have a drink, he settles down 'hip to haunch' with their captain to talk. Many Browning monologues are exercises in self-justification – not Browning justifying himself, but his characters justifying to their listeners a certain course of action, a set of beliefs, even their entire life. The Duke in *My Last Duchess* manipulates his self-justification so that he can also relay to his intended new Duchess a code of behaviour she will be expected to follow. Bishop Blougram, who 'believed, say, half he spoke', justifies his ecclesiastical position and personal beliefs while at the same time destroying Gigadibs' beliefs and way of life. Often a Browning character will indulge in 'special pleading', and will defend 'his actions as he must have defended them to himself in the inner recesses of his mind';[7] or he begins 'with an established point of view, and is not concerned with its truth but with trying to impress it on the outside world'.[8] Often a Browning monologuist will take his eyes off his listener, forget his conscious attempt to justify himself to another, and begin with obscure emotional urgency to talk to himself and seek 'his way to a clearer understanding of himself'.[9] Cleon's vision of an afterlife comes at such a moment when he forgets his reasonable answers to Protus and expresses a deep spiritual need. Blougram, for all his urbane casuistry, occasionally relaxes his skilful argument to voice sincerely and eloquently his own doubts and his need for faith. Much of the richness and much of the psychological reality of *Fra Lippo Lippi* grows out of his various reasons for talking, for giving voice to his frustrations, his anger, his love of sensual pleasure, his ideas on art, his slight sense of guilt at his un-monkish behaviour.

When Fra Lippo sits down to talk with the captain of the guard, he has already used his considerable rhetorical powers to rout the local constabulary. Sensing an amused sympathy for his escapades in the eyes of the captain, he gives a lively account of how he came to be among the ladies at carnival time instead of at the Medici house painting 'saints and saints/And saints again' and most appropriately painting St Jerome 'knocking at his poor old breast/With his great round stone to subdue the flesh'. This excuse leads him to a memory of torments of the flesh he had known as an orphan child in the streets trying to live on 'fig-skins, melon-parings, rinds and shuck,/Refuse and rubbish'. At eight years, his aunt put him in a Carmine convent, where he 're-nounced' the world in exchange for

> ... the good bellyful,
> The warm serge and the rope that goes all round,
> And day-long blessed idleness beside!

The account of his childhood is not a plea for sympathy – Lippo tells it with too much humorous gusto – but he can draw two lessons from it:

> You should not take a fellow eight years old
> And make him swear to never kiss the girls.

And:

> ... mind you, when a boy starves in the streets
> Eight years together, as my fortune was,
> Watching folk's faces to know who will fling
> The bit of half-stripped grape-bunch he desires,
> And who will curse and kick him for his pains, –
> Which gentleman processional and fine,
> Holding a candle to the Sacrament,
> Will wink and let him lift a plate and catch
> The droppings of the wax to sell again,

Or holla for the Eight and have him whipped, –
How say I? – nay, which dog bites, which lets drop
His bone from the heap of offal in the street, –
Why, soul and sense of him grow sharp alike,
He learns the look of things. . . .

Hence, he early became a realist; but when he transfers his sense of reality to art by including recognizable human faces in his paintings, his superiors admonish him to follow the more stylized and didactic examples of Giotto and Fra Angelico.

As Lippo tells of this conservative reception of his first realistic painting, his voice changes from that of an amused and amusing raconteur to a voice of anger: anger at the ecclesiastics who inhibit him even now while he paints for the Medici and anger at himself for compromising his realistic vision of 'the value and significance of the flesh':

> . . . I swallow my rage,
> Clench my teeth, suck my lips in tight, and paint
> To please them – sometimes do and sometimes don't;
> For, doing most, there's pretty sure to come
> A turn, some warm eve finds me at my saints –
> A laugh, a cry, the business of the world . . .
> And my whole soul revolves, the cup runs over,
> The world and life's too big to pass for a dream,
> And I do these wild things in sheer despite,
> And play the fooleries you catch me at,
> In pure rage!

Fra Lippo has moved a long way from merely excusing himself for his midnight escapades among the ladies: his anger and frustration, warmed by the memories of his childhood and his life in the Carmine cloister, force him to articulate what he himself is, his love of the physical world, the nature and function of his realistic art. His sensuality is not just a lovable weakness in a licentious monk but is itself a profoundly religious attitude towards the beauty of God's world:

> . . . you've seen the world
> – The beauty and the wonder and the power,
> The shapes of things, their colors, lights and shades,
> Changes and surprises, – and God made it all!
> – For what? Do you feel thankful, ay or no,

For this fair town's face, yonder river's line,
The mountain round it and the sky above,
Much more the figures of man, woman, child,
These are the frame to? What's it all about?
To be passed over, despised? or dwelt upon,
Wondered at?

Fra Lippo now sees that his role as a realistic painter is to bring other
men to a love of this world:

... don't you mark, we're made so that we love
First when we see them painted, things we have passed
Perhaps a hundred times nor cared to see;
And so they are better, painted – better to us,
Which is the same thing. Art was given for that;
God uses us to help each other so,
Lending our minds out.

After this eloquent testimony, Fra Lippo's speech moves to a lower
plane: to anger at those who misapprehend his art, to apology for
having spoken so strongly, to a plan to make amends for his night's
foolery by painting something for the nuns of St Ambrogio:

I shall paint
God in the midst, Madonna and her babe,
Ringed by a bowery, flowery angel-brood,
Lilies and vestaments and white faces, sweet
As puff on puff of grated orris-root
When ladies crowd to Church at midsummer.
And then 'i the front, of course a saint or two. . . .

He remains rebellious, and perhaps his rebellion has been strengthened
by the act of 'talking it out' to himself and to the captain. He intends to
put himself in that painting he will do for the nuns: the artist himself,
holding hands with a pretty woman right there in the presence of
God.

Fra Lippo Lippi was a personal favourite of Browning's. He read it
aloud from manuscript at Tennyson's in September 1855, after Tennyson had read his rather Browningesque 'monodrama' *Maud*, which
Rossetti called an 'odd De Balzacish sort of story. . . .' Rossetti was at
the reading and sketched the Poet Laureate as well as Browning.
Talking about that evening, the great Browning scholar William

DeVane rightly emphasizes the relationship of Fra Lippo to his creator. Browning, DeVane says,[10]

> could not have chosen a better poem with which to challenge the orthodox conception of poetry in mid-nineteenth century, or one that better expresses the new elements in poetry which he was to introduce. Browning found in the Renaissance painter a very sympathetic character; like himself highly individualistic, suffering from the tyranny of artistic convention, and like himself energetic and instinct with seemingly well thought out aesthetic and religious opinions which chimed with Browning's own.

The evening at the Tennysons' suggests something of the anomaly Browning found himself in by 1855. It had been a full twenty years since his *Paracelsus* had placed him among the 'acknowledged poets of the age'. During those years he had gained the respect and often the friendship of many of the leading literary men of his time – Landor, Dickens, Carlyle, Tennyson, Lowell, Ruskin – and he had attracted the warm admiration of younger writers – Rossetti, Morris, George Eliot. Yet his books did not sell and his poetry remained, in a phrase favoured by reviewers, '*caviare* to the multitude' while he himself was often thought of as 'Mrs Browning's husband'. At the same time, Browning was not a 'poet's poet' in the sense that those writers who admired him studied his poetry for the purpose of imitating his techniques in their own work. Only a handful of Victorian poems could be said to have felt the 'challenge' DeVane sees in *Fra Lippo Lippi*: Rossetti's *Jenny* (1870), a monologue spoken to a London prostitute, doubtless owes much to Browning. The basic quality of Rossetti's poetry, however, was and remained quite different from the dramatic realism of Browning's monologues he admired so much. Years later Browning described Rossetti's poems this way:

> poetical they are, – *scented* with poetry, as it were – like trifles of various sorts you take out of a cedar or sandal-wood box: you know I hate the effeminacy of his school... how I hate 'Love', as a lubberly naked young man putting his arms here and his wings there, about a pair of lovers, – a fellow they would kick away in reality.

In 1858, in *The Haystack in the Floods* and the monologue, *The Defence of Guenevere*, Morris invested his medieval settings with an air of physical and psychological reality he certainly learned from Browning, but Morris's subsequent poetry moves away from the Browningesque. In the same year (1870) that he expressed his dislike of Rossetti's poetry, Browning found Morris's *The Earthly Paradise* 'sweet, pictorial, clever always . . . a laboured brew with the old flavour but not *body*'. Although his *Maud* is close in spirit and method to Browning's monologues, Tennyson was secure in his own mature style. In 1859 Tennyson would publish the first of his *Idylls of the King*; when Tennyson added more *Idylls* in 1869, Browning noted how different their conceptions of poetry were:

> We look at the object of art in poetry so differently! Here is an idyll about a knight being untrue to his friend and yielding to the temptation of that friend's mistress to assist him in his suit. I should judge the conflict in the knight's soul the proper subject to describe: Tennyson thinks he should describe the castle, the effect of the moon on its towers, and anything *but* the soul.

By the time *Men and Women* was published in 1855 Browning's poetic achievement was acknowledged, privately, by many of the famous names in Victorian literature; publicly, they remained silent. Carlyle and Leigh Hunt sent letters congratulating Browning; Rossetti opened a letter to William Allingham with 'What a magnificent series is *Men and Women*!' – but the letter was not made public until 1896. Rossetti spent an entire night instructing Ruskin in the beauties of *Men and Women*; in the morning Ruskin sent off a bulky letter of praise to Browning, but Rossetti never carried his course of instruction to the wider public. Morris's warmly appreciative review was unsigned, and he was an unknown Oxford undergraduate anyway. George Eliot was only slightly better known, and her favourable review was also unsigned. The regular reviewers were generally hostile as they made a variety of what Browning called 'zoological utterances' condemning his obscurity, 'perversity, carelessness, and bad taste' and his obstinate refusal to correct his earlier faults in accordance with their earlier criticisms. When, in 1853, Browning was in the process of writing many of the poems which would go into *Men and Women*, he wrote to Joseph Milsand: 'I am writing – a first step towards popularity for me – lyrics with more music and painting than before, so as to get people to hear and see. . . .' Few saw the vivid psychological portraiture of his characters or heard the subtly orchestrated tones of their speech. Few of those who did hear and see spoke out. Browning had good cause to complain that the 'half-dozen people who know and could impose their opinions on the whole sty of grunters say nothing to *them* ... and speak so low in my own ear that it's lost to all intents and purposes'.

Browning's letters from this period reveal his deep disappointment at having failed to achieve something of that 'popularity' which he had sought and which he fully expected. Ruskin's long letter drew from Browning an eloquent defence of his methods while at the same time expressing his bitterness:

> Do you think poetry was ever generally understood – or can be? Is the business of it to tell people what they know already, as they know it, and so precisely that they shall be able to cry out – 'Here you should supply *this* – *that*, you evidently pass over, and I'll help you from my own stock'? It is all teaching, on the contrary, and the people hate to be taught. They say otherwise, – make foolish fables about Orpheus enchanting stocks and stones, poets standing up and being worshipped, – all nonsense and impossible dreaming. A poet's affair is with God, – to whom he is accountable, and of whom is his reward; look elsewhere, and you find misery enough.

Writing a bit later to Leigh Hunt, Browning replaces his defiance with a sad resignation: 'I know', he said of his poems, 'they err in obscure and imperfect expression, – wishing it were not so, and trying always for the future it may be less so.' But Browning had very nearly given up trying. He wrote very little poetry between 1855 and 1862–3, by which time Elizabeth was dead, and he was living again in London. 'I began pretty zealously,' Browning says of one of his rare fits of writing during these years, 'but it's no use now; nor will the world very greatly care.' A few months before she died, Elizabeth sent this vignette to Browning's sister:

> I wanted his poems done this winter very much – and here was a bright room with three windows consecrated to use. But he had a room all last summer, and did nothing. Then, he worked himself out by riding for three or four hours together. ... He was not inclined to write this winter.

He published only one small poem in a literary annual and two letters to the editor of the *Athenaeum* denying that he and Elizabeth supported the opinions of a certain lady lecturing in America on the events surrounding Orsini's attempt to assassinate Napoleon III. In a reply, Horace Greeley and Henry Ward Beecher defended the lady.

American friends were numerous in the Brownings' life in Italy. Instead of writing poetry after 1855, Browning took up drawing and sculpting in the studio of his close friend William Wetmore Story. The Browning and Story families had been intimate from 1848 onwards. Another close friend was Hiram Powers, the American sculptor who had gained fame with his popular *The Greek Slave*, and who, to Browning's amusement, was in 1853 embodying the California Gold Rush in an allegorical figure with a dubious smile, a rod of thorns in one hand and tempting gold in the other. The Brownings came to know the American actress Charlotte Cushman, the painters William Page and Hamilton Wild, the historian Motley, and 'that miraculous Mr Fields', as Browning called the Boston publisher who made a success of *Men and Women* when his London publisher could not. Three talented and 'emancipated' (Elizabeth's word) American women were particularly close to the Brownings: Margaret Fuller, the sculptor Harriet Hosmer, and Kate Field, who was to become a successful journalist in Washington. Miss Fuller and Miss Hosmer would find their way into Nathaniel Hawthorne's novels: Miss Hosmer in *The Marble Faun* and Miss Fuller in *The Blithedale Romance*, the Hawthorne novel Browning liked most – and he pleased the author by telling him so in 1858. Another good friend of the Brownings entered two of Hawthorne's later novels, *Dr. Grimshawe's Secret* and *The Dolliver Romance*. He was Seymour Kirkup, an Englishman but long an eccentric fixture in Florentine life. A connoisseur, collector, and alleged necromancer, Kirkup shared Robert's interest in Florentine art and fed Elizabeth's intense interest in spiritualism.

As much as Browning enjoyed in Florence and Rome the friendship of American artists and as much as he was pleased by the public reception of his poetry in America, he was almost as equally irritated by American spiritualists like Mrs Eckley who lived in Florence, Daniel Home who visited there, or Harriet Beecher Stowe who corresponded with Elizabeth about her 'manifestations'. The Americans were not the only nationality caught up in the cult of proving the immortality of the human personality by table-rapping, but they had a good slice of the export market. Boston is the appropriate setting for Browning's *Mr. Sludge, 'The Medium'*. Just as appropriate is the figure who appeared to Elizabeth in the one manifestation she believed to be authentic: the figure was the Boston Unitarian minister Dr Channing. The late Dr Channing assured her that he now knew that God was incarnate in Jesus Christ. America was also the source of other irritations. Since the early 1840s Elizabeth's poetry had been popular there and Edgar Allan Poe had even dedicated a book to her; after *Men and Women* Browning sold well there, but they received little money from American sales because there was no copyright law to protect British authors. Yet more painful was the American poetess Julia Ward Howe's public sarcasm about Elizabeth's addiction to morphine. Browning was to support the Union side in the coming American Civil War, but it was not out of friendship for Harriet Beecher Stowe, author of *Uncle Tom's Cabin*, or for Julia Ward Howe, author of *The Battle Hymn of the Republic*.

The Brownings' close acquaintances in Italy were largely American or English, although their Prussian physician Grisanowski, the German painter Lehmann, and the Italian historian Villari were often at Casa Guidi. The English women (Isa Blagden, the novelist, and the art historian Anna Jameson) were as talented and independent as their American counterparts. The less talented brothers of Tennyson and Trollope were also there, as was Bulwer-Lytton's son and the young Frederic Leighton, who would later become president of the Royal Academy. On visits to Rome the Brownings met the actress Frances Kemble, Thackeray and his daughters, Sir Walter Scott's biographer and son-in-law Joseph Lockhart, and Browning's early friend the Comte de Ripert-Monclar. While on a visit to Paris, Browning would attend an Italian play with Dickens, and afterwards argue with Dickens, Macready, and Lord Houghton about the play's merits. In Paris Browning would search out material for Carlyle to use in his *Life of Frederick the Great*; in Florence he would discover a Papal Nuncio's manuscript collection that he hoped Houghton, with his immense fortune and library, would purchase. During their marriage the Brownings lived a full and interesting life punctuated by quiet intervals at Casa Guidi. They raised their son and taught him languages, drawing, music, horseback riding, and swimming. If he wrote little poetry after 1855, Browning worked hard at preparing for the press successive editions of Elizabeth's highly popular volumes: the collected poems of 1853 and 1856, the verse novel *Aurora Leigh* (1857) and *Poems Before Congress* (1860), poems ('more political than poetical', said a reviewer) expressing her passionate concern over the fate of Italy now that Napoleon III and Victor Emmanuel had beaten the Austrians at Magenta and Solferino. That was 1859. Two years later she was dead; within weeks Browning closed the house in Florence and moved with his son to London.

5

The Eighteen-Sixties: I

Dramatis Personae

I suppose that what you call 'my fame within these four years' comes from a little of this gossiping and going out, and showing myself to be alive: and so indeed some folks say – but I hardly think it: for remember I was uninterruptedly (almost) in London from the time I published Paracelsus – till I ended that string of plays with Luria: and I used to go out then, and see far more of merely literary people, critics &c – than I do now, – but what came of it? There were always a few people who had a certain opinion of my poems, but nobody cared to speak what he thought, or the things printed twenty five years ago would not have waited so long for a good word – but at last a new set of men arrive. . . .

Browning to Isa Bladgen, 1865

Browning, himself, was among the new set of men who had arrived. Within four years of his return to London, Browning's life had taken on a pattern it would follow for the remaining twenty-five years of his life. Two selected editions of his earlier work and the eighteen new poems collected in *Dramatis Personae* (1864) brought him public fame and critical recognition. The general manner of Browning's poetry did not change with the new poems, but Browning's mode of writing, though still difficult, had become familiar to the new set of men and women who bought, read, and praised his books. When *Men and Women* had appeared a decade earlier, the readers – to Browning's mind – had grunted like hogs at the pearls cast before them. Another animal metaphor for readers came to Walter Bagehot's mind in his famous review of *Dramatis Personae*. Bagehot compared them to racehorses:

> many of Mr. Browning's works make a demand upon the reader's zeal and sense of duty to which the nature of most readers is

unequal. They have on the turf the convenient expression 'staying power': some horses can hold on and others cannot. But hardly any reader not of special and peculiar nature can hold on through such composition. There is not enough of 'staying power' in human nature.

Bagehot did not like Browning's 'grotesque' poetry, but in the essay he gave Browning equal billing with Wordsworth and Tennyson. And a more numerous and hardier breed of reader, willing to undertake the rigours of Browning's poetry, had evolved by the mid-1860s. Swinburne, who was converted to admiration for Browning by *Dramatis Personae*, would warn readers that the 'proper mood to study for the first time a book of Mr Browning's is the freshest, clearest, most active mood of the mind in its brightest and keenest hours of work'. The *study* of Browning's poetry would become a collective enterprise with the founding of the London Browning Society in 1881.

Browning's return to London and his new public fame also made him a personality in London society. Perhaps his many hostesses did not spend their 'brightest and keenest hours of work' studying his poetry, but they found his genial nature and sparkling conversation an ornament at table. Less than a year after Elizabeth's death, he wrote to Isa Blagden from his new home in Warwick Crescent:

> Let's see: I dined two days ago with Mrs Fitz-Patrick: I sate by my old friend Mrs Cust – who confirmed what I had heard six months before of Gertrude having refused Mr Beaumont and 80,000 a-year. At the same place I found Mad^e B. de Burg, of whom I have a fear, besides an unanswered letter praying me to go and see her she having been daily with Lytton at Vienna, consumed with the study of my things, and all that. Kingslake sat next her – sucking in authentic news about cessions of territory and so on. Yesterday I met the Storys at a dinner, and afterward went with them to the Athenaeum, where I saw nothing worth the trouble of going but the Parsee girls, – prettier to my corrupt and rotten cheese loving taste than any of the English fineness and loveliness (aquiline nose between two pudding cheeks with lightish hair and eyes, and 'fine' complexion – give me these coal black little bitter-almonds!) To day I dine at the Martin's – as I did last week – charming people they are, – Thackeray and his girls to be there. I was at a House four days ago, where an English young bride of a year's standing began the dinner by getting

hold of her husband's hands, with other significances before us all, – me, an entire stranger; by the evening she was resting her head on his shoulder, and *I* did not stay for the little more that could well happen, and which probably *did*, for the edification of boys and girls: Thackeray was there too, and I mean to ask him what he thought of it – expecting to hear great plainess of speech: she was very pretty, too. I saw Rossetti on Monday, – mean to go and see him soon, and meet his sister and mother. Hatty and Gibson arrive in a week. Story's success continues: he refuses £1500 for the Sibyl (I know) and there is a talk about his getting £2000 for the Cleopatra: such prices mean nothing, properly understood – but I like his being able to give just the answer most folks require when they ask 'what are the works worth?'

If one were to read this letter in the way we read Browning's monologues, one would find in the character of the speaker a clear fore-shadowing of the public face Browning revealed during the last twenty-five years of his life. This is the Robert Browning documented by scores of diarists, memoirists, and letter-writers who saw, talked with, or overheard the loud voice of the Robert Browning who became an 'inveterate diner-out', who took 'the three loveliest ladies in London' to hear the pianist Rubenstein play, who attended art exhibitions, literary salons, country-house weekends, and who went on holidays to the French Alps or seaside. This rather conventional, sociable Robert Browning was a disappointment to some who expected to meet at dinner a romantic, bohemian artist or the bereaved widower of Elizabeth Barrett Browning. The cult of the alienated and unconventional life of the artist had grown during the romantic movement, and *la vie de la Bohême* was in full flower in Paris; it was making headway along Cheyne Walk in Chelsea where Rossetti and Swinburne shared a house. A few houses down the Walk, living less flamboyantly but none the less unconventionally, were George Eliot and George Lewes, whom Browning visited often in the early 1860s. Tennyson, in his moody desire for privacy, his black beard, cape and sombrero, fulfilled public expectations of 'the poet' in a way that Browning, with all 'this gossiping and going out' did not. Browning was too mundane to pass for the popular image of the *poète maudit*. Those who studied both his public personality and his poetry were not so much disappointed as puzzled: 'Browning's personality,' said Thomas Hardy, 'is the literary puzzle of the nineteenth century.' In his short story *The Private Life*,

Henry James explored the puzzle and posited two Robert Brownings: one to whom one talked in drawing-rooms and at table; one who withdrew out of sight to write subtle psychological and dramatic poetry. That theoretical dichotomy has persisted among Browning's biographers, and Maisie Ward's recent two-volume study has the appropriate subtitles – *The Private Life* and *Two Robert Brownings*? 'One goes out, the other stays home. One is the genius, the other is the bourgeois, and it's only the bourgeois whom we personally know. He talks, he circulates, he's awfully popular; he flirts with you', the narrator of James's story explains.

Frequently in Browning's letters or in anecdotes by others there are suggestions of the larger social forces at work in the 1860s. We see Browning walking to catch the Underground train at Paddington Station; we hear him complaining about the suburban sprawl around Florence or the destruction of a Breton fishing village to make way for a resort building. Now that he is a householder, Browning can serve on a jury, and one assumes that the fifty-year-old poet has for the first time a right to vote. His son is not barred on religious grounds, as he had been, from entering Oxford. Browning leaves his old publisher, whose methods of accounting had been no more efficient than had his promotion and advertisement of books; one thinks of Zola learning the art of public promotion of books while working for Hachette and Company during the 1860s. Browning develops a close friendship with Julia Wedgwood, the intelligent niece of Darwin, whom the biologist praised because she 'understood my book completely'. While riding the train in 1863 Browning learns from the American Ambassador Francis Adams that Vicksburg has fallen to the Union forces; late in the summer of 1870, Browning hurriedly leaves Normandy by cattle boat to avoid being mistaken as a spy for the invading Prussian forces. The American Civil War and the Franco-Prussian War open and close the 1860s. The Crimean War of the 1850s was fought by professional armies however badly administered; its 'theatre' of operations was as limited as were its objectives. The American and Franco-Prussian Wars mobilized entire populations, became wars of attrition against the civilian populations, and were won largely by the efficient use of conscript armies and new weapons delivered to the front by networks of railways.

Browning was a constant, and according to Carlyle's testimony, a skilful user of railways from 1846 onwards. He did not, however, make any literary use of the railway. The one time the railway enters his work with any prominence is *The Inn Album* (1875) when it is treated, much as he must have treated it in his own life, as a convenient mode of getting somewhere. The fact that Browning did not make literary use of this important agency of change in nineteenth-century life is, in itself, of no more importance in judging Browning's achievement than is the fact that he failed to note the formation of the First International in London in 1864 or the publication of *Das Kapital* in 1867. It might, however, serve as a test to contrast Browning's cast of mind to that of a number of other nineteenth-century writers. Railways became a constant source of metaphor for writers after 1830. Pausing to speak with the reader in an early chapter of *Cousin Pons* (1848), Balzac begs us to 'borrow a metaphor from the railways, even if only to recoup ourselves for the sums they have borrowed from us'. Carlyle had borrowed to suggest that the universe had become 'one huge, dead, immeasurable Steam-engine'. Thoreau and Ruskin used railways as symbols of mindless and destructive technology. To Matthew Arnold they served as indices to the 'illiberal, dismal life' of the middle-class philistine who 'thinks it is the highest pitch of development and civilization when his letters are carried twelve times a day from Islington to Camberwell, and from Camberwell to Islington, and if railway trains run to-and-fro between them every quarter of an hour'. Hawthorne modernized *Pilgrim's Progress* into *The Celestial Railway*. Dickens in *Dombey and Son* and Tolstoi in *Anna Karenina* make the locomotive an instrument of retribution against transgressing characters. Zola would close *La Bête Humaine* with a driverless train, cattle-cars crammed with tired and drunken conscripts destined for the humiliating defeat of the Franco-Prussian War. For Zola, it was not just a train, but the very 'image of France'. All of these writers, in their own way, make of the technological, economic, and social reality of the railway a symbol for large collective or universal forces. In the twentieth century Hart Crane in *The Bridge*, and then T. S. Eliot in *Four Quartets* would turn the Underground into a symbol for the mythical underworld or inferno. Browning rode the Underground and he took the railway to country houses or to French seaside or Alpine resorts; but when he withdrew to write his poems, he created individual human beings who were not shaped by large collective or universal forces but who were caught in their own particular situations, ideas, weaknesses and strengths. In Balzac, money has a life of its own; it is a force in and of itself. To Andrea del Sarto money was something to buy a house with; to Mr Sludge, 'Twenty V-notes' will get him passage from Boston to Liverpool. Browning did not have an 'institutional' imagination as did Dickens, who in *Bleak House* (1852–3) could merge the fog off the River Thames into the obstructions of the British legal system, and then allow the same fog to obscure and injure the innermost lives of unsuspecting victims. In *Our Mutual Friend* (1864–5) Dickens makes the Thames-turned-sewer into a symbol of the corrupt and rotten greed of a city, where even the fishing of corpses from the river has become an economic activity. A few years later in Thomson's *The City of Dreadful Night* the Thames becomes the River of Suicides, a haven to those who need no longer fear damnation for they have received the 'tidings of great joy' that there is no God. In the penultimate poem in *Dramatis Personae*, Browning works with quite similar material but to a much different effect. Browning's river is the Seine and his suicides are part of the human refuse of Paris, men who the previous night had slept under 'Some arch' or on 'the plain asphalt'. Now, in the poet's memory, they lie on the copper slabs of the morgue, a building soon to be pulled down to make way for one of the splendid and easily policed boulevards being built by Baron Haussmann for Napoleon III. The poet (or speaker of the poem) had visited the morgue in the same year that he had watched Napoleon III's son baptized, had observed the Congress convened to settle the Crimean War and had heard Cavour's appeal to the Congress to further Italian unity. The poet imagines the three suicides to be a young boy thwarted in his ambition to have the power of a Buonaparte, an old socialist with his fist still clenched, a third man who needed money for 'women, cards, and dice' but has gotten instead

> The copper couch and one clear nice
>   Cool squirt of water o'er your bust,
> The right thing to extinguish lust!

Dickens might have made these men into pathetic victims of inhuman social forces; Thomson might have made them victims of cosmic despair. To Zola their lives may have been determined by heredity and environment; Hardy might have seen them as the inconsequential playthings of the Immanent Will. They draw from Browning only the ironic comment that

> It's wiser being good than bad;
>   It's safer being meek than fierce:
> It's fitter being sane than mad.

The causes of these men's deaths can only be imagined; the failure of their lives is only 'apparent', as the title of the poem, *Apparent Failure*, suggests. The poem is only a short sketch compared to the fuller, detailed portraits of personality Browning supplies in his dramatic monologues. But here, as in the monologues, the agents of human behaviour and fate are obscure, complex, and come from within the individual and not from some external, deterministic force which can be symbolized by a railway train or a polluted river. Like Flaubert in *A Sentimental Education* (1869) or Dostoievski in *Crime and Punishment* (1865–6), Browning was more interested in psychology than sociology. He pursued, in Swinburne's words, 'the inner study of an individual mind, the occult psychology of a single soul, the personal pathology of a special intelligence . . .'

The poems collected in *Dramatis Personae* address themselves more directly to contemporary moods and lively intellectual issues than had any previous volume of Browning's poems. The volume opened with *James Lee's Wife*, a study of a disintegrating modern marriage; the *Epilogue* to the volume is a debate with Ernest Renan who had just published his criticism of the Gospels as *La Vie de Jésus* in 1863. *A Death in the Desert* was a yet more ambitious refutation of biblical criticism; *Caliban upon Setebos* merges notions about the primitive origin of religious belief with Darwinian ideas. Browning challenged the melancholy disillusionment of Edward Fitzgerald's *The Rubáiyát* (1859) with *Rabbi Ben Ezra*. In *Mr. Sludge, 'The Medium'*, he exposed a charlatan spiritualist and at the same time portrayed a society whose values have become so confused that an egregious quack like Sludge might well be its priest. With the possible exception of Walt Whitman's expanded version of *Leaves of Grass*, no other volume of poems in English published in the 1860s so clearly reflects the life of the decade as does *Dramatis Personae*. To William DeVane, this contemporaneity is the chief feature of the volume;[1]

in an age when the poets were mainly interested in escaping to the past – Tennyson to Arthur's medieval kingdom, Arnold to Greece, Rossetti and Morris to the Middle Ages, the young Swinburne to Greece and Elizabethan England – Browning almost alone wrote of contemporary ideas and contemporary life, often in colloquial language and contemporary phrase.

James Lee's Wife was the first poem in *Dramatis Personae*. Its language is more lyrical than colloquial, but it catches very well that mood of boredom, lassitude, and grey disillusionment which had been growing during the century and found frequent expression in particular in the work of Baudelaire and Flaubert, who described the malady as 'that modern ennui which gnaws at a man's entrails, and turns an intelligent man into a walking shadow, a thinking phantom'. In Browning's poem it is the woman who recognizes the disease that has caused her marriage to run to

> Rot and rust,
> Run to dust,
> All through worms i' the wood, which crept,
> Gnawed our hearts out while we slept:
> That is worse.

The poem is constructed on a series of scenes set in and around the couple's house on the coast of Brittany. The woman sees images of the certain decay of her married love in the 'shipwreck wood' burned in the fireplace, in the coming cold of winter, in the rocky cliffs. The opening stanzas of the section entitled *On The Cliff* measure her estrangement and disillusionment:

> I leaned on the turf,
> I looked at a rock
> Left dry by the surf;
> For the turf, to call it grass were to mock:
> Dead to the roots, so deep was done
> The work of the summer sun.

> And the rock lay flat
> As an anvil's face:
> No iron like that!
> Baked dry; of a weed, of a shell, no trace:
> Sunshine outside, but ice at the core,
> Death's altar by the lone shore.

Like the 'thinking phantom' of Flaubert, the woman puzzles over the loss of joy and love but finally resigns herself. Browning, in a letter written to Julia Wedgwood soon after the poem was published, was quite insistent that something like *ennui* was intended as the cause of the woman's tragedy:

> I misled you into thinking the couple were 'proletaire' – but I
> meant them for just the opposite – people newly married, trying

to realise a dream of being sufficient to each other, in a foreign
land (where you can try such an experiment) and finding it break
up, – the man being *tired* first, – and tired precisely of the love . . .

James Lee's Wife is a particularly bleak poem, and it becomes bleaker
when set in the context of the nineteenth-century literary tradition
which saw love between man and woman as final refuge of peace and
certainty in a world otherwise stripped of meaning. Matthew Arnold
gave that mood definitive expression in the closing lines of his *Dover
Beach* of 1867:

> Ah, love, let us be true
> To one another! for the world, which seems
> To lie before us like a land of dreams,
> So various, so beautiful, so new,
> Hath really neither joy, nor love, nor light,
> Nor certitude, nor peace, nor help for pain;
> And we are here as on a darkling plain
> Swept with confused alarms of struggle and flight,
> Where ignorant armies clash by night.

In an irreverent twentieth-century parody, Anthony Hecht has Arnold's
woman complain about being turned into a kind of 'cosmic last resort'.
In *James Lee's Wife* even the prop of human love, the possibility of a
man and woman 'being sufficient to each other', has been removed.

Browning had opened *Men and Women* with a poem (*Love Among
the Ruins*) which asserted the supremacy of human love above all other
achievement. This attitude appears often in Browning's poetry; and it
finds varied expression in *The Last Ride Together, The Statue and the
Bust, By the Fireside*. The 'love' poems collected in *Dramatis Personae*,
however, are studies in frustration and failure: *The Worst of It*, a husband's speech to his unfaithful wife; *Too Late*, a remorseful meditation
by a man who has learned that the woman he once loved is dead;
Youth and Art and *Dîs Aliter Visum, or, Le Byron de nos Jours* are laments
by people who failed to act on their love, married the wrong person,
and thus ruined four lives instead of fulfilling two. Often these poems
are given a contemporary flavour by a kind of drawing-room dropping of names: 'Schumann's our music-maker now . . . Ingres's the
modern man that paints . . . Heine for songs.' Browning gains much
the same effect in *A Likeness* by mentioning popular prints of the
famous racehorse Cruiser and the prizefighter Sayers. In *Mr. Sludge*

Browning makes elaborate use of circumstantial contemporary detail; but in the less ambitious and less successful examinations of modern love like *Youth and Art*, the 'contemporary' atmosphere depends largely on a jaunty tone and conversational phrasing. The woman in *Youth and Art* ends her speech to the man she should have married:

> But you meet the Prince at the Board,
>   I'm queen myself at *bals-paré*,
> I've married a rich old lord,
>   And you're dubbed knight and R.A.
>
> Each life unfulfilled, you see;
>   It hangs still, patchy and scrappy:
> We have not sighed deep, laughed free,
>   Starved, feasted, despaired, – been happy.
>
> And nobody calls you a dunce,
>   And people suppose me clever:
> This could have happened but once,
>   And we missed it, lost it forever.

This poem, and *Too Late*, *The Worst of It*, and *Dîs Aliter Visum* are easy and slight achievements. One almost suspects that Browning may have written them to refute the old charge that he wrote obscurely about obscure, historical people. To their credit, reviewers of *Dramatis Personae* preferred Browning's richer and more solid accomplishments: *Mr. Sludge*, *Caliban*, *A Death in the Desert*, *Abt Vogler*.

In *Mr. Sludge* Browning stretched his understanding if not his sympathy to include a modern confidence-man *par excellence*. Sludge is as skilful in defending his spiritualist chicanery as he is in calling up the spirits of the dead: a beloved mother, a dear departed child, Benjamin Franklin to advise on the purchase of telegraph shares, or Shakespeare to write new songs. If during a seance the medium had tried to contact Francis Bacon and roused P. T. Barnum instead, the mistake can be explained; so can the odd form Beethoven's music might take if the late composer tried to relay a thirty-third sonata through the medium of Sludge:

> Suppose, the spirit Beethoven wants to shed
> New music he's brimful of; why, he turns
> The handle of this organ, grinds with Sludge,
> And what he poured in at the mouth o' the mill

As a Thirty-third Sonata, (fancy now!)
Comes from the hopper as bran-new Sludge, naught else,
The Shaker's Hymn in G, with a natural F,
Or the 'Stars and Stripes' set to consecutive fourths.

After all, he is only a means, a medium, human and subject to error.
Further, he is most put upon and subjected to the pressures of a society
eager to fool itself, desperate to prove immortality by table-rapping,
willing to see Providence in signs and omens, bored with its flat,
routine life and impatient for a Sludge to slap colour and mystery back
into the world with his 'harlequin's pasteboard sceptre'. Sludge is, and
audaciously declares himself to be, a modern surrogate for lost religion:

As for religion – why, I served it, sir!
I'll stick to that! With my *phenomena*
I laid the atheist sprawling on his back,
Propped up Saint Paul, or, at least Swedenborg!

On a less blasphemous level, the varied tricks of his trade are no worse
than those of other artists and entertainers:

Really mere novel-writing of a sort,
Acting, or improvising, make-believe,
Surely not downright cheatery. . . .

People admire and praise the lies of Homer, why shouldn't Sludge's
'inventions' be treated the same? Why shouldn't he receive the same
homage as 'wondrous Longfellow,/Surprising Hawthorne' or one of
the contemporary school of 'scientific' historians who

. . . states the law and fact and face o' the thing
Just as he'd have them, finds what he thinks fit,
Is blind to what missuits him, just records
What makes his case out, quite ignores the rest.
It's a History of the World, the Lizard Age,
The Early Indians, the Old Country War,
Jerome Napoleon, whatsoever you please,
All as the author wants it.

If in spinning out his spiritualist inventions Sludge sometimes exceeds
his skill and makes mistakes, it is his patrons, not he, who are to blame.
For his patrons, being children of their century, are 'for progress' and
demand improvement, newer and more stupendous demonstrations of
his powers.

These patrons, and particularly Hiram H. Horsefall of Boston to whom Sludge is talking, have created Sludge out of their own needs; and they now encourage and exploit him in the hope of satisfying those needs. At the same time he has become their possession, their 'discovery', their treasure, and as such their social vanity protects him from exposure. Any guest who might be inclined to doubt the authenticity of Sludge's demonstrations would be inhibited by either etiquette or ostracism:

> Pray do you find guests criticise your wine,
> Your furniture, your grammar, or your nose?
> Then, why your 'medium'?

Here Sludge characterizes himself as a valued piece of personal property, but like so many possessions he firmly controls his possessors. He is an intelligent, subtle, informed rogue who successfully preys upon fools on whichever side of the North Atlantic he finds them. His speech to Hiram H. Horsefall is, in itself, a demonstration of his audacious and self-confident superiority. As with so many of Browning's monologues, this poem begins with the speaker enmeshed in a difficult situation which requires that he defend, explain, justify his actions to another. As the poem opens, Horsefall, having caught Sludge at cheating, threatens to expose him with a letter to Horace Greeley's *New York Tribune*. Momentarily taken aback and confused, Sludge makes some lame excuses for his trickery: it was caused by drinking too much champagne which Sludge mistook for mere Catawba water; or the vindictive spirit of a Negro or an Irish emigrant has interfered with the seance. These preliminary excuses do not appease Horsefall's anger any more than do Sludge's appeal to Horsefall's 'sainted mother' or the return of a gift of shirt-studs. These early skirmishes do, however, give Sludge time to collect his very considerable wits. He has soon struck a compromise; and, while Horsefall pours him out eggnog and lights his cigars, Sludge reveals the tricks of his trade and justifies his life as a medium. So thoroughly and so acutely does Sludge analyse himself and the society Horsefall represents that Sludge easily wins the day. He ends humbly accepting from a penitent Horsefall 'Twenty V-notes more, an outfit too,/And not a word to Greeley'. Perhaps *Mr. Sludge* was among the poems Mark Twain and his friends read aloud and studied during the 'Browning class' Twain conducted at his home during the 1890s. The American humorist certainly understood the type and the phenomenon of the modern charlatan.

Sludge has adapted himself quite successfully to the society in which he must survive. His adaptability, intelligence, and clear-sightedness, however, compound rather than redeem the ugliness of his character and his moral deformity. Sludge is a 'grotesque', a word used by Bagehot to distinguish Browning's poetry from the 'pure' mode of Wordsworth and the 'ornate' mode of Tennyson. From his earliest poems, Browning had displayed a keen interest in the ugly, the twisted and deformed, the exaggerated, the eccentric, the insane. A childhood poem described the ravage of Egyptian children by famine, plague and disease. The title of another childhood poem, *The Dance of Death*, suggests an early fascination with the morbid, the macabre, or the sinister, which so frequently attracted the romantic imagination of Shelley, Byron, and Coleridge. Even Keats puts a severed, rotting head into his *Isabella*. Browning's fascination for grotesque subjects can be seen in the sick and twisted minds of Johannes Agricola and Porphyria's lover, in the scenes of carnage in *Sordello*, in the lurid, diseased landscape over which Childe Roland rides, or in the 'rotten-runged rat-riddled stairs' down which the organist must stumble at the close of *Master Hugues of Saxe-Gotha*. In *Christmas Eve*, ugly physical details lend a note of realism to the characters; in *The Flight of the Duchess* Browning gains a coarse and vulgar, but none the less grotesque, humour by calling the dowager duchess' breasts an 'udder'' Browning was fond of debasing human characters by comparing them to animals. Sludge offers an excellent example of this process when he explains how it is that he knows so much surprising personal information about people who attend his seances. First, Sludge compares himself to a hunchback political informer who gathers his treacherous information by simply sitting on a sidewalk in Rome and keeping his ears open. The hunchback is then compared to an ant-eater and the ants to the information he gathers:

> His trade was, throwing thus
> His sense out, like an ant-eater's tongue,
> Soft, innocent, warm, moist, impassible,
> And when it was crusted o'er with creatures – slick,
> Their juice enriched his palate.

Later in the monologue, Sludge comes back to the comparison to describe his selfish method of getting along in, and feeding upon, society:

> Be lazily alive,
> Open-mouthed, like my friend the ant-eater,
> Letting all nature's loosely-guarded motes
> Settle and, slick, be swallowed! Think yourself
> The one i' the world, the one for whom the world
> Was made, expect it tickling at your mouth!
> Then will the swarm of the busy buzzing flies,
> Clouds of coincidence, break egg-shell, thrive,
> Breed, multiply, and bring you food enough.

Sludge can, in part, justify his rapacious preying upon society because the ethical authority of God, the First Cause, 'The Word', has been eroded or forced to recede by biologists in search of the simple life forms at the origin of human evolution. So, Sludge lives in a world in which 'The Word comes close behind a stomach-cyst'. When Sludge declares 'I somehow vomit truth to-day', the reader must feel the aptness of the statement.

Caliban upon Setebos was Bagehot's prime example of Browning's grotesque art. Lying 'flat on his belly in the pit's much mire' letting his 'rank tongue blossom into speech' as he speculates upon the cruel, capricious nature of God and the Universe, Caliban might seem a figure of playful humour to twentieth-century readers, steeped as they are in images of horror and grotesque violence. To an informed, intelligent, and tough-minded man like Bagehot, however, Caliban was 'a nasty creature – a gross animal, uncontrolled and unelevated by any feeling of religion or duty'. Bagehot's reaction to Browning's version of the primitive mind in Caliban, is not dissimilar to the reaction of other Victorians to Darwin's supposed implication that man had descended from the monkey. It is of the same order of indignation that led the cartoonist in *The Hornet* to portray the eminent biologist as a stooping ape or which led Bishop Wilberforce in the Oxford debate with Thomas Huxley to imply that whatever the family history of his scientific opponent Huxley, his own ancestry did not include the great apes. Bagehot's attitude towards Caliban may even suggest something of Carlyle's gruff rejection of the Darwinian theory: 'If true, it was nothing to be proud of, but rather a humiliating discovery, and the less said about it the better.' Bagehot did not charge Browning's grotesque manner with being 'untrue'; he did, however, believe that the only justification for portrayal of ugliness and imperfection was to remind the reader of the beautiful and the perfect. Basically,

Bagehot thought poetry should idealize and ennoble its subjects. And Browning was 'the most of a realist, and the least of an idealist of any poet' Bagehot could think of. By acknowledging Browning's 'realism' while at the same time condemning what has been portrayed, Bagehot reveals a division of mind that Oscar Wilde would attribute to nineteenth-century man in general:

> The nineteenth century dislike of Realism is the rage of Caliban seeing his own face in a glass.

> The nineteenth century dislike of Romanticism is the rage of Caliban not seeing his own face in a glass.

The attitudes of both Wilde and Bagehot indicate a growing tendency in the nineteenth-century literary mind to associate 'realism' with portrayals of the harsher, more sordid and degraded aspects of human life. The new documentary 'naturalism' of the Goncourts in *Germinie Lacerteux* (1865) and of Zola in *Les Rougon-Macquart* series during the succeeding decades, became the most notorious embodiment of that attitude. Zola called his series 'a natural and social history', but to a French critic it was 'a pessimistic epic of human animality'. Tennyson, enraged by the shift in literary focus by 1886, saw readers

> . . . wallowing in troughs of Zolaism –
> Forward, forward, aye, and backward, downward too into
>   the abysm!
> Do your best to charm the worst, to lower the rising
>   race of men;
> Have we risen from out the beast, then back into the
>   beast again?

It would be wrong to view Browning's man-beast Caliban as a character from a naturalistic novel or even as a realistic version of the mind of primitive man. Browning uses Caliban as a vehicle by which he can satirize contemporary religious issues; consequently Browning endows his savage, as George Bernard Shaw told the Browning Society, 'with the introspective powers of a Hamlet, and the theology of an evangelical Churchman'. But by embodying contemporary ideas within this 'nasty creature', Browning had provided a measure for post-Darwinian man. After the *Origin of Species* came out in 1859, animals rather than angels seemed the more accurate measure. Charles Lyell's *The Antiquity of Man* (1863), important archeological

excavations like those among the stones of Carnac in Brittany (which
Browning made a special trip to see in 1866), the accumulating
information about primitive societies recorded by missionaries and
travellers, all contributed to a fascinating if ill-understood picture of
early man. In a letter in 1859, the naturalist John Evans reveals
something of the puzzled excitement the Victorians felt about new
evidences of primitive man:

> Think of their finding flint axes and arrowheads at Abbeville in
> conjunction with bones of Elephants and Rhinoceroses 40 feet
> below the surface in a bed of drift. In this bone cave in Devonshire
> now being excavated by the Geological Society they say they
> have found flint arrowheads among the bones, and the same is
> reported of a cave in Sicily. I can hardly believe it.

Whatever else he was, primitive man was no longer seen as the simple,
noble savage of Rousseau or the bumptious clown that was Shakespeare's Caliban in *The Tempest*. Bagehot called Browning's poem a
description of a '*mind in difficulties*'. It is Caliban's tortuously difficult
attempt to puzzle out his universe and his relation to that universe
that creates the dramatic interest of the poem and is also the source of
much of the satiric humour.

Caliban's method (one might almost say his 'methodology') for
understanding his world is what Browning calls (in the subtitle to the
poem) 'Natural Theology', i.e., the notion that by studying man and
nature one can discover the nature of God. At its simplest it is the act
of creating God in one's own image, an act which Browning considered
humorously futile rather than blasphemous. Caliban, lying in the 'cool
slush' of his cave and laughing as 'small eft-things' scamper over his
body, evolves a portrait of his god Setebos as cruel, vindictive, envious
and capricious as is Caliban himself:

> He is strong and Lord.
> 'Am strong myself compared to yonder crabs
> That march now from the mountain to the sea;
> 'Let twenty pass, and stone the twenty-first,
> Loving not, hating not, just choosing so.
> 'Say, the first straggler that boasts purple spots
> Shall join the file, one pincer twisted off;
> 'Say, this bruised fellow shall receive a worm,
> And two worms he whose nippers end in red;
> As it likes me each time, I do: so He.

Caliban's formula is 'as I: so He'. Contemporary readers would see in the formula similarities to continuing Victorian attempts, in the tradition of Paley's *Evidences*, to deduce the divine from the study of the natural; and they would also see similarities to the assertions of the Higher Critics that the Christus was the product of human myth-making. Coming as it does from the mouth of Caliban, however, the formula can only provoke horror or laughter. Contemporary readers would also recognize, as Shaw did, the 'theology of an evangelical Churchman' in Caliban's speculations. Setebos is the stern Calvinistic God still preached from many a Victorian pulpit. He is the God whose inscrutable ways and power are not to be questioned. He is also puritanical, and the 'best way to escape His ire/Is, not to seem too happy'. To be safe Caliban

> ... mainly dances on dark nights,
> Moans in the sun, gets under holes to laugh,
> And never speaks his mind save housed as now:
> Outside, 'groans, curses.

If Setebos were to catch Caliban chuckling and speculating upon His identity, Caliban plans to appease the wrath of this Old Testament God by sacrificing his best goat or cutting off a finger

> Hoping the while, since evils sometimes mend,
> Warts rub away and sores are cured with slime,

Setebos' vigilance will relax and Caliban will be left in peace. If God can be deduced from the brutal and violent world which informs the whole of *Caliban upon Setebos*, then it would be well if, like a wart or a sore, He would disappear.

A Death in the Desert is a poetic strategy by Browning to combat forces threatening man's belief in a God of love. The enemies are, again, those scholars who challenged the authenticity of the scripture as revealed truth. Browning's method of attack is similar to the one he used in *An Epistle* and *Cleon*, both mock-documents from the early Christian era. In the new poem, however, Browning used a more elaborate machinery to create his document. The central section of the poem consists of the dying words of St John, whom Browning takes to be the author of *Revelation* as well as of the Gospel which bore his name. John reaffirms his witness of Jesus' life and his certainty that God embodied his love for man in Christ. He foresees the coming of a time when men will doubt whether he, John, lived at all; he anticipates the charge that the Christ was a 'mere projection from man's inmost mind'; he traces man's past and future spiritual growth. John's speech foreshadows the less dramatic, more argumentative style of many of Browning's later poems. It is not a dramatic monologue, for John's utterance is surrounded by a number of other voices designed to create the physical setting for John's dying words, to testify to their authenticity, to question and clarify those words. As a result the poem purports to exist as a manuscript awaiting discovery in some Mediterranean cave or monastic library. When some nineteenth-century biblical scholar discovers it, he will find it properly labelled and preserved:

> [Supposed of Pamphylax the Antiochene:
> It is a parchment, of my rolls the fifth,
> Hath three skins glued together, is all Greek,
> And goeth from *Epsilon* down to *Mu*:
> Lies second in the surnamed Chosen Chest,
> Stained and conserved with juice of terebinth,
> Covered with cloth of hair, and lettered *Xi*,
> From Xanthus, my wife's uncle now at peace:
> *Mu* and *Epsilon* stand for my own name.
> I may not write it, but I make a cross
> To show I await His coming, with the rest,
> And leave off here: beginneth Pamphylax.]

Then follows a realistic narrative describing how several men cared for the dying John. Some of John's words are recorded, and the square brackets return as the preparer of the manuscript supplies a commentary to clarify what John has said. When John's more prolonged utterance ends, the reader is given an account of the saint's death and burial, and the information that the narrator (Pamphylax) has dictated to one Phoebus this account of his experience the night before he must enter the arena in Rome. Once again there are square brackets: an early sceptic, Cerinthus, whose implied attitude towards Christ is that of a Strauss or a Renan, is allowed to muse over the manuscript; but an unknown writer of glosses quickly and heatedly refutes the sceptic.

A Death in the Desert could not, of course, seriously compete with the carefully argued theses of Strauss, Renan, or the contributors to *Essays and Reviews* (1860). The poem was, however, an ingenious if deadly serious parody of 'documentary evidence'; and Browning managed to create a human context for what was otherwise a rather abstract theological dispute. T. S. Eliot would do much the same thing when he opened his *Journey of the Magi* with a 'discordant' note of realism:

> 'A cold coming we had of it,
> Just the worst time of the year
> For a journey, and such a long journey:
> The ways deep and the weather sharp,
> The very dead of winter.'
> The camels galled, sore-footed, refractory,
> Lying down in the melting snow.
> There were times we regretted
> The summer palaces on slopes, the terraces,
> The silken girls bringing sherbet.
> Then the camel men cursing and grumbling
> And running away, and wanting their liquor and women,
> And the night-fires going out, and the lack of shelters,
> And the cities hostile and the towns unfriendly
> And the villages dirty and charging high prices:
> A hard time we had of it.

Further, the unusual construction of *A Death in the Desert* suggests that Browning was attempting to make his poem more understandable and accessible to the reader than would be a strict dramatic monologue by the subtle and argumentative John. The information about the history of the purported manuscript, the clarifying commentary, the refutation of the sceptical Cerinthus, all are aids to help the reader understand the message of St John.

As early as 1845, Elizabeth had asked Browning about an unnecessary obscurity in his poems: 'Would it not be well if you were to stoop to the vulgarism of prefixing some word of introduction as others do, you know . . . a title . . . a name?' A representative complaint by a reviewer of the 1855 *Men and Women* was that Browning had the habit of 'presenting incidents so allusively as to baffle ordinary penetration to discover what he means – of printing poems having reference to some facts or conversation not given and needed to explain them. . . .' In a number of poems in *Men and Women* he had, in fact, adopted various devices to act as aids to the reader. To *Cleon*, for example, Browning had prefixed a quotation from St Paul – 'As certain of your own poets have said' – to alert the reader to the irony that Cleon's desperate spiritual needs could be met by Paul's message. To *Holy-Cross Day*, Browning affixed an entry from a fictional diary to explain that, by tradition, the Jewish inhabitants of Rome had to attend an annual Christian sermon aimed at their conversion. This preparatory information must have been welcomed by readers who otherwise would have had to enter the poem with the opening stanza:

> Fee, faw, fum! bubble and squeak!
> Blessedest Thursday's the fat of the week.
> Rumble and tumble, sleek and rough,
> Stinking and savoury, smug and gruff,
> Take the church-road, for the bell's due chime
> Gives us the summons – 't is sermon-time.

Confused readers of *Bishop Blougram's Apology* must have been equally grateful to Browning: at the close of that poem, after the Bishop has ended his difficult and convincing argument, Browning himself steps in, in *propria persona*, to describe for the reader Blougram's general method of arguing, to warn the reader not to take seriously all that Blougram has said, and to reveal the effect Blougram's argument has had upon his listener, Gigadibs. In *Mr. Sludge* Browning also broke the strict dramatic mode of the monologue form by allowing Sludge to reveal more candidly his spiteful nature once his listener, Horsefall, has left the stage. The title, subtitle, and quotation

CALIBAN UPON SETEBOS; or, NATURAL
THEOLOGY IN THE ISLAND
'Thou thoughtest that I was altogether such a one as thyself'

signal to the reader the contemporary issue, inform him that Caliban (who in the poem itself often hides behind the third-person pronoun 'he') will be talking *about* Setebos, and suggest the kind of logic Caliban will follow. All of these extra-dramatic devices serve as guideposts to the reader who would otherwise, as George Eliot said in her 1855 review, have 'to trace by his own mental activity the underground stream of thought that jets out in elliptical and pithy verse'.

Abt Vogler represents another shift away from the strictly dramatic mode: here, as in *Rabbi Ben Ezra*, the dramatic mask has become rather transparent, and Browning himself is more visible. Vogler is more a mouthpiece for the poet and less a fully independent dramatic character.[2] In *My Last Duchess*, *The Bishop Orders His Tomb*, or *Andrea del Sarto*, Browning is almost completely hidden from the reader's view. In those poems Browning had been similar to the artist James Joyce describes in his *Portrait of the Artist as a Young Man*: 'The artist, like the God of creation, remains within or behind or beyond or above his handiwork, invisible, refined out of existence, indifferent, paring his fingernails'. Abt Vogler, the eighteenth-century organist and inventor of the Orchestrion, was an historical personage; but Browning makes no real effort to draw him as a particular individual living in a particular time and place. The extemporizing organist becomes, instead, a vehicle through which many of Browning's own strongly held ideas can be expressed. Browning's notion that music, above all other arts, can express the eternal and the absolute; his preference for *process* over *completion*; his belief that the imperfections of this world imply the perfection of the next – all these ideas receive powerful rhetorical expression in *Abt Vogler*. The language itself matches the abstract ideas being expounded:

> There shall never be one lost good! What was, shall live as before;
>   The evil is null, is naught, is silence implying sound;
> What was good shall be good, with, for evil, so much good more:
>   On earth the broken arcs; in the heaven, a perfect round.

The language is not the less powerful because abstract, but it exists in sharp contrast to Browning's more typical colloquial style. The abstract quality of music itself is carefully infused into the monologue, nowhere more effectively than in the closing lines when Vogler can no longer sustain the vision of the eternal his extemporizing has brought him:

> Give me the keys. I feel for the common chord again,
>   Sliding by semitones, till I sink to the minor – yes,
> And I blunt it into a ninth, and I stand on alien ground,
>   Surveying awhile the heights I rolled from into the deep;
> Which, hark, I have dared and done, for my resting place is found,
>   The C Major of this life: so, now I will try to sleep.

In two poems about musicians in *Men and Women* Browning had been more interested in the effect of the music on the characters. In *A Toccata of Galuppi's*, a fugue by the eighteenth-century Venetian composer brings a chilling awareness of life's transcience to a complacent nineteenth-century British scientist. The organist in *Master Hugues of Saxe-Gotha* is frustrated in his attempt to discover some richer meaning to life in the barren, mathematical music of a 'dry-as-dust' imitator of Bach. Abt Vogler, too, is personally engaged in the musical combinations which can reveal the very 'finger of God', but the eloquent expression of Browning's own ideas competes with the emotional involvement of his character. In keeping with a growing willingness to deliver himself of his own opinions through poetry, Browning would in the late poem *Parleying with Charles Avison* (1887) declare his own musical tastes and opinions on 'to-day's music manufacture, – Brahms, Wagner, Dvorak, Liszt. . . .'

With *Dramatis Personae* Browning had become 'the interpreter of our modern life' to an extent that would surely have pleased the 1855 reviewer for *Fraser's* magazine. The volume was free of the 'Italianesque pedantry . . . of olives and lizards, artists and monks' of which Kingsley had earlier complained. As a foreign setting for poems, contemporary France or America had replaced historic Italy; Browning had relaxed his former inhibition about speaking out in his own voice, and he was willing to make some concessions to readers who found his poems difficult to understand. His earlier work was receiving more careful reading and belated praise; he had himself become a public figure. Samuel Smiles, the journalist who had had a sure finger on the public pulse since the publication of his best-selling *Self Help* in 1859, must have been confident of general public assent when he announced in his *Brief Biographies* of 1868: 'We are confident that Mr Browning's dramas and lyrics will long continue to find appreciative readers, and that, as culture and taste and love of pure art make progress, the number of his constant admirers will steadily increase.' In the same year Browning began publishing *The Ring and the Book*, an infinitely complex version of an obscure seventeenth-century Roman murder. One reviewer, slightly exaggerating the approval of other reviewers, would call the new poem 'the supremest poetical achievement of our time . . . the most precious and profound spiritual treasure that England has produced since the days of Shakespeare'.

6

The Eighteen-Sixties: II

The Ring and the Book

We saw the other day, in a paper set at one of our public schools, this question asked – 'Why are epic poems not written nowadays?' The questioner, if he had seen Mr. Browning's poem, would surely have thought his inquiry somewhat premature. For, though you may, if you please, restrict the term epic to such quasi-historical records as the Iliad and the Niebelungen-Lied, yet if *Paradise Lost* is to be termed an epic, why not the *Ring and the Book*? It at least professes to be of pure fact, which cannot be said for a large part of *Paradise Lost*.

The Saturday Review, 1868

The idea that epics have 'died out with Agamemnon and the goat-nursed gods', is one which is obviously absurd, even without practical evidence to the contrary, and has arisen from the false notion that 'heroic' is a term applicable only to wars and large actions. Now that Walt Whitman has written the Epic of Democracy on the other side of the Atlantic, and Browning, on this side, has furnished what may be fitly termed the Epic of Psychology, the idea of the decease of the epic is more than ever a dead idea.

F. B. Forman, *London Quarterly Review*, 1869

The Ring and the Book is Browning's masterwork. Here his quick intelligence and jocular humour, his love of argument and delight in historical detail, his genius for the creation of character through the dramatic monologue, all receive their most extensive and richest expression. The sheer bulk of the poem led many reviewers to compare it to the great epic poems of the past – nearly twenty-two thousand lines divided into the traditional twelve books and published in four monthly instalments from November 1868 to February 1869. The length alone gave *The Ring and the Book* a superficial resemblance to the traditional epic poem. Homer had sung the heroism and glory of the Greeks at Troy; Virgil the founding of the Roman state; Dante had charted the mind of the medieval world; Milton had given eloquent and consciously epical expression to the English Protestant version of the justice of the ways of God to man. As his subject Browning chose a sordid and forgotten murder that took place in the historically unimportant final decade of seventeeth-century Italy. Carlyle thought it 'an Old Bailey story that might have been told in ten lines and only wants forgetting'. A modern reader looking for an *epic* work published in the 1860s would likely fix, not on *The Ring and the Book*, but on the grand sweep of Russian life during the Napoleonic Wars provided by Tolstoi in *War and Peace* (1865–9); or on Whitman's new edition of *Leaves of Grass* (1867) with its celebration of democratic man, the westward course of the new American Empire, the tragedy of its Civil War and the death of its heroic President Lincoln; perhaps on Flaubert's history of the disillusionment of an entire generation in *Sentimental Education* (1869) or on Tennyson's account of the legendary rise and fall of British civilization in the *Idylls of the King* (1869). But Browning, by recreating the obscure Italian criminal case through the words of town gossips, buffoonish lawyers, a monstrous villain, an ineffective hero, a child-like heroine, and a wise old Pope, achieved a grandeur and scope which made the comparison to traditional epics inevitable to his contemporaries. Browning 'feels deeply with the men of his own generation', one reviewer calmly reflected upon *The Ring and the Book*: 'A resolute keeping to the reality which he knows, a resolute abandonment of all the customary fictitious ornaments and appendages of poetry ...' G. K. Chesterton would call the poem 'the great epic of the nineteenth century, because it is the great epic of the enormous importance of small things'. Robert Langbaum opens the most influential essay on Browning of the past twenty-five years with these words:[1]

> In the same sense that Dante's great poem can be said to derive its meaning from a Catholic, and Milton's from a Protestant, ethos – so Browning's *The Ring and the Book* derives its meaning from the relativist ethos predominant in Western culture since the Enlightenment.

Other recent students of nineteenth-century culture have found the poem to be the central document in related important cultural currents of the century: the phenomenon of 'the disappearance of God',[2] the evolution of the philosophical attitude William James would call 'pluralism',[3] the 'historicization of European culture',[4] and the great wave of Comtian positivism that became so pervasive in the intellectual life of the century.[5]

Browning found his great subject significantly but paradoxically among the refuse of the Florentine flea-market in June of 1860. In the first book of his poem, Browning recreates his discovery. There, among the odds and ends of cast-off furniture, cheap and broken art objects, used clothing and second-hand books, he found and purchased an Old Yellow Book:

> Small-quarto size, part print part manuscript;
> A book in shape but, really, pure crude fact
> Secreted from man's life when hearts beat hard,
> And brains, high-blooded, ticked two centuries since.

Contained in the forgotten book was a great human drama which, under the resuscitating hand of the poet, becomes an intricate narrative of passion and violence, the highest holiness and the deepest evil, of heroic action and cruel torture, of deception, self-deception and the nearly impossible search for truth. The old book contained, as its title-page announced, an account of

> 'Romana Homicidiorum' – nay,
> Better translate – 'A Roman murder-case:
> Position of the entire criminal cause
> Of Guido Franceschini, nobleman,
> With certain Four the cutthroats in his pay,
> Tried, all five, and found guilty and put to death
> By heading or hanging as befitted ranks,
> At Rome on February Twenty Two,
> Since our salvation Sixteen Ninety Eight:
> Wherein it is disputed if, and when,
> Husbands may kill adulterous wives, yet 'scape
> The customary forfeit.'

The trial testimony, the legal depositions, and the correspondence bound into this volume revealed to Browning the story of Pompilia, bastard of a Roman prostitute, deceitfully reared as the daughter of an old Roman burgher couple, married at the age of twelve to a down-at-the-heels count. She fled from the count's impoverished palazzo at

Arrezzo and returned to Rome in the company of a young priest, Giuseppe Caponsacchi. Soon after Pompilia had given birth to a son, Count Guido and four peasants from his estate brutally stabbed to death the young mother and the old burgher couple. The murderers were caught, tried, and found guilty. Pope Innocent XII refused to quash the court's verdict, and they were executed to the edification and diversion of the public. This was the historic, factual, sordid reality out of which Browning would create *The Ring and the Book*. 'How do you like The Ring and the Book?' Rossetti asked William Allingham in a Christmas letter of 1868. 'It is full of wonderful work, but it seems to me that, whereas other poets are the more liable to get incoherent the more fanciful their starting-point happens to be, the thing that makes Browning drunk is to give him a dram of prosaic reality, and unluckily this time the "gum tickler" is less like pure Cognac than 7 Dials gin.'

Intoxicated fascination with the old document is displayed in a lively fashion in the opening book of Browning's poem. The poet tosses the book exuberantly into the air, offers it to the reader for examination, then asks for it back because 'The thing's restorative/I' the touch and sight'. He describes his absorption in the book while walking back through the flea-market and through the Florentine streets:

> And on I read
> Presently, though my path grew perilous
> Between the outspread straw-work, piles of plait
> Soon to be flapping, each o'er two black eyes
> And swathe of Tuscan hair, on festas fine;
> Through fire-irons, tribes of tongs, shovels in sheaves,
> Skeleton bedsteads, wardrobe drawers agape,
> Rows of tall slim lamps dangling with gear, –
> And worse, cast clothes a-sweetening in the sun:
> None of them took my eye from off my prize.
> Still read I on, from written title-page
> To written index, on, through street and street,
> At the Strozzi, at the Pillar, at the Bridge;
> Till, by the time I stood at home again
> In Casa Guidi by Felice Church,
> Under the doorway where the black begins
> With the first stone-slab of the staircase cold,
> I had mastered the contents, knew the whole truth. . . .

That evening, standing on the terrace of Casa Guidi in a rapt, imaginative vision, the poet 'fused' his own creative energy with the dead facts of the document and perceived the deeper, spiritual truths inherent in the story of Guido, Pompilia and Caponsacchi.

Despite the excited sense of discovery on 'That memorable day' it would nevertheless be over four years before Browning would begin to think seriously of turning the Old Yellow Book into a poem. He is known to have offered the document to two prose writers, one a novelist. Perhaps he sensed that the sordid murder-case was more suited to the novelist's art than to the poet's. (Towards the end of the first book, in a pun, he refers to the subject as 'A novel country'. And, Carlyle had, since the 1840s, urged him to write prose. After Browning's death, Henry James would describe in an essay called 'The Novel in *The Ring and the Book*' how he would have treated the same material.) Browning sought more documentary evidence about the case while in Rome during the winter of 1860–1. In the opening book of the poem he claims he was rebuffed in his search by Catholic authorities, perhaps at the Vatican library, because he was not Catholic and because he had a reputation for writing against the Church. That episode leads Browning into atrocious puns on the Catholic hierarchy in England as the authorities in Rome advise him:

> 'Go get you manned by Manning and new-manned
> By Newman and, mayhap, wise-manned to boot
> By Wiseman, and we'll see or else we won't.'

Elizabeth died in June 1861; and Browning returned to London where he was busy educating his son Pen, taking up his varied and full social life, and preparing for publication not only his own *Selections* and *Dramatis Personae* but also two volumes of Elizabeth's work. It was not until the late summer of 1864, while reviewers were giving unaccustomed but long-awaited praise to his poetry, that Browning, on holiday in the French Pyrennees, began to think seriously about transforming the documents of the old Roman murder story into what was to be his master-work.

The method Browning chose was a natural one for a poet who had made the dramatic monologue his characteristic poetic mode, but the method was much more ambitious and revolutionary than anything Browning had attempted before: the facts of the Old Yellow Book would be related and individually interpreted from ten distinct points of view in ten dramatic monologues. The same story ten times over.

The dramatic speakers would be two street gossips and another gossip bent on entertaining High Society with his clever account of the sensational events. Then the principals in the case – Count Guido, the priest Caponsacchi, and the victim Pompilia – would give their versions. The legal involutions of the prosecuting and defending lawyers would be followed by the wiser assessment of Pope Innocent XII; at last would come an anguished cry from the by now condemned Guido. Further, in opening and concluding books which frame the ten monologues, Browning himself becomes the dramatized speaker. In the first book he provides the reader with a variety of information not only about his discovery of the Old Yellow Book but also justifications of his selection of so harsh and sordid a subject, an account of the creative process he used to transform the inert historical facts into a poem, a straightforward narrative summary of the events which the other speakers would elaborate and complicate; he also supplies short descriptions of the monologues to come, thus alerting the reader to the special conditions which will influence each speaker's interpretation of the murder-case. In the final book the poet gives an account of the executions and the public reaction to them; then, he suggests to the 'British Public' the significance of his poem.

Why Browning chose this novel and revolutionary method of arranging his material is, if anything, less certain than when the conception came to him. A memoir by his friend Rudolf Lehmann, suggests that the idea came to Browning upon his first reading of the Old Yellow Book, and probably the method of presenting conflicting points of view came from the trial testimony itself. Lehmann has Browning say that he arranged twelve pebbles in a circle to indicate the twelve books of the poem. Rossetti's brother William records in his diary that the idea came to Browning while he was vacationing near the Pas de Roland in the summer of 1864. At any rate, the poem was begun in October of 1864 and the bulk of it was completed by the following autumn. Near the end of the first book, the poet comments that he might have treated his subject differently. He might, for example, have given his disparate materials a more obvious but ultimately sterile unity by selecting a traditional and appropriate seasonal setting:

A novel country: I might make it mine
By choosing which one aspect of the year
Suited mood best, and putting solely that

On panel somewhere in the House of Fame,
Landscaping what I saved, not what I saw:
– Might fix you, whether frost in goblin-time
Startled the moon with his abrupt bright laugh,
Or, August's hair afloat on filmy fire,
She fell, arms wide, face foremost on the world,
Swooned there and so singed out the strength of things,
Thus were abolished Spring and Autumn both,
The land dwarfed to one likeness of the land,
Life cramped corpse-fashion.

Such selectivity and imposition of a false unity would not only be
sterile and untrue to the historic reality, but it would also pander to
the reader's weakness for absolute black-and-white judgments. Browning wished to portray the dynamic, changing, rich and baffling multiplicity of human experience he had found in the lives of his historical
characters. Hence, he advises his readers:

Rather learn and love
Each facet-flash of the revolving year! –
Red, green and blue that whirl into a white,
The variance now, the eventual unity,
Which make the miracle. See it for yourselves,
This man's act, changeable because alive!
Action now shrouds, nor shows the informing thought;
Man, like a glass ball with a spark a-top,
Out of the magic fire that lurks inside,
Shows one tint at a time to take the eye:
Which, let a finger touch the silent sleep,
Shifted a hair's-breath shoots you dark for bright,
Suffuses bright with dark, and baffles so
Your sentence absolute for shine or shade.
Once set such orbs, – white styled, black stigmatized, –
A-rolling, see them once on the other side
Your good men and your bad men every one,
From Guido Franceschini to Guy Faux,
Oft would you rub your eyes and change your names.

The primary facets which go to make up 'the eventual unity' of *The
Ring and the Book* are the speeches of the ten monologuists. Through
their words the varied incidents which make up the tragedy are

recreated, and through their experiences and characters the reality of the world of the old documents comes to life. G. K. Chesterton, with characteristic suggestive hyperbole, says of these speeches:

> One of the most important steps ever taken in the history of the world is this step, with all its various aspects, literary, political, and social, which is represented in *The Ring and the Book*. It is the step of deciding, in the face of many serious dangers and disadvantages, to let everybody talk. The poet of the old epic is the poet who had learnt to speak; Browning in the new epic is the poet who has learnt to listen. This listening to truth and error, to heretics, to fools, to intellectual bullies, to desperate partisans, to mere chatterers, to systematic poisoners of the mind, is the hardest lesson that humanity has ever been set to learn.
> *The Ring and the Book* is the embodiment of this terrible magnanimity and patience. It is the epic of free speech.

Browning's decision to include himself as the speaker in the opening and closing books was nearly as revolutionary as was the device of retelling the story ten times through individual monologues. No reader of Browning's earlier poetry could have expected so much helpful information and commentary as the poet provides in the opening book. The psychological realism he had accomplished in his earlier monologues rested largely on his remaining 'dramatic in principle' and resolutely refraining from overt commentary in his own voice. At the same time, the strictly dramatic principle had disadvantages. As early as 1845 Browning had complained in a letter to Elizabeth:

> What easy work these novelists have of it! A Dramatic poet has to make you love or admire his men and women, – they must *do* and *say* all that you are to see and hear – really do it in your face, say it in your ears, and it is wholly for *you*, in *your* power, to *name*, characterize and so praise or blame, *what* is so said and done ... if you don't perceive of yourself, there is no standing by, for the Author, and telling you.

In the opening book of *The Ring and the Book* Browning takes something of the novelist's licence and plays 'the Author ... telling you' (the reader) things you should know before you begin to listen to the voices of the monologuists. The strict dramatic principle had also been the source of much of the 'obscurity' contemporary readers complained of. 'That is a fact', Carlyle had written to him soon after the publication of *Men and Women*; 'you are dreadfully difficult to understand; and that is really a sin. If you took up some one *great* subject, and tasked all your powers upon it for a long while, vowing Heaven that you *would* be plain to mean capacities, then – !' The old Roman murder case was not Carlyle's idea of 'one *great* subject' but it was Browning's. And when he took up that subject and began to task his powers upon it he wrote to Julia Wedgwood from his holiday spot in the Pyrenees: 'I keep trying to be quite intelligible next poem.' Four years later, after she had read the early proofs of the first six books of *The Ring and the Book*, Miss Wedgwood wrote to Browning: 'You seem to me hardly, if at all, liable in this work to the stock reproach against you; the design is perfectly clear. . . .'

The design is perfectly clear largely because Browning openly and fully announces that design in the first book. He gives away the plot in a lucid summary of the narrative and in lurid cinematic previews of the major actions – Pompilia's marriage, her sufferings at Guido's palazzo, her flight with Caponsacchi to Rome, the murders, the trial, the executions. This information is a convenient measure for the reader once he begins to listen to the special and prejudiced interpretations given by the various monologuists. Browning was not writing a detective story in the manner of, say, Wilkie Collins's *The Moonstone* (1868) or Dickens's unfinished *Mystery of Edwin Drood* (1870). As a story of crime, *The Ring and the Book* is closer to Dostoievski's *Crime and Punishment* (1865–6). In that novel the reader soon knows all the information about the 'crime', i.e., when, where, how and even why Raskolnikov kills the old woman. The author and reader are then free to concentrate their attention on the 'punishment', i.e., the mental suffering caused by Raskolnikov's guilt. The question is not 'who done it?' but what was the psychological effect and the moral significance of doing it. Browning achieves something of the same effect by revealing his 'story' in the first book and thus shifting the reader's attention away from the plot and towards the psychology of the individual speakers and the varied use they will make of that plot. *The Saturday Review*, which had at other times complained about Browning's obscurity, now complained that he had given his plot away too early. The writer in *Cornhill* made a further complaint: the poet had in the opening book declared his own moral judgments of the characters in his story. And so he had. Nearly ten thousand lines of *The Ring and the Book* are devoted to always ingenious and sometimes profound defences of the murderer Guido; nevertheless, the reader knows in the first book that

Browning has judged Guido a wolfish monster from hell equal in hate and evil to Lucifer himself. The poet's sentiments candidly and un-equivocally favour the innocent, pure and long-suffering Pompilia and the 'young good beauteous priest' Caponsacchi, whom the poet implicitly compares to St George and the archangel Gabriel. The short *précis* of the subsequent monologues further condition the reader's expectations and further direct his interest away from the mere story to the characters and to the odd way even factual truth has of taking on the colouring of the eye which perceives it.

The first three speakers – Half-Rome, Other Half-Rome, and Tertium Quid – form a balanced symmetry of the public version of the murder-case. Half-Rome 'found for Guido much excuse'; to Other Half-Rome 'Pompilia seemed a saint and martyr both'; with simple Hegelian logic 'One and one breed the inevitable three', so Tertium Quid selects the more entertaining circumstances and interesting argu-ments from both sides. All three speakers pervert and distort the truth because they are predisposed, either by circumstance or personality, to interpret human events from single conditioned, and therefore inade-quate points of view. They (and by extension 'the world') are afflicted with the 'plague of squint'; and it is the reader's task and delight to observe the various symptoms of that plague. Half-Rome sympathizes with the husband Guido, and condemns both the wife who ran away and the gallant young priest who helped her largely because Half-Rome finds himself in a position potentially like that of Guido – he, too, keeps a wife who is being courted by 'a certain what's-his-name and jacka-napes'. Because he is talking to the cousin of this rival, Half-Rome makes his narration of the tragic murder-case into an object lesson about the terrible vengeance a wronged husband must take to preserve the institution of marriage. Half-Rome reveals himself at the end of his monologue to be a strategist much like the Duke in *My Last Duchess*. Other Half-Rome is a bachelor afflicted with an idealized vision of love and marriage, a weakness which leads him in the opposite direc-tion in his 'feel for truth'. His idolatry of the 'flowerlike' Pompilia, his contempt for the cruel Guido, his envious admiration of the gallant Caponsacchi, all derive from his habit of viewing the world as though it were a book of romance. In contrast to the sentimentally quixotic Other Half-Rome, the tough-minded and opportunistic Tertium Quid uses the sensational murders as a means of gaining the admiration and approval of influential members of the upper class. He searches not for truth but for ways to display his considerable wit, eloquence, and ability to flatter the class prejudices of 'Eminence This and All-Illustrious That/Who take snuff softly, range in well-bred ring . . .'

Tertium Quid believes that he has not 'advanced' himself socially by his amusing recitation, but the reader has certainly advanced a good distance during these three opening monologues. The speakers themselves are interesting representatives of Roman public opinion, while at the same time they illustrate the difficult road truth must travel in this world. The story itself has been given fuller, more detailed, and sometimes deliberately false exposition. Perhaps more important, Browning has created the atmosphere of seventeenth-century Rome a-buzz with rumour and has built up by accumulated detail a realistic context for the tragedy. Half-Rome speaks the day after the murders. He stands just off the crowded Corso and near the entrance to the church of San Lorenzo where the bodies of the putative parents of Pompilia lie. Thus stationed, he can describe the jostle of the crowd intent on viewing the spectacle, and he can report on the obstinate vigil of old Luca Cini who, man and boy, has for seventy years watched the laying out of bodies but finds the wounds on these bodies (triangular punctures of a Genoese dagger with hook-teeth) superior to his previous experience. Old Luca stays close in order to instruct the less experienced viewer, all the while hoping that the dying Pompilia, with her twenty-two stab wounds, will soon be on display. Tertium Quid's monologue gives off much of that 'glitter and gold-dust of the Roman *salon*' which Henry James so valued in the poem; it also provides a lascivious and snobbish account of how and in what obscure Roman street the transaction to buy the babe Pompilia from her prostitute mother took place. Modern readers may weary of the intricate involutions of the known facts; even the Victorian reading public, addicted as it was to three-decker novels, may have been in danger of foundering on the rich diversity of these opening books. John Addington Symonds gave counsel to such readers as have 'the patience and the intellect to follow the elaborate and subtle working of the most profound of living artists . . .' His advice was: 'As in a novel of Balzac's, their patience will be rewarded by the final effect of the accumulated details grouped together by the artist, and their intellect will be refreshed with the exhibition of prodigious power carefully exerted and marvellously sustained.'

The original readers of *The Ring and the Book* – those who read it as it came out three books at a time in monthly instalments – read first the poet's version of the case in Book I, then the diametrically opposed views of Half-Rome and Other Half-Rome. They had to wait a full month to read Tertium Quid's 'reasoned statement of the case', as the poet sneeringly described it in the opening book. Immediately following Tertium Quid come the audacious defence of Count Guido Fransechini and the impassioned utterance of Caponsacchi. Guido would be allowed to speak yet a second time (in Book XI) so that his evil might be seen to 'rise to limit conceivable', as Browning informed his somewhat anxious bluestocking correspondent Julia Wedgwood. When Guido speaks this first time, however, his malicious hatred and hellish nature are carefully masked behind words strategically and skilfully designed to justify himself. His speech marks the opening of the trial, and his listeners are the judges 'ranged there to slay him or to save . . .' He knows, as he says upon declining more than a single sip of wine,

> I want my head
> To save my neck, there's work awaits me still.

His 'work' consists of admitting the murders, then justifying all his actions because they were perpetrated in an honourable cause. Feigning humility, flattering the judges' class and professional prejudices, portraying himself as a long-suffering victim finally moved to righteous vengeance, Guido subtly builds his self-defence. The main line of his argument begins with the fact that he is 'representative of a great line'. His marriage to Pompilia was a dutiful attempt to perpetuate the family, but his discovery that Pompilia was base-born and finally adulterous brought such a blemish to his noble line that he made the difficult but honourable decision to remove the blemish. By murdering Pompilia and her supposed parents (the deceitful old burgher couple, Violante and Pietro) he had upheld not only his own honour but the ancient traditions of Italian and Christian society. As his monologue closes, Guido asks the judges to make the 'brave decision' to approve his action and thereby conserve and strengthen the threatened social order. His acquittal will assure a

> Rome rife with honest women and strong men,
> Manners reformed, old habits back once more,
> Customs that recognise the standard worth, –
> The wholesome household rule in force again,
> Husband's once more God's representative,
> Wives like the typical Spouse once more, and Priests

No longer men of Belial, with no aim
At leading silly women captive, but
Of rising to such duties as yours now . . .

Against the blatant posturing and calculated rhetoric of Guido, Browning placed the powerful emotive outcry of the priest Caponsacchi. Nearly broken by grief because Pompilia is dying, angry at a legal system that failed to prevent the murders, confused by the mixture of masculine passion and priestly adoration he feels towards Pompilia, and filled with hatred for Guido, Caponsacchi tries to explain to the judges the great experience that has transformed his life. The nature of that transforming experience is not easy for Caponsacchi to put into words. Early in his utterance he describes Pompilia as

The glory of life, the beauty of the world,
The splendour of heaven . . . well, Sirs, does no one move?
Do I speak ambiguously? The glory, I say,
And the beauty, I say, and the splendour still say I,
Who, priest and trained to live my whole life long
On beauty and splendour, solely at their source,
God, – have thus recognised my food in her . . .

The burden of Caponsacchi's monologue becomes a need to make understandable to the human comprehension of the judges the 'miracle' that Caponsacchi had recognized in Pompilia the glory, beauty, and splendour of God, and that service to Pompilia (i.e., aiding her flight from Guido) was service to God. He must explain how, as a gifted young nobleman, he became a social ornament to the Church, and how he became dissatisfied in his role as 'coxcomb, fribble, and fool' for cynical superiors. The call to a higher duty, outside the conventions of Church and class, came to him instantaneously and intuitively when he saw Pompilia at her window in Guido's palazzo:

. . . there at the window stood,
Framed in its black square length, with lamp in hand,
Pompilia; the same great, grave, griefful air
As stands i' the dusk, on altar that I know,
Left alone with one moonbeam in her cell,
Our Lady of all the Sorrows.

So he was initiated 'Into another state, under new rule'. Pompilia, whom Caponsacchi frequently describes as a Raphael *Madonna*, becomes

the object of his priestly adoration and service. At the same time,
Pompilia's persecution by Guido enlists Caponsacchi's sense of chivalric
duty and attracts his masculine ardor. Rather late in the monologue,
he self-consciously and uneasily identifies his action with the legend of
St George and the Dragon:

> Can I assist to an explanation? – Yes,
> I rise in your esteem, sagacious Sirs,
> Stand up a renderer of reasons, not
> The officious priest would personate Saint George
> For a mock Princess in undragoned days.
> What, the blood startles you? What, after all
> The Priest who needs must carry sword on thigh
> May find imperative use for it? Then, there was
> A Princess, was a dragon belching flame,
> And should have been a Saint George also?

Caponsacchi knows, in the way that Other Half-Rome for example
does not know, that complex human experience cannot be rendered
in the terms of romantic legend. The legend may 'assist to an explana-
tion' and it may help describe a part of that mysterious coil of 'man
and priest' which is Giuseppe Caponsacchi. Saint George's legend,
however, is a story of heroic success; Caponsacchi knows too well that
he lives in 'undragoned days' and that he was an ineffective hero who
failed to slay the dragon Guido who now has slain the Princess.

Pompilia, who speaks next to round out the trio of monologues by
the principal actors in the tragedy, talks with greater simplicity and
serenity. The horrors of her life with Guido and his final murderous
assault have so overwhelmed her that they have taken on an air of
unreality, blankness, 'Sheer dreaming and impossibility ...' But
gradually she develops her version and interpretation of the experience,
motivated as she is by a pious obedience to the injunction of her Confessor that she tell her story so he may advise her how to forgive, and
motivated also by a desire to free Caponsacchi of any public suspicion
that the priest and she were lovers. The act of remembering and
coming to some understanding of her tragic life is difficult and painful.
However, by identifying herself with simple and familiar objects – a
broken clay Virgin, an Andromeda-like figure in an old tapestry,
flowers and helpless animals – she finds she can express what had seemed
inexpressible. The telling out of her story brings Pompilia a sense of
catharsis in much the same way as Caponsacchi purges himself of his

grief, anger and hatred of Guido by his resolve, as he tells the judges, to 'Burn my soul out in showing you the truth'.

The reviewer for *St. Paul's* magazine, searching for some common element among the various speakers in *The Ring and the Book*, found that 'they are all alike in one thing: their excessive love of talk'. Certainly as a death-bed utterance, Pompilia's speech would be *excessive* if it were to be measured by the standards of realistic narrative or drama. But *talk* is the important action in all of Browning's monologues. And important things happen to characters while they are in the process of talking. The rich complexity of Browning's method can be illustrated by a single thread in Pompilia's monologue: her consideration of the birth of her child, Gaetano. For the other speakers in the poem, the child is the object of much speculation, idle gossip, and legal manoeuvring. To Guido and his defenders the child might be proof of Pompilia's adulterous relationship with Caponsacchi; but that would be awkward for Guido, who wishes to claim the child as his own in order to receive Pompilia's property. All of the speakers make some use of the child; all, that is, excepting Caponsacchi, who likes to think of Pompilia as an innocent distressed maiden or the Virgin Mary. In the final book, Browning makes the subsequent history of Gaetano into an amusing historical puzzle thus frustrating the expectations of readers accustomed to finding in The Concluding Chapter of the conventional novel a tidy summary of the fates of various minor characters. In Pompilia's monologue, Browning uses the fact of Gaetano's birth to enrich his psychological portraiture of his heroine while also illustrating one of his favourite philosophical notions – the notion that evil is only apparent and that good can and often does arise out of evil. One of the things Pompilia cannot or will not remember about her past experience is that she had sexual relations with Guido. Now that she is dying, she considers the birth of her child to be the one great good that has come to her in life; yet, she denies that Guido, the greatest evil in her life, was father to this good. Gradually she is able to admit that, on the orders of the Archbishop to whom she had vainly appealed for help, she had allowed Guido sexual relations albeit she still wishes she had resisted. By the end of her monologue she acknowledges Guido's fatherhood while at the same time recognizing the natural enmity between the goodness in herself and the evil in Guido. Armed with this deeper understanding, Pompilia finds she can forgive Guido because in killing her he has purged her soul of the bodily corruption caused by their sexual relations:

His soul has never lain beside my soul:
But for the unresisting body, – thanks!
He burned that garment spotted by the flesh.
Whatever he touched is rightly ruined: plague
It caught, and disinfection it had craved
Still but for Guido; I am saved through him
So as by fire; to him – thanks and farewell!

Victorian readers immediately recognized Pompilia as one of Browning's most sublime creations even if some did suggest that the poet had
endowed his heroine with an eloquence and philosophical understanding not quite in keeping with an illiterate, seventeen-year-old girl.
Modern readers are as likely to be put off by what Philip Drew has
called 'the poet's faintly oppressive reverence for the innocence of
Pompilia'.[6] As a literary character, Pompilia has probably suffered
more than any other character in *The Ring and the Book* from shifting
taste and fashion during the past one hundred years. Her sweetness,
innocence, vulnerability to masculine treachery and her demure acceptance of Caponsacchi's gentlemanly worship, align her with the Victorian heroine-wife-mother-fiancée-daughter – fragile and forgiving,
as attractive on her death-bed as on the bench of the new pianoforte.
Dickens's Esther Summerson in *Bleak House* is a better known example
of the species. So is Amelia in *Vanity Fair*, but she exists under Thackeray's ironic observation. It is unfair to use a single sentence to charac-
terize so complex a creation as Browning's Pompilia; nevertheless,
when Pompilia, dying of twenty-two stab wounds inflicted by her
constant tormentor, Guido, says of him – 'I could not love him, but
his mother did', – a twentieth-century reader has no choice but to
laugh or to hope desperately that Browning intends the line to indicate
Pompilia's simple acceptance of the sanctity of motherhood. The
pathetic and innocent nature of Pompilia is, however, created mainly
through the testimony of three characters – the romantic bachelor
Other Half-Rome, Caponsacchi, and Pompilia herself. More cynical
versions of her character are provided by Half-Rome, Tertium Quid,
both lawyers, and, of course, by Guido, who in the final monologue
describes her as 'a nullity in female shape', who has 'milk for blood'.
Caponsacchi portrayed her as a gentle Raphael Madonna; Guido
prefers Titian's women:

Give me my gorge of colour, glut of gold
In glory round the Virgin made for me!

Titian's the man, not Monk Angelico
Who traces you some timid chalky ghost
That turns the church into a charnel: ay,
Just such a pencil might depict my wife!

For the Pope, who finds Pompilia 'perfect in whiteness' and Guido
the 'midmost blotch of black', she becomes a symbol of surviving and
persisting virtue in a world threatened by moral anarchy because
individuals (Caponsacchi as well as Guido) are moved by 'mere
impulse' instead of submitting to the carefully evolved code of the
Church. These varied interpretations of Pompilia do not alter the
obvious and nearly sentimental reverence Browning has for his
heroine; but with them, he provides alternative perspectives towards
her. Julia Wedgwood, who complained of Browning's excessive
interest in evil and of his 'photographic impartiality', playfully warned
the poet that when she brought out an abridged edition of *The Ring
and the Book* she would 'only keep enough of Guido and the Lawyers
to make an ebony frame for that pearly image of Pompilia'. Miss
Wedgwood never got around to her edition, but numerous anthologists along with twentieth-century theatrical, operatic and cinematic
versions of *The Ring and the Book* have used only elements that fit the
pearly image of a Victorian heroine.

After the sublime heights of Pompilia's monologue, the reader is
dropped suddenly down to listen to the written briefs of the lawyers
as they manipulate the 'patent truth-extracting process' of legal argument
and procedure. Both Guido's defender (Archangelis) and Pompilia's
advocate (Bottinius) exploit factual evidence and contrive perverse
interpretations in order to further their own personal and professional ends. Both are satiric creations at whom the reader is invited
to laugh and through whom Browning condemns the dehumanizing
system of legal interpretation of vital human motives and relationships.
Though Bottinius is the more fluent of the two, both lawyers are men
of

> . . . ready smile and facile tear,
> Improvised hopes, despairs at nod and beck,
> And language – ah, the gift of eloquence!
> Language that goes, goes, easy as a glove,
> O'er good and evil, smoothens both to one.

Archangelis's defence of Guido's monstrous crime exists banally side-by-side with his familial affections and his gluttonous anticipation of his little son's birthday feast. And his words, regularly translated into hopefully impressive and certainly obfuscating court Latin, are

A-bubble in the larynx while he laughs,
As [if] he had fritters deep down frying there.

Bottinius's professionalism and extravagant egotism are equally humourous and perhaps more sinister than those exposed in his rival. Bottinius will concede any false imputation, engage in any specious logic, so long as the 'wheels of argument run glibly on', so long as he can display his mastery of his profession, and so long as he can sustain his utopian vision of a world becoming 'one lawsuit', in which he ('Law's son') can find a lucrative and honourable position. The 'rule of law', so valued by most nineteenth-century men and so passionately sought by those classes who suffered from its arbitrary exercise, is derisively dismissed by Browning in these two monologues. Much like Dickens, who had in *Bleak House* figuratively portrayed the ultimate self-destruction of the iniquitous Court of Chancery, Browning expresses in these monologues the optimistic 'confidence that men without artificial restraints would live more honestly and more generously'.[7] He had also provided comic-relief between the 'serene song' of Pompilia and the majestic judgment of Pope Innocent XII.

The Pope's monologue is 'wonderfully grand – a fitting organ peal to close such a book of mighty music', or so said Robert Buchanan, who would soon damn Browning's friends and supporters, Rossetti and Swinburne, as leaders of *The Fleshly School of Poetry*. Posterity has been more inclined to agree with Buchanan's eulogy to Browning's Pope than with his priggish and self-serving indictment of Rossetti and Swinburne as dangerous pornographers. Browning had himself, in the opening book, recommended to the reader Pope Innocent's account of the tragedy as 'the ultimate Judgment save yours'. The Pope, with his hard-won wisdom and quick insight into the moral issues of the case, speaks with more convincing authority than does any other monologuist. As such he is often taken to be Browning's spokesman or 'mouthpiece'. Henry James complained that the Pope was 'too high above the whole connection functionally and historically for us to place him within it dramatically'. J. Hillis Miller suggests that aesthetic presuppositions of *The Ring and the Book* are that by multiplying perspectives (points of view) the limited, single, individual perspective can be transcended; however, the 'Pope is somehow beyond the limitations and distortions of the other monologuists. He speaks for Browning. He speaks for God himself. To include such a character is to betray the presuppositions of the poem'.[8]

Browning's Pope, seen from these lines of interpretation, might be made to echo the words of the Judge-Penitent in Albert Camus's *The Fall*: 'I was concerned with no judgment; I was not on the floor of the courtroom, but somewhere in the flies like those gods brought down by machinery from time to time to transfigure the action and give it its meaning'. But like Camus's ironic monologuist, Browning's Pope is deeply and personally involved in the judgment he must make. Not only must he struggle with the mass of evidence – 'this coil of statement, comment, query and response' – which will lead him either to quash or to approve the court's verdict that Guido is guilty and must die. He must also struggle with the knowledge that his judgment is not infallible and that the terrible act of condemning to death 'Another poor weak trembling human wretch' may be the final act of his life. Further, he is highly conscious of his institutional position as Christ's Vicar; and in that role he realizes he must act decisively to curb the rising individualism which threatens the institutionalized values of the Church. If the reader assents more fully to Pope Innocent's profound meditations on the moral meaning of Pompilia's tragedy, that assent is based on Browning's success in engaging the reader's sympathy for a wise, experienced, and imaginative old man.

The Pope's highly wrought meditation might have been a fit close to *The Ring and the Book*, as Buchanan had suggested; but Browning had decided to let his villain Guido speak 'yet a second time'. Guido is the only character in all of Browning's poetry to be so privileged as to have a second chance to justify himself. When he had spoken the first time, Guido worked with great rhetorical skill to defend his actions, but he had failed to save himself. When he speaks a second time he does so in the terrifying knowledge that he will soon be executed and that the enormous elemental life he feels within himself will soon be annihilated. Consequently, a grotesquely honest revelation of his evil nature replaces the whining and ingratiating character who had first appeared before the court. The poet had prepared the reader for this dramatic change of personality in the first book:

While life was graspable and gainable,
And bird-like buzzed her wings round Guido's brow,
Not much truth stiffened out the web of words

> He wove to catch her: when away she flew
> And death came, death's breath rivelled up the lies,
> Left bare the metal thread, the fibre fine
> Of truth, i' the spinning: true words shone last.
> How Guido, to another purpose quite,
> Speaks and despairs, the last night of his life,
> In that New Prison by Castle Angelo
> At the bridge-foot: the same man, another voice.

Terrified and outraged that he must soon die, Guido's speech becomes a reckless and desperate search for some inner justification, 'something changeless at the heart of me/To know me by, some nucleus that's myself'. He finds that he contains within himself a primitive amoral force which had been naturally opposed to the pale virtue of Pompilia. In his earlier speech he had pretended to be a conservator of traditional social values. For a short time in the second monologue he tries to excuse himself on the grounds that he is an Hobbesian individualist or a kind of calculating Utilitarian who tortured and killed while acting out a sinister pleasure–pain principle. Eventually, however, he admits that his cruel and voracious nature is more akin to that of predatory animals, and particularly to the wolf. At one point he can imagine himself metamorphosed after death into a wolf:

> Let me turn wolf, be whole, and sate, for once –
> Wallow in what is now a wolfishness
> Coerced too much by the humanity
> That's half of me as well! Grow out of man,
> Glut the wolf-nature . . .

In his own eyes, Guido is not the morally deformed monster a Christian reading of the tragedy might make of him; he is a natural force of the kind his aboriginal Etruscan ancestors worshipped. He has in him, too, something of the Nietzschean superman, coerced and maddened by narrow human ethical codes and the sickeningly effeminate virtue of Pompilia.

Guido's vision of himself as a fiery, surging life-force beyond the judgment of conventional moral codes allies him with other examples of nineteenth-century romantic diabolism – Byron's rebellious outcasts, Melville's maddened and defiant Captain Ahab, Dostoievski's nihilistic Raskolnikov. He remains defiantly unrepentant of the murders nearly to the end:

Nor is it in me to unhate my hates, –
I use up my last strength to strike once more
Old Pietro in the wine-house-gossip-face,
To trample underfoot the whine and wile
Of beast Violante, – and I grow one gorge
To loathingly reject Pompilia's pale
Poison my hasty hunger took for food.

But when the torches appear at the cell door, Guido collapses back into 'Another poor weak trembling human wretch', claiming that all he has said of himself has been madness and pleading pathetically to be allowed to live. Miss Wedgwood thought she saw in Guido's closing words some 'hope' for Guido's soul, but Browning chided her: 'Guido "hope"? – do you bid me turn him into that sort of thing? No indeed!' Yet when we see Guido again, in the final book through the eyes of a Venetian visitor to Rome,

'He begged forgiveness on the part of God,
And fair construction of his act from men,
Whose sufferage he entreated for his soul,
Suggesting that we should forthwith repeat
A *Pater* and an *Ave*, with the hymn
Salve Regina Coli, for his sake.
Which said, he turned to the confessor, crossed
And reconciled himself, with decency,
Oft glancing at Saint Mary's opposite,
Where they possess, and showed in shrine today,
The blessed *Umbilicus* of our Lord,
(A relic 't is believed no other church
In Rome can boast of) – then rose up, as brisk
Knelt down again, bent head, adapted neck,
And, with the name of Jesus on his lips,
Received the fatal blow.'

So Guido, now the main actor in a public spectacle, is restored to human dimension and historical context; the Venetian visitor closes by voicing his disappointment at Guido's unheroic physiognomy and stature and the meanness of his costume.

Browning ends *The Ring and the Book* by once more openly addressing the 'British Public'. The lesson is an odd one to come at the end of one of the longest poems in the English language:

143

> This lesson, that our human speech is naught,
> Our human testimony false, our fame
> And human estimation words and wind.

This rather despairing assertion of the powerlessness of language to convey truth, is quickly countered by the more optimistic assertion that 'Art remains the one way possible/Of speaking truth, to mouths like mine at least'. As in the opening book, Browning once again asks the reader to find the 'meaning' of his poem in his artistic method rather than in his subject. The 'meaning' of *The Ring and the Book* does not lie in resolving disputes over Pompilia's virtuous innocence, Caponsacchi's chivalric heroism or Guido's monstrous evil. It was Browning's decision to present those characters and actions through nine distinct individual consciousnesses that led Forman in 1868 to call *The Ring and the Book* an appropriate nineteenth-century Epic of Psychology and that led Chesterton in 1903 to call it 'the epic of free speech'. It is the arrangement of the story rather than the story itself that makes *The Ring and the Book* an important cultural document reflecting the age in which it was written: to Robert Langbaum it expresses the 'relativist ethos' which was becoming predominant in western culture during the century; to J. Hillis Miller it is a rather desperate epistemological experiment aimed at regaining some certainty in an increasingly uncertain world. Another aspect of Browning's method was his reliance upon documentary evidence and historical fact. In the opening and closing books Browning reveals his delight and faith in man's ability to retrieve the past and breathe life back into long dead and nearly forgotten human beings. Nearly all nineteenth-century historians shared Browning's faith. Browning's sometimes shrill insistence on the factual basis for his poem further marks him as a man living in a world which, as Park Honan has said, was 'becoming Comtian with a vengeance ... In a continuing landslide caused by the tremors of scientific rationalism and the higher criticism, what could remain in place for long but primary documents and provable facts?'[9]

7

The Eighteen-Seventies and Eighties

He never thinks but at full speed; and the rate of his thought is
to that of another man's as the speed of a railway to that of a
waggon or the speed of a telegraph to that of a railway.

Swinburne, 1875

Browning is not merely a great dramatist but a great thinker.
'Browning is the greatest thinker in poetry since Shakespeare',
we have heard it said; and the remark appears to us no
exaggeration.

The London Quarterly, 1886

Mr. Browning's poetry, to describe it in a word, is a galvanic
battery for the use of spiritual paralytics. At first the shock
and the tingling frightened patients away; now they crowd to the
physician and celebrate the cure.

Edward Dowden, *Fortnightly*, 1887

By 1875 Robert Browning had become an eminent Victorian. He was
over sixty years old, but the poet who as a young man had been 'eager
for success, eager for fame' at last got his due. A book-length study of
his poetry had been published; accompanied by Carlyle and Lyell, he
had an audience with Queen Victoria; he had noted that his tailor paid
more careful attention to fittings; and he was, with the alarming
industry of Victorian authors, publishing a new book every year. The
young Robert Louis Stevenson, who believed that 'Compression is the
mark of careful workmanship', feared that Browning might begin to
bring out new books 'month after month'. Balliol College, Oxford,
made him an Honorary Fellow in 1867; and in 1881 Cambridge,
following the lead of the London Browning Society, advertised their

intention 'to develop the society into one for the more thorough study and deeper appreciation of modern literature, making Browning, as *the* representative modern English poet, the centre of the society's work'. A decade earlier the directors of the Chicago and Alton Railway had already decided to print 'everything of Mr Browning's' in their timetables; by 1888 the Boston-based *Atlantic Monthly* encouraged the women of the 'great West' with the hope that their 'Browning clubs will have their influence not less than the grain elevators'. Numerous parodies of Browning's poetry – such as Bayard Taylor's parody of *The Ring and the Book* printed in the *New York Daily Tribune* in 1875 – testify to a large public able to recognize the Browningesque manner.

Browning's wider fame was in no way the result of any shift in his poetry after 1870 towards a more easily understood or 'popular' style. If anything, the poetry written during the final two decades of his life is more difficult than anything he had written since *Sordello*. Though there is a rich and astonishing variety of subject, mood and style among the fifteen new volumes published after *The Ring and the Book*, Browning tends to become more argumentative, discursive and digressive. Two short quotations from *Fifine at the Fair* (1872) may suggest this tendency. The first exemplifies Browning's use of abstract language to express an abstruse idea:

> Each lie
> Redounded to the praise of man, was victory
> Man's nature had both right to get, and might to gain,
> And by no means implied submission to the reign
> Of other quite as real a nature, that saw fit
> To have its way with man, not man his way with it.

On the other hand, a philosophical speculation might be expressed in language which one reviewer described as 'those uncouth shrouds of diction, the complicated parentheses and inharmonious syllables':

> Here gape I, all agog
> These thirty years, to learn how tadpole turns to frog;
> And thrice at least have gazed with mild astonishment,
> As, skyward up and up, some fire-new fabric sent
> Its challenge to mankind, that, clustered underneath
> To hear the word, they straight believe, ay, in the teeth
> O' the Past, clap hands, and hail triumphant Truth's outbreak –
> Tadpole-frog-theory propounded past mistake!

Here Browning uses harsh sounds and rough rhythm to mockingly deride the ultimate importance of new biological theories. It is the style he would habitually use for humourous or satiric purposes as when in *Pacchiarotto* (1876) he openly attacked those critics who continued to carp about his lack of clarity and melody. After reading that poem one can better understand why Browning nicknamed the two pet geese he kept at Warwick Crescent *Quarterly* and *Edinburgh*. Browning's main retort to his criticis was that however small and easily expressed their own ideas, his thoughts were so new and large that language had to be wrenched to fit them. But here is how Browning put it:

> But had you to put in one small line
> Some thought big and bouncing – as noddle
> Of goose, born to cackle and waddle
> And bite at man's heel as goose-wont is,
> Never felt plague its puny *os frontis* –
> You'd know, as you hissed, spat and sputtered,
> Clear cackle is easily uttered!

Earlier in the poem the critics had appeared as chimney-sweeps come to accuse the poet of the polluting of the neighbourhood with his smokey obscurity. He warns them to leave before his housemaid empties the chamber-pots over their heads.

Browning had always been ruggedly independent in pursuing his own way in poetry. He had 'never pretended to offer such literature as should be a substitute for a cigar, or game of dominos to an idle man', as he told his friend the painter Kingsland. He had, as Henry James mused after Browning's burial in Westminster Abbey in 1890, 'broken at every turn' with the tradition represented by the older poets whom he joined in the Poet's Corner of the Abbey. Still, by some stroke of institutional wisdom, his memorial slab was placed alongside that of Chaucer; and next to Browning's stone is that of T. S. Eliot, whose debt to Browning was greater than Eliot would ever acknowledge. James emphasized the 'tremendous and incomparable modern' nature of Browning's achievement: 'moderness – by which we mean the all-touching, all-trying spirit of his work, permeated with accumulations and playing with knowledge'. Browning's delight in 'playing with knowledge' remained strong in his old age. One senses in this later work that with *The Ring and the Book* behind him and his fame secure, Browning felt freer to indulge his fancy, to deliver himself of his own opinions, and to cast whatever subjects he might choose into strange new forms. His first new poem, *Balaustion's Adventure* (1871), he described in the dedication as 'the most delightful of May-month amusements'. This poem, which is built upon a retelling of Euripides's *Alcestis*, led into further recreation and translation of Greek drama in *Aristophanes' Apology* (1875) and *The Agamemnon of AEschylus* (1877) where he displayed his considerable erudition; and, when classical scholars criticized, he was able to defend himself with obvious gusto. After the defeat of France by Prussia and the crushing of the Paris Commune, Browning would allow, in *Prince Hohenstiel-Schwangau* (1872),a garrulous Napoleon III to defend his career to a London courtesan. With greater ingenuity a Breton Don Juan in *Fifine at the Fair* (1872) pleads to his wife a case for infidelity. In *Red Cotton Night-Cap Country* (1873) Browning narrates, sometimes with jarring levity, the story of a Norman suicide he had taken from the French newspapers; in *Ferishtah's Fancies* (1884) he dons the mask of a Persian dervish to expound his ideas on such subjects as prayer, divine incarnation, asceticism, the balance of good and evil. Though none of these poems has had the lasting appeal of Browning's great dramatic monologues, they testify to the continued fertility and restlessness of Browning's imagination; and one can understand why the young Stevenson undertook to lecture the elder Browning in this manner:

> why does he always come before us in an Indian war-paint and cutting fantastic capers? Let him wash the red off his nose and the green off his ears; let him uncurl his legs from about his neck, and sit down quietly for a moment in this easy-chair, and then we shall see what he is, and tell him candidly whether he is Apollo or Quasimodo.

Browning remained nearly as puzzling and unpredictable in old age as he had been throughout his career. It was a quality which protected Browning the poet, if not Browning the man-about-town, from becoming an institutional eminent Victorian. By the Seventies and Eighties reactions against the institutions and values of the 'Victorians' had already set in; and the word itself was beginning to be uttered in derisive tones by younger men. Samuel Butler in *Erewhon* (1872), or so one reviewer complained, 'held us up to ridicule and treated our most cherished opinions with biting scorn'. Gilbert and Sullivan made ridicule of 'cherished opinions' into public entertainment. When W. H. Mallock published his irreverent *The New Republic* (1877), an earnest George Eliot labelled it as the work of 'a young man who has no solid contribution to make, [who] sets about to ridicule the men who are most prominent in serious effort to make such a contribution'. Seriousness, earnestness, a persistent though cautious optimism about human progress and an ultimate meaning to the universe, a belief in the moral function of art and the need for individuals to struggle energetically to 'contribute', these were some of the values challenged by a deepening cynicism and disillusionment. In England this new mood often took the form of satire, masquerading as refreshing candour or irreverent frivolity.[1] It also took the form of aestheticism or art-for-art's sake, an attitude which replaced the moral function of art with a 'religion of art'. John Ruskin, whose commitment was more serious and earnest (and admirable) than the following quotation suggests, captured that mood with these words: 'Does a man die at your feet, your business is not to help him, but to note the colour of the lips; does a woman embrace her destruction before you, your business is not to save her, but to watch how she bends her arms.'

It was in a religion of art that William Butler Yeats was instructed as a child by his father while they lived in London during the 1870s and early 1880s. In the provincial English resort town of Bournemouth, the French poet Paul Verlaine, already disgraced by first loving then shooting Arthur Rimbaud, was teaching French and feeling some of the same impulses. In France the reaction to *bourgeois* (i.e., now *Victorian*) values could take on more dramatic proportions. When Balzac answered criticism of the ugliness of his portraits of middle-class life with 'So the bourgeois are!' he had expressed an attitude which would lead to a rejection of 'western', bourgeois values and send Rimbaud to Abyssinia and the former bank clerk Gauguin to Tahiti.

Browning was an ambivalent figure to his readers in these decades. He had never held to a 'smug Christian optimism', of which Hardy accused him, but he was more in step with the values of an earlier generation than he was with the more sombre and sceptical moods of the newer generation. When Fra Lippo Lippi asserts in Browning's poem of 1855 that

> This world's no blot for us,
> Nor blank; it means intensely, and means good:
> To find its meaning is my meat and drink,

the licentious monk speaks largely for his creator, Robert Browning. In *The Ring and the Book*, he had dramatized the hard and awkward way modern man has when trying to disentangle truth from falsehood; and he organized a poetic form by which the various points of view could be heard. Still, he insisted, in the opening and closing books of that poem, upon his own absolute moral judgment. He anticipated much of the scepticism apparent at the end of the century. 'But Browning, united with the decadents on this point', Chesterton rightly said soon after the close of the century,

> is divided from them sharply and by a chasm in another equally important point. He held that it is necessary to listen to all sides of a question in order to discover the truth of it. But he held that there was a truth to discover. He held that justice was a mystery, but not, like the decadents, that justice was a delusion. He held, in other words, the true Browning doctrine, that in a dispute every one was to a certain extent right; not the decadent doctrine that in so mad a place as the world, every one must be by the nature of things wrong.

Hardy, whose sombre pessimism had been expressed in a series of novels after 1871, was puzzled that Browning, whose sensitivity and intelligence Hardy admired, could continue to hold to more hopeful versions of man and the universe. In *La Saisiaz* (1878) Browning engaged in earnest debate about the immortality of the human soul and concluded that he 'believed in Soul, was very sure of God!' In the *Epilogue* to his final volume (*Asolando*, 1889) Browning carries his cheerful optimism into the after-world itself:

> ... at noonday in the bustle of man's work-time
>   Greet the unseen with a cheer!
> Bid him forward, breast and back as either should be,
> 'Strive and thrive!' cry 'Speed, – fight on, fare ever
>   There as here!'

Ten years later Hardy would look back upon the century through which Browning had lived:

> The land's sharp features seemed to be
>   The century's corpse outleant,
> His crypt the cloudy canopy,
>   The wind his death-lament.
> The ancient pulse of germ and birth
>   Was shrunken hard and dry,

And every spirit upon earth
Seemed fervourless as I.

The sad, elegiac lament of Hardy contrasts sharply with the energetic celebration of hope by Browning. The contrast might also measure the distance between the Victorian Browning and the modern Hardy.

In the early decades of the twentieth-century it became the fashion to laugh at the 'easy optimism' of the kind that one can find in Browning's *Epilogue*. In the 1870s and 1880s, however, the young men did not laugh at Browning, even if they did often ridicule the Browning Societies which were beginning to emphasize the religious and moral instruction to be taken from Browning's poetry. Max Beerbohm's cartoon of Browning taking tea with the Society lampoons the severe moral earnestness of the devotees who surround the poet, but Browning himself sits among them ruddily healthy, enjoying their admiration, but sharply and enigmatically separated from those who have gathered around their prophet. Two of the most irreverent young men in London in the Eighties were Bernard Shaw and Oscar Wilde; both were profound and admiring students of Browning's poetry. Shaw enjoyed attending Browning Society meetings and wittily debunking notions about Browning's poetry, but he warmly defended Browning's neglected plays and the Wagner-like cacophony of his verse. Like Shaw, Wilde objected to the growing tendency to portray Browning as a philosopher and moral prophet, preferring instead to view Browning as a psychologist and creator of character:

> He has been called a thinker, and was certainly a man who was always thinking, and always thinking aloud; but it was not thought that fascinated him, but rather the processes by which thought moves . . . The method by which the fool arrives at his folly was so dear to him as the ultimate wisdom of the wise . . . He will be remembered as a writer of fiction, as the most supreme writer of fiction, it may be, that we have ever had.

Shaw and Wilde, ready to laughingly reject much held dear by Browning's generation, continued to take Browning seriously. If more and more of Browning's widening reading public found in his poetry 'a moral tonic' against increased scepticism, Browning could also number among his fervent admirers James Thomson, author of the despairing atheistical poem *The City of Dreadful Night*. On the other hand, a truly religious poet like Gerard Manley Hopkins failed to finish reading *The Ring and the Book* on the grounds that 'the tale was not edifying'.

Hopkins would probably have found some of the long poems Browning published in the early 1870s even coarser and less edifying than he found *The Ring and the Book*. *Prince Hohenstiel-Schwangau*, *Red Cotton Night-Cap Country*, and *The Inn Album* are all attempts to mould into poetic form essentially 'unpoetic' subjects drawn from contemporary European life which could be both morally ambiguous and coarse. In the first of these the subject is the private motive behind the public career of Napoleon III. Browning had distrusted the Emperor ever since he had watched him parade down the Champs Elysée after the *coup d'état* of 1851; the poet's distrust deepened after Napoleon compromised the cause of Italian unity with the treaty of Turin in 1860. Writing from Normandy a month before the French surrender at Sedan in 1870, Browning said: 'Not one human being could venture to approve the conduct of the Emperor, – for what was ever more palpably indefensible?' Yet, within a year Browning gave over to Napoleon a long dramatic monologue by which the Emperor could defend himself with sufficient complexity to cause one reviewer to read the poem as a 'scandalous attack on the old constant friend of England', while to another it was a 'eulogium on the Second Empire'. There is no heroic dimension to this man who had for two decades controlled the destiny of Europe. Now exiled in London, he opens his monologue by playfully suggesting that he is the Sphinx who finally must yield up his secrets to Œdipus, cast here in the form of a London courtesan who like himself has 'seen better days'; she listens quietly 'Under a pork-pie hat and crinoline . . . in Leicester Square' while the Emperor presents his apologia. His defence consists, in part, of admitting that he lacked the capacity to be a great leader who could dramatically change the course of history; he scorns the idealism and utopianism of a Fourier or a Comte, a Proudhon or a Hugo. Still, he considers he has been adequate 'for the age's need'. He has been a pragmatist, not attempting what might be best for his people but accomplishing what was possible, bringing them 'the sweets of ease and safety'. Building boulevards and bridges was preferable to the wars of liberation fought during the First Empire. Trade wars – to be won 'by forbidding neighbours to sell steel/Or buy wine, not by blowing out their brains' – would be a more prosperous and safer policy. But if there must be war, as there was with Austria in 1859 and would be with Prussia in 1870, it would be 'war for the hate of war', or, in twentieth-century parlance, 'a war to end wars'. Napoleon's case, that he brought peace and prosperity to France, is given an ironic wrench at the close of the poem. The reader discovers that Napoleon is not in exile in London after all. He has been engaging in a 'ghostly dialogue' sometime previous to the Emperor's abdication. He has been imagining how he might, in the future, defend his actions. The reader of Browning's poem, when it came out in December 1871, could measure that defence against the humiliating surrender at Sedan, the siege of Paris, and the brutal crushing of the Commune.

Red Cotton Night-Cap Country is set 'twelve months since, the Commune had the sway', and in Normandy where there are

> ... woe's me, still placards of the Emperor
> His confidence in war he means to wage,
> God aiding and the rural populace.

Browning's subject this time was an 'old tale of town and country life'. The town was Paris and the country was the area near the Norman resort village of St Aubin, where Browning frequently took a long autumn holiday. It was not, however, an 'old tale'; on the contrary, the story of the suicide of the scion of a rich Parisian jeweller's family had only been resolved in the French courts one month before Browning announced to his friend Isa Blagden that he had 'a capital brand-new subject for my next poem'. Browning had been alerted to the subject by his French friend Joseph Milsand; and he had followed the case in the provincial French Press and read the court proceedings of a civil case arising out of the incident. The affair was recent enough that Browning, on the advice of the Chief Justice, changed the names of the persons and places to avoid a possible libel suit. In taking his subject from a recent sensational news-story, Browning was following a practice honoured among novelists, at least, since Stendhal had written *Le Rouge et le Noir*. As in *The Ring and the Book*, he was working with factual and documented events, and he was again interested in the way such events can be interpreted. This time, however, the poet himself would be the only interpreter.

The story as Browning found it (but using the changed names) is that of Léonce Miranda who, though accustomed to hard, earnest work in the family business and to the severe Catholic piety of his mother, took up as a young man the dissolute life of the boulevards of Paris. Falling in love with a married woman, Clara de Millefleurs, Miranda left the operation of the family business to cousins and went to live with Clara at the family estate in Normandy. There he busied himself restoring the old house and building a tower from which he could view the Church of the Ravissante – a pilgrimage church nearly as celebrated then for its miraculous cures as was Lourdes. Called to Paris by his widowed mother to account for extravagant expenses, Miranda was severely rebuked by her for his sinful liaison with Clara; as a result, he attempted to drown himself in the Seine. Miranda had barely recovered from this breakdown when he was summoned by telegraph to Paris where he found his mother dead. An officiating priest accused him of killing her by his sinful life, and he once more broke down under the burden of guilt. He now resolved to break off the liaison. As a step in that direction he placed love-letters from Clara in a box and placed the box in the fireplace. He also left his hands in the fire until they were charred and the fingers burned off. Upon recovery, Miranda returned to Clara and to Normandy. On 13 April 1870, a gardener saw him fall or jump from the tower to his death. He left a will giving his property to the Church and the income to his mistress. The Franco–Prussian War interrupted a court case brought at Caen by cousins to disallow the will on the grounds that Miranda was insane. When the case was completed in 1872, the court ruled that Miranda had been sane. Browning agreed, but for his own special reasons.

Browning read Miranda's fall as a leap of faith, a desperate testing of his belief in an active providence through the agency of the Virgin mounted atop the Church of the Ravissante. Browning arranged the poem so that he might analyse Miranda's action and comment upon its significance. Against the grotesque events of Miranda's life, Browning sets himself as a cheerful, playful, amusing raconteur. For the first one thousand lines, he talks pleasantly with Miss Ann Thackeray, daughter of the novelist, as they stroll along the beach or in the countryside near a small Norman bathing-place, quiet enough (Browning mentions) to have so far escaped mention in Murray's guidebooks. The story Browning will eventually tell Miss Thackeray has all the brutal and sordid elements of a naturalistic novel after the manner of Zola; but in these opening pages the poet and his companion exhibit something of the carefree and pleasant holiday life that Boudin and Monet were painting in these years a few miles down the coast at Trouville. Because of the somnolence of the countryside, Miss Thackeray had nicknamed it *White* Cotton Night-Cap Country; but Browning, hinting at the bloody tragedy of Miranda, prefers the adjective *Red*. There are digressions on the deceptiveness of appearances and on the variety of human experiences and night-caps. The poet extravagantly suggests that a 'Night-cap-show' might be organized to rival the exhibition of stringed instruments then on show at the Kensington Museum. Gradually the story of Miranda begins to be told: how he was conditioned as a child to believe tales of miracles; how the Castillian temperament he had inherited from his father lent passionate firmness to his religious faith; how he fell into dissipation and profligacy. All the while Browning elaborates a metaphor of 'Turf and Towers', the subtitle of the poem which names the symbols of Miranda's divided nature. The 'turf' stands for earthly delights and pleasures Miranda sought in his life in the Parisian boulevards and his luxurious life with Clara at his Norman estate; the 'towers' stands for his aspirations towards purity and spiritual peace and certainty. Throughout, the poet maintains a mocking, bantering tone. The central events are described quickly and almost comically. When Miranda, filled with guilt and remorse, tries to drown himself in the Seine, Browning describes the suicide attempt this way:

Monsieur Léonce Miranda flung at last
Out of doors, fever-flushed: and there the Seine
Rolled at his feet, obsequious remedy
For fever, in a cold autumnal flow.
'Go and be rid of memory in a bath!'
Craftily whispered Who besets the ear
On such occasions
              Done as soon as dreamed.
Back shivers poor Léonce to bed – where else?

When Miranda burns off his hands, Browning brings in an anti-clerical physician to describe the charred fingers and angrily attribute the tragedy to those priests who had preyed upon Miranda's sense of guilt. The physician looks forward to the next Republic, when these priests will get their due; but – 'the Commune ruled/Next year, and ere they shot the priests, shot him'. Several times Browning, in a callously indifferent manner, draws the reader's attention to Miranda's grotesquely mutilated hands:

Benevolent? There never was his like:
For poverty, he had an open hand
... Or stop. – I use the wrong expression here –
An open purse, then ...

When Miranda finally throws himself from the tower to test whether the Virgin of the Ravissante will catch him and confirm his faith, Browning describes the leap in four drily anti-climatic lines:

> A sublime spring from the balustrade
> About the tower so often talked about,
> A flash in middle air, and stone-dead lay
> Monsieur Léonce Miranda on the turf.

Despite his frequent levity and occasional callousness, the poet draws a serious lesson from the pathetic case of Miranda. Judged against the influences of his domestic and religious environment and his inherited temperament, Miranda's leap was not only a sane act but a nearly heroic challenge against religious uncertainty which had become a cancer in the contemporary world:

> ... sane, I say.
> Such being the conditions of his life,
> Such end of life was not irrational.
> Hold a belief, you only half-believe,
> With all-momentous issues either way, –
> And I advise you imitate this leap,
> Put faith to proof, be cured or killed at once!
> Call you men, killed through cutting cancer out,
> The worse for such an act of bravery?
> That's more than *I* know. In my estimate,
> Better lie prostrate on his turf at peace,
> Than, wistful, eye, from out the tent, the tower,
> Racked with doubt ...

It was an extreme cure for spiritual sickness. Dostoievski had examined a similar sickness in *The Devils*, published in 1871 two years before *Red Cotton Night-Cap Country*. Also drawing upon newspaper accounts of a sensational trial, Dostoievski posited through the character of Kirolov the dark metaphysic that in the absence of belief in God, suicide becomes the one way man can assume god-like control over his life. Dostoievski's enigmatic hero, Stavrogin, commits suicide at the end of the novel; the closing line of *The Devils* is: 'The verdict of our doctors after the post-mortem was that it was most definitely not a case of insanity'. In James Thomson's *City of Dreadful Night*, published a year after Browning's poem, suicide becomes a joyful release from the misery of this world; a release possible only by the discovery that 'There is no God'. *Red Cotton Night-Cap Country* is an odd amalgam of materials and of the poet's attitude towards them. In it Browning shares a morbid interest in religious despair and suicide with Dostoievski and Thomson; in his use of documented contemporary events and his analysis of the influence of environment and heredity, Browning shares the 'naturalistic' impulse of Zola. The juxtaposition of the grotesque events of the story with the bantering and playful tone of the narrator's voice almost prefigures the dark comedy and theatre of the absurd of the twentieth century. At the same time, Browning could be rather flatly commonsensical about his hero's tragic fate. Alluding to Miranda's prayer to the Virgin to '"suspend the law of gravity"', Browning says:

> Miranda hardly did his best with life:
> He might have opened eye, exerted brain . . .
> Also, the sense of him should have sufficed
> For building up some better theory
> Of how God operates in heaven and earth . . .

In the opening pages, the poet had asked Miss Thackeray not to mock his 'sturdy effort to redeem/My pledge to wring you out some tragedy/ From even such a perfect commonplace!' Victorian reviewers did not believe that Browning had redeemed that pledge; he had been too 'indefensibly whimsical' while telling the 'uncleanly history of M. Miranda's intrigue and lunacy', to have created a tragedy drawn from modern life.

The Inn Album (1875) is constructed in a more orderly and traditional mode, although this poem was the immediate cause of Stevenson's questioning whether Browning was 'Apollo or Quasimodo'. Here the poet again tells the story, but he is not the intrusive, digressive raconteur he had been in *Red Cotton Night-Cap Country*. Browning's intense interest in classical Greek tragedy clearly made itself felt in this new dramatic poem. Four characters gradually assemble on the stage and by degrees reveal to the reader and discover for themselves the intricacies of their relationships. The action climaxes in the violent deaths of two of the characters. The setting (an inn near a country railway station) and the situation are contemporary. When he had finished the poem, Browning announced to his publisher that it

is on so very modern a subject that it concerns last Whitsuntide –

and English country life, – and moreover means to be abundantly passionate and pathetic: – I did it with a will in two months exactly: it is some 3,500 lines in length, and, in fact, is a tragedy in a new style.

Browning's tone here is reminiscent of the time, thirty years earlier, when he had assured Macready that *A Blot on the 'Scutcheon* was a 'spick and span new Tragedy [with] *action* in it, drabbing, stabbing, et autres gentillesses ...' Browning based his poem in part upon the unscrupulous career of Lord de Ros, who in the late 1830s had been disgraced for cheating at cards, and who figured frequently in the *Greville Memoirs* published in 1874. The infamous peer becomes the Elder Man of *The Inn Album*. The Elder Man meets a rich Younger Man, who had once been his protégé in the devious ways of the world, at a country inn. The Younger Man has come to the country to see his fiancée, but as he talks with the Elder Man he discovers that this man had once seduced and abandoned another woman whom the Younger Man had subsequently loved but lost. As the plot unravels, the woman arrives in the country to advise the young man's fiancée on love and marriage. The plot climaxes by the Younger Man killing the Elder Man, after which the fallen woman takes poison.

'Once admit that such subjects are to be handled at all,' argued *The Athenaeum*, 'and who is there but Mr Browning able to handle them?' Browning was the only major nineteenth-century poet to attempt to work such materials into a modern tragedy. It was the stuff of 'penny dreadfuls' and 'sensation novels'. Earlier in the century the novelist Bulwer-Lytton, whom Browning knew and whose work he admired, had argued for the use of such materials in serious literature: 'In the portraiture of evil and criminal characters lies the widest scope for an author profoundly versed in the philosophy of the human heart'. From *Porphyria's Lover* (1835) to *The Ring and the Book* (1868–9) Browning had successfully drawn 'evil and criminal characters'. *The Inn Album* was an attempt to fit such characters into the mould of classical tragedy rather than to reveal them through dramatic mono-logues. The result was simpler characters than those revealed through monologues (e.g., the characters remain nameless, known only as the Elder Man, the Younger Man, the Elder Woman, the Young Woman); there is also greater emphasis upon the story and dramatic action. To a recent student of the poem Browning was working in a 'genre of modern macabre';[2] the reviewer for *The Spectator*, however, accused

Browning of falling into that peculiarly Victorian pitfall – the melodrama.

Browning's ability to tell a macabre story simply and powerfully
shows itself in several poems written when the poet was nearing the
age of seventy. *Ned Bratts*, *Iván Ivánovitch*, *Martin Relph*, and *Halbert
and Hob* are all tales of sin or guilt or dark brutality. All are dramatic,
as Browning was careful to point out, 'because the story is told by
some actor in it, not by the poet himself'. The focus of attention,
however, is on the events of the narrative, not, as was usual with
Browning, upon the personality of the speaker. Also, these short
stories in verse are told chronologically so that a suspense is built up
about what happens next and what happens finally. In *The Ring and
the Book* Browning had given away his plot in the opening pages; the
narrative line of *Red Cotton Night-Cap Country* reminded one nineteenth-century commentator of 'a sort of looking-glass country, where
the end is always reached before the beginning'. By contrast, the events
of these later narratives are given a straightforward and clear account
in language that, if often roughly vigorous, is nevertheless lucid. *Ned
Bratts*, the story of a pub-keeper and his wife who unexpectedly confess to crimes and beg to be hanged, begins with a leisurely mood-
setting passage:

'T was Bedford Special Assize, one daft Mid-summer's day:
A broiling blasting June, – was never its like, men say.
Corn stood sheaf-ripe already, and trees looked yellow as that;
Ponds drained dust-dry, the cattle lay foaming around each flat.
Inside town, dogs went mad, and folk kept bibbing beer,
While the parsons prayed for rain.

The tale of a Russian peasant woman who loses her children to
wolves and is then executed by Iván Ivánovitch, begins with a catalogue
of the varied uses Russian carpenters have for their axes and continues
by setting a dark and savage landscape in which the quick justice Iván
deals out with his axe would be appropriate:

In the deep of our land, 't is said, a village from out the woods
Emerged on the great main-road 'twixt two great solitudes.
Through forestry right and left, black verst and verst of pine,
From village to village runs the road's long wide bare line.
Clearance and clearance break the else-unconquered growth
Of pine and all that breeds and broods there, leaving loth
Man's inch of masterdom, – spot of life, spirt of fire, –

To star the dark and dread, lest right and rule expire
Throughout the monstrous wild, a-hungered to resume
Its ancient sway, suck back the world into its womb . . .

Iván Ivánovitch, although written in a realistic mode, achieves the sombre simplicity and remoteness of myth or legend quite different from the careful recreation of historical particulars in *The Ring and the Book* or the crowded contemporary details of *Red Cotton Night-Cap Country*. In *Halbert and Hob*, the beast-like father and son who fight on Christmas Eve on their farm in 'a wild part of North England', are acting a ritual of conflict between generations which is mythic. Martin Relph, publicly confessing, as a white-bearded old man, his youthful failure to prevent the execution of the girl he loved, takes on a similar quality. These and other poems collected in *Dramatic Idyls* (1879–80) find Browning the old man looking away from the crowded and ambiguous world of history and the newspapers and finding simple, moral tales in the world of folklore, anecdote, or Greek, Hebrew and Arabic legend. This tendency would continue in *Jocoseria* (1883), *Ferishtah's Fancies* (1884), and *Asolando* (1889).

While Browning was publishing these volumes, the London Browning Society and similar groups throughout England and America were engaged in regular discussions of his work.[3] The Society represented an unprecedented form of public recognition for a living writer. Earnest men and women gathered to explicate the obscurities of Browning's poems, to hunt down allusions and discover sources, and to draw religious and spiritual lessons from the body of his work. Their purpose, as the final report (1891) of the London Browning Society declared, was 'popularization'. Frederick J. Furnivall, the main instigator of the society, was active in the Workingmen's College movement; and Furnivall rather naïvely hoped that Browning's poetry, which had never attracted a large following even among the educated classes, could be made available to the masses by means of study guides and cheap editions. Many members were clearly attracted to Browning's supposed message of robust optimism and stalwart faith in a troubled world. Other members – among them Arthur Symons, James Thomson, and Bernard Shaw – stressed Browning's richly complex artistic achievement. Although the Society was often the object of gentle satire, much excellent criticism and basic scholarship was inspired by the Society: Arthur Symons's sensitive and highly appreciative *An Introduction to the Study of Browning*, the *Handbook* and *Life* by

Mrs Orr, the biographies by William Sharp and W. H. Griffin, and the bibliographies by Furnivall and Thomas J. Wise. The full titles of two books by another member of the Society, Dr Edward Berdoe, describe much of the activity of the Society: *The Browning Cyclopaedia: A Guide to the Study of the Works of Robert Browning with Copious Explanatory Notes and References on All Difficult Passages* and *Browning's Message to His Time: His Religion, Philosophy and Science*. Never before had a living poet's work been subjected to such intense collective scrutiny.

Throughout most of his career Browning had been reluctant to comment upon and interpret his own work to curious readers. In 1872 he published a selection of his earlier work and, in a dedicatory preface to Tennyson, he commented that he was happy with his rising popularity which he attributed to more studious readers who had begun to meet the poet 'fully half-way'; he emphasized, however, his 'disinclination to write the poetry and the criticism besides'. But in later years, as more puzzled Browningites applied to the master for help, Browning often relented and supplied what help he could. Once upon learning that the Society was mightily exercising itself upon the poem *Numpholeptos*, the poet sent Furnivall an interpretation which he obviously intended as helpful. Browning's comment suggests two things about the poet: (1) he was highly conscious of the complex patterns he wove into his poems, and (2) he was a bit impatient with readers who failed to recognize 'a common image'. Browning began by insisting that the title of the poem, i.e., 'caught or entranced by a nymph', was the 'key':

An allegory, that is, of an impossible ideal object of love, accepted conventionally as such by a man who, all the while, cannot blind himself to the demonstrable fact that the possessor of knowledge and purity obtained without the natural consequences of obtaining them by achievement – not inheritance – such a being is imaginary, not real, a nymph and no woman; and only such an one would be ignorant and surprised at the results of a lover's endeavour to emulate the qualities which the beloved is entitled to consider as pre-existent to earthly experience, and independent of its inevitable results.

I had no particular woman in my mind; certainly never intended to personify wisdom, philosophy, or any other abstraction; and the orb, raying colour out of whiteness, was

altogether a fancy of my own. The 'seven spirits' are in the
Apocalypse, also in Coleridge and Byron: a common image.

Browning's willingness to be helpful to those readers who at last
were friendly to his poetry was often mixed with an impatience, even
exasperation, at the way some readers went about trying to interpret
a poem. The serious study of Browning's poetry coincided with a
growing tendency in literary studies to emphasize sources, allusions,
historical background and the writer's own life. The New Shakspere
Society and the Chaucer Society, both creations of Furnivall, fostered
this method of study as did the strong tradition of literary scholarship
growing up in Germany and being transplanted into American 'gradu-
ate' schools. The drift of the reader's interest away from the poetry
itself and towards 'extraneous matter' disturbed Browning as much as,
nearly fifty years later, it disturbed I. A. Richards and other New
Critics who wished to return the student's attention to the poem itself.
When *Jocoseria* was published in 1883, Browning's good friend Mrs
Thomas FitzGerald applied to the poet for 'background' information
to help her understand the poems. Browning's rather testy reply is
worth quoting at some length for it remains good advice. Mrs Fitz-
Gerald had written disparagingly of her own intelligence, baffled as it
was by many of the poems. 'May I venture to say', Browning advises,

> that all its fault is in the exercise of industry in a wrong direction –
> so far as regards my poems, at least. If you would – when you
> please to give them your attention – to confine it to the poems
> and nothing else, no extraneous matter at all, – I cannot but think you
> would find little difficulty: but your first business seems to be
> an inquiry into what will give no sort of help. . . . there was no
> need to 'know *d'avance* all the Talmudic stories' – which, – such
> of them as I referred to, are all sufficiently explained in the
> poem itself – indeed every allusion needing explaining is
> explained. But you begin by asking a friend 'Who Jochanan was:'
> why, *nobody*. 'John' (as the name is in English) was no more the
> 'John' mentioned by your friend than he was St. John of the
> Gospels: the poems *tells* you *who* he was, what he was, where he
> lived, and why he was about to die: what more do you want? . . .
> all the other stories are told at just as much length as is
> requisite for the purpose, and years of study of dictionaries and
> the like would make the student learned enough in another direction
> but not one bit more in the limited direction of the poem itself.

The Society did much to help the already devoted reader of Browning's poetry. In their larger aim of 'popularization', however, they failed. A British reading public which had bought within a few weeks of publication nearly 50,000 copies of Tennyson's *Enoch Arden* and nearly a million copies of Longfellow's verse, made *Ferishtah's Fancies* (1883) Browning's best-selling volume by a purchase of less than 7,500 copies. His fame as a great poet was disproportionately wider than his readership. His burial in the already crowded Poets' Corner at Westminster Abbey in January 1890, was public recognition of that wide fame. Yet, when the sixteen-volume *Complete Works* was published a few weeks later, one reviewer could with justice comment that 'to a large majority of the English-reading public, including not a few gifted and accomplished persons, this kingly poet remains a name only and for certain of them not even that, being actually known to some eager thinkers and readers solely through the parodist's sneer ...' After the deluge of public eulogy for the dead poet subsided, reassessment of Browning's fame and an inevitable deflation of his reputation began. First to come under attack was his role as a thinker, as a moral and spiritual guide. In the summer of 1890 Oscar Wilde, still a warm admirer of Browning's genius for the creation of fictional characters, charged that Browning's 'work is marred by struggle, violence and effort, and he passed not from emotion to form, but from thought to chaos'. The following year Sir Henry Jones in a carefully argued book, *Browning's Reputation as Philosophical and Religious Teacher*, warned that Browning by 'casting doubt upon the validity of knowledge, ... degraded the whole spiritual nature of man; for a love that is ignorant of its object is a blind impulse, and a moral consciousness that does not know the law is an impossible phantom – a self-contradiction'. By 1900, in an influential essay, George Santayana asked readers to be on their guard against the dangerous 'barbarism' of Browning's thought and art which he characterized as 'a volcanic eruption that tosses itself quite blindly and ineffectually into the sky'. After the turn of the century, when the general reaction against all things 'Victorian' had set in, Browning's hard and briefly won status as a Victorian Sage continued to decline. Even the brilliant and sympathetic studies by Percy Lubbock and G. K. Chesterton, as Philip Drew has recently remarked, were 'unable to halt the decline in Browning's reputation. . . .'[4] Yet, if less and less Browning was considered a reliable guide to how one might live in the modern world, more and more he was studied by younger men – Hardy, Yeats, E. A. Robinson,

Frost, Pound, Eliot – as a guide to how one might write poetry in the modern world.

8

Browning among the Modern Poets

Robert Browning was not, as many Victorian reviewers were fond of noting, a member of any recognizable 'school' of poetry. Nor did he become the founder of a literary tradition as did that other 'barbarian' against whom Santayana warned – Walt Whitman, whose acknowledged debtors range from Hart Crane and William Carlos Williams to Allen Ginsberg and Robert Duncan. Only Ezra Pound, among the major poets of the twentieth century, has openly acknowledged Browning as 'son père'. Still, as Lord David Cecil has said, 'Browning may be looked upon as the original English ancestor of the "modernist" school of English poetry.'[1] And the contemporary British poet Edward Lucie-Smith argues well his assertion that he 'cannot think of any other nineteenth-century poet whose work is still so much alive in the mid-twentieth. Browning moves within contemporary English and American poetry like yeast in dough'.[2] From the 1860s, when Thomas Hardy began imitating the rough cacophony of Browning's language, to the 1950s, when Robert Lowell turned the Browning monologue into a new kind of confessional poetry, Browning's work has supplied poets with possibilities of language, form and subject no other nineteenth-century English poet could offer. Most modernist poets have held to a darker, more tragic version of human experience than did Browning; such poets have found they could learn from Browning's technique but had to ignore his 'optimism'. In the early 1930s T. S. Eliot conceded Browning's lessons in the use of 'non-poetic material', of the dramatic mode, and of the 'relation of poetry to speech'. Eliot placed Browning alongside John Donne and the French poets Laforgue and Corbière as a technical model for younger poets. 'The place of Browning in this group', Eliot went on, 'is obscured by several accidents: by the fact that he is often tediously longwinded, that he is far less a wit and ironist, and perhaps more than anything by the fact that his knowledge of the particular human heart is adulterated by an optimism which has proved offensive to our time . . .'[3]

Thomas Hardy was a young apprentice architect and aspiring poet in London in the early 1860s when Browning began to gain a public reputation. Hardy probably first read Browning's roughly colloquial and realistic poetry in the *Selections* (1863) or *Dramatis Personae* (1864). From the first the relationship between the younger and the older poet was an ambivalent one: Hardy admiring and imitating Browning's language and verse forms but distrusting Browning's apparent cheerful confidence. The process was already at work in one of Hardy's earliest poems, *Hap* (1866). Among Browning's new poems of 1864 was *Rabbi Ben Ezra*, a favourite of Hardy. Browning's old Rabbi robustly asserts that the care and doubt of this imperfect world are but tests to prepare man for the perfect joy of the next. The Rabbi can strenuously ask:

Irks care the crop-full bird? Frets doubt the maw-crammed beast?

Hardy adopts a voice of similar 'grating cacophony' but finds this life a meaningless and painful pilgrimage in which

– Crass Casualty obstructs the sun and rain,
And dicing Time for gladness casts a moan . . .

Readers in the 1860s were at last willing to tolerate Browning's idiom, but Hardy's imitation of it was, perhaps, a major reason why publishers consistently rejected the poems of the younger man.[4] Hardy turned, with greater success, to fiction. In his first novel, *The Poor Man and the Lady* (1868), he began the practice of quoting from Browning poems, a practice he would continue through *Tess of the D'Urbervilles* in which Angel Clare reversed Pippa's famous formula by announcing that 'God's *not* in His heaven; all's *wrong* with the world!'

After Hardy began to publish his poetry in 1898, the influence of Browning was apparent in many aspects of Hardy's verse. The rhythms of *The Statue and the Bust* are taken over in *The Waiting Supper*; there are Browning evocations of historical situations as in *The Peasant's Confession*, echoes of *Childe Roland* in *The Something that Saved Him* and of *Cleon* in *In Paul's A While We Go. In a Waiting Room* opens with a careful attention to prosaic contemporary detail which Browning had brought into English poetry:

There were few in the railway waiting-room.
About its walls were framed and varnished
Pictures of liners, fly-blown, tarnished.
The table bore a Testament
For travellers' reading, if suchwise bent.

Many Hardy poems are dramatic monologues, but like most modernist poems, Hardy's monologues tend to be shorter, less 'longwinded' than Browning's. The amplitude of a Browning monologue allows the gradual and detailed revelation of the speaker's character. Poems like Hardy's *The Collector Cleans His Picture* and *The Wood Fire* aim less at a Browningesque exploration of character than at an ironic commentary upon a situation. In *The Wood Fire* we are more interested in the fact that the speaker has purchased for firewood, 'bargain-cheap', Christ's cross than we are in the personality of this man who has thriftily taken advantage of the authorities' desire to get 'the crosses out of sight/By Passover'. Hardy allows himself more Browningesque fullness of detail in *Panthera*. As the story of the ageing Roman officer unfolds so too does a realistic context for the life of Jesus. Panthera, while commanding the soldiers who executed Jesus, recognizes Mary as the woman he had loved more than thirty years ago. In old age he relates his experiences out of a tragic awareness that he may have crucified his own son:

> The impalements done, and done the soldiers' game
> Of raffling for the clothes, a legionary,
> Longinus, pierced the young man with his lance,
> At signs from me, moved by his agonies
> Through naysaying the drug they had offered him.
> It brought the end. And when he had breathed his last
> The woman went. I saw her never again. . . .
> Now glares my moody meaning on you, friend? –
> That when you talk of offspring as sheer joy
> So trustingly, you blink contingencies.
> Fors Fortuna! He who goes fathering
> Gives frightful hostages to hazardry!

Panthera imitates the form and language of poems like *Karshish*, *Cleon*, and *A Death in the Desert* while at the same time it denies their message. Both men drew upon the Higher Criticism of the Bible for their subjects: Browning created mock-documents to refute the corrosive scepticism of a Strauss, Feuerbach or Renan and to affirm that God's love was incarnate in Christ; Hardy allows his poem to stand as an ironic commentary upon the Incarnation itself. Hardy was not the profound pessimist many of his contemporaries thought him to be; nor was Browning the easy optimist Hardy sometimes took him for. Perhaps in Hardy's quarrelling fascination with Browning lies a way to see both poets more clearly. During the dark days of World War I Hardy re-read Browning's robust assertion of faith in the 'Epilogue' to *Asolando*. He then rather nostalgically confided to his notebook: 'Well, that was a lucky dreamlessness for Browning.' Still, the night before he died in 1928 Hardy insisted that his wife read to him all thirty-two stanzas of *Rabbi Ben Ezra*.

The final poem of the last volume William Butler Yeats saw through the press, *New Poems* (1938), concludes with the old poet suggesting that he might live out his remaining days by trying to

> . . . demonstrate in my own life
> What Robert Browning meant
> By an old hunter talking with Gods;
> But I am not content.

The poem, *Are You Content?*, is an invitation to Yeats's forefathers to judge his achievement and an announcement that he himself is still discontented. Yeats's allusion is, appropriately, to *Pauline*, Browning's early Shelleyan poem. Shelley, then Blake, not Browning, were the nineteenth-century poetic forefathers of Yeats. Nevertheless, from youth onward Yeats was an admiring reader of Browning's poetry.[5] When he entered art school in Dublin in 1884 he was surprised at his fellow students' ignorance of poetry; Yeats was an enthusiastic reader of English poetry, 'especially of Browning, who had begun to move me by his air of wisdom'. In 1887 one of Yeats's poems was mutilated by the typesetter for the *Gael*; Yeats published a humorous letter denying the poem was his and attributing it to 'an imitator of Browning'. An early poem, *How Frencz Renyi Kept Silent*, about a Hungarian nationalist and published in the Fenian exile journal *Boston Pilot*, is 'obviously an imitation of Browning's dramatic dialogues'.[6] Shortly after Browning's death, the young Yeats published an essay about Browning in that same Fenian journal. He objected to the flood of public eulogies that emphasized Browning's optimism, praised the 'great reverie of the Pope in *The Ring and the Book*', and described Browning's poetry in a manner that would have pleased the older poet: 'To Robert Browning the world was simply a great boarding house in which people come and go in a confused kind of way. The clatter and chatter to him was life, was joy itself.' Browning was one of the 'great Victorians' with whom Yeats and other members of the Rhymers' Club had to quarrel in the 1890s. A close companion in the Club was Arthur Symons, whose appreciative book on Browning had appeared in 1886 and whose essay of 1890 specifically linked Browning to Verlaine and the French symbolist poets. Yeats was more profoundly influenced by Symons' book *The Symbolist Movement in Literature* (1899) than by Symons' enthusiasm for Browning. However, it was Yeats who organized at the Abbey Theatre the 1912 centennial observance of Browning's birth. Soon, he had his young secretary Ezra Pound reading *Sordello* aloud to him. He preferred *Sordello* and *The Ring and the Book*, for which he retained an 'admiring astonishment', to the contemporary writing Pound wished to bring to his attention. By 1929, when Yeats was sixty-four years old and busily re-writing and revising his poetry with an eye towards a collected edition, he announced: 'I have turned from Browning – to me a dangerous influence. . . .'

The influence that Yeats considered dangerous is but dimly discernible in Yeats's *Collected Poems*. There is an occasional, almost incidental, similarity of language and a shared attitude towards the sources of poetic inspiration. In old age Yeats recognized that his poetic themes often arose out of

> A mound of refuse or the sweepings of a street,
> Old kettles, old bottles, and a broken can,
> Old iron, old bones, old rags, that raving slut
> Who keeps the till. Now that my ladder's gone,
> I must lie down where all the ladders start,
> In the foul rag-and-bone shop of the heart.

Browning frequently found his tawdry, often sordid subjects, as he had *The Ring and the Book* 'Mongst odds and ends of ravage' where the poet 'May chance upon some fragment of a whole,/Rag of flesh, scrap of bone in dim disuse. . . .' Yeats was particularly interested in Browning's early, more romantic poetry – *Pauline, Paracelsus, Sordello*. There Browning explored, as Yeats often explored, the theme of creative men divided within themselves and struggling to unify their aspirations towards knowledge and power, love and intellect, a life of aesthetic contemplation and a life of heroic action. In his 'doctrine of the mask' Yeats provided a formal aesthetic for the poet's need to speak dramatically through the masks of other personalities; Browning had long practised a poetry 'dramatic in principle' in which he donned the masks of personalities totally unlike his own. Both men shared an interest in the arcane, the occult, the mystical. Browning tended to hide his interests behind the masks of his characters, whereas Yeats more openly avowed a bewildering variety of occult and mystical notions. (Yeats himself tells the anecdote of the man who said to Browning: 'Sir, you are a mystic.' 'Yes,' replied Browning, 'but how did you find out?') Common subjects and ways of expressing those subjects can also be found in what one recent commentator has called 'the way Browning and Yeats use the Pagan-Christian dualism to project an underlying squabble between soul and sense'.[7] Only as a young man, however, was Yeats an 'imitator' of Browning in the manner of Thomas Hardy. Yeats remained an appreciative reader of the older poet, but the great original achievement of Yeats's own poetry transforms and transcends the influence he thought 'dangerous'.

The year Hardy died and a year before Yeats 'turned from Browning', Ezra Pound once more affirmed his debt to Browning. 'Uberhaupt ich stamm aus Browning. Pourquoi nier son père?' Pound wrote in that polyglot with which he was attempting to enrich English and American poetry.[8] 'Ma reforme', he had written earlier: '1. Browning – denué des paroles superflus.' In his first volume, A Lume Spento, published shortly after the young American had established himself in London in 1908, Pound began his 'reforme' of poetry by consciously imitating Browning in poems like La Fraisne, Cino, Fifine Answers, and Scriptor Ignotus. To the young poet, Browning was the 'old mesmerizer':

> Thought's in your verse-barrel,
> Tell us this thing rather, then we'll believe you,
> You, Master Bob Browning, spite your apparel
> Jump to your sense and give praise as we'd lief do.
> . . . .
> Here's to you, Old Hippety-hop o' the accents,
> True to the Truth's sake and crafty dissector,
> You grabbed at the gold sure; had no need to pack cents
> Into your versicles.
> Clear sight's elector.

During that first year in London, Pound wrote to his former university friend, William Carlos Williams, to describe the kind of poems he was writing. The letter suggests how Pound drew upon, while at the same time innovated upon, Browning's 'dramatic lyrics':

> To me the short so-called dramatic lyric – at any rate the
> sort of thing I do – is the poetic part of a drama the rest of
> which (to me the prose part) is left to the reader's imagination or
> implied in a short note. I catch the character I happen to be
> interested in at the moment he interests me, usually a moment
> of song, self-analysis, or sudden understanding or revelation.

Pound worked for greater economy than Browning, but he retained the essential form and tone and often the subjects of his master. When his enlarged collection of poems, *Personae*, appeared in 1910, the reviewer for *Punch* made the obvious connection: 'His verse is the most remarkable thing in poetry since Robert Browning.'

The dramatic monologues of Browning became a bench mark by which Pound measured the poetry of past cultures as well as the contemporary poetry he so effectively influenced. He noted T. S. Eliot's similarity to Browning in his enthusiastic review of *Prufrock and Other Observations* (1917). He pauses in his essay on 'Chinese Poetry' (1918) to say:

> If the reader detests fairies and prefers human poetry, then that
> also can be found in the Chinese. Perhaps the most interesting
> form of modern poetry is to be found in Browning's 'Men and
> Women'. This kind of poem, which reaches its climax in his
> unreadable 'Sordello', and is most popular in such poems as
> 'Pictor Ignotus', or the 'Epistle of Karshish', or 'Cleon', has had a
> curious history in the west. . . . From Ovid to Browning this sort
> of poem was very much neglected.

Pound rescued Browning's *Sordello* from the neglect to which it had been assigned. Since its publication in 1840 three other poets – Rossetti, Swinburne, and Yeats – had admired the poem; critics and general readers, however, had ignored that ambitious and bafflingly obscure work. Pound's championship of the poem which those 'Victorian halfwits' found obscure is tied to his own attempt to write a long poem which could take all history as its matter if not its subject. The second of his continuing *Cantos* opens:

> Hang it all, Robert Browning,
> There can be but one 'Sordello'.
> But Sordello and my Sordello?

Pound is not here announcing so much a theme or subject for his *Cantos* as he is asking if he cannot write a poem structured like Browning's. Pound had been interested in the subject of Sordello since he had given a series of lectures on medieval Provençal and Italian poetry at the London Polytechnic in 1909. When he began to write his *Cantos* during the First World War, however, it was the compendium-like form of *Sordello* that he hoped to use. Throughout the nineteenth century, the growing complexity of human knowledge had challenged poets who wished to write for their own times an epic work which could embrace the diversity of their culture. Writing to his publisher in 1797, Coleridge reveals some of the pressures that rapidly expanding knowledge brought upon a poet:

> I should not think of devoting less than 20 years to an Epic Poem.
> Ten to collect materials and warm my mind with universal
> science. I would be a tolerable Mathematician, I would
> thoroughly know Mechanics, Hydrostatics, Optics, and
> Astronomy, Botany, Metallurgy, Fossilism, Chemistry, Geology,
> Anatomy, Medicine – then the *mind of man* – then the *minds of
> men* – in all Travels, Voyages and Histories. So I would spend
> ten years – the next five to the composition of the poem –
> and the five last to the correction of it.

Henry James had noted that Browning's work was marked by an incomparable 'moderness – by which we mean the all-touching, all-trying spirit of his work, permeated with accumulations and playing with knowledge'. Pound saw in *Sordello* a form capable of holding the rich and diverse material he poured into his *Cantos*. In an early (1917) version of the *Cantos* he defended Browning's poem because

> . . . the modern world
> Needs such a rag-bag to stuff all its thought in.

Many modern readers are as baffled by the highly allusive monologues which make up the *Cantos* as were Browning's contemporaries when they faced *Sordello*. Many would also sympathize with Pound's father, who told a reporter for the *Philadelphia Evening Bulletin*: 'Ezra told me unless I read Browning's "Sordello" I couldn't expect to understand the Cantos. So I waded through that. Ever read it? Well, I don't advise you to. I found it didn't help me much with Ezra's Cantos either.'

T. S. Eliot's relation to Browning is more problematical than is Pound's. No Eliot poem follows the rugged conversational speech and dramatic form of Browning's monologues so closely as do Pound's *Marvoil, In Durance,* and *Near Perigord.* In *The Love Song of J. Alfred Prufrock, Gerontion, The Journey of the Magi,* and the various monologues woven into *The Waste Land,* Eliot made radical innovations upon the dramatic monologue form which Browning had practised. Eliot was justifiably reluctant to admit any debt to Browning as Pound had so openly done. Towards the end of his life, Eliot commented that among the poets who 'could have been of use to a beginner in 1908 ... Browning was more of a hindrance than a help, for he had gone some way, but not far enough, in discovering a contemporary idiom'. The voice of Prufrock is more allusive and elliptical than the voice of any Browning character, and it reveals an underground stream of human consciousness with greater subtlety than the openly spoken thought and emotion which Browning strove to capture. Eliot's *personae* speak with a more intense 'thought-tormented music', a phrase that Gabriel Conroy uses to describe Browning's poetry in James Joyce's *The Dead.* The naturalistic description of the journey by Eliot's Magi is close to the idiom of Browning's Karshish, but the incorporation of suggestive symbols into the second stanza creates an idiom far different from that of either Browning or Hardy:

> Then at dawn we came down to a temperate valley,
> Wet, below the snow line, smelling of vegetation;
> With a running stream and a water-mill beating the darkness
> And three trees on the low sky,
> And an old white horse galloped away in the meadow.
> Then we came to a tavern with vine-leaves over the lintel,
> Six hands at an open door dicing for pieces of silver....

When Browning's St John in *A Death in the Desert* describes how he refused to acknowledge Christ when He was arrested in Gethsemane, John turns the incident into an argument that truth is never safe in this world:

> Even a torchlight and a noise,
> The sudden Roman faces, violent hands,
> And fear of what the Jews might do! Just that,
> And it is written, 'I forsook and fled':

There was my trial, and it ended thus.
Ay, but my soul had gained its truth, could grow:
Another year or two, – what little child,
What tender woman that had seen no least
Of all my sights, but barely heard them told,
Who did not clasp the cross with a light laugh,
Or wrap the burning robe round, thanking God?
Well, was truth safe forever, then? Not so.

Eliot opens the fifth section of *The Waste Land* with a quite similar description of Christ's arrest; but whereas Browning attempts to provide a realistic human dimension to John, Eliot's voice turns to a sad prophetic lament for the loss of faith in the modern world:

After the torchlight red on sweaty faces
After the frosty silence in the gardens
After the agony in stony places
The shouting and the crying
Prison and palace and reverberation
Of thunder of spring over distant mountains
He who was living is now dead
We who were living are now dying
With a little patience

Eliot's old man Gerontion also laments the decay of vital faith. The poem is a parody of Cardinal Newman's dramatic monologue *The Dream of Gerontius* (1866), but the idiom Eliot adopts is that of Browning's Caliban who tried to puzzle out the nature of his god, Setebos, and his universe:

'Thinketh He made it, with sun to match. . . .
'Thinketh, it came of being ill at ease:
He hated that He cannot change His cold,
Nor cure its ache. . . .
'Thinketh, such shows nor right nor wrong in Him,
Nor kind nor cruel: He is strong and Lord.

Gerontion is a kind of shrunk-shanked Caliban bewildered by historical changes and without hope:

Think now
History has many cunning passages. . . .

> Think now
> She gives when our attention is distracted. . . .
> Think
> Neither fear nor courage saves us. . . .
> Think at last
> We have not reached conclusion. . . .

Although Eliot's idiom is distinctly his own and distinctly modern, it frequently echoes back to the varied conversational phrasing and use of disparate materials Browning, alone among nineteenth-century English poets, wove into his poetry. This is particularly true of Eliot's deliberate mixture of profound prophetic announcements, snatches of bawdy songs, allusions to Elizabethan or classical literature, descriptions of urban refuse, references to fertility myths, and snatches of inane conversation. A reviewer of Browning's *Men and Women* noted a similar potpourri of tone and material in 1856 when he complained of Browning writing in a mode of 'violent contrast and provoking incongruities – fine irony and coarse abuse, subtle reasoning and halting twaddle, the lofty and the low, the refined and the vulgar, earnestness and levity, outpoured pell-mell. . . .' Pound's old university teacher, Cornelius Weygandt, recognized the similarity of Browning's and Eliot's styles, and he noted also their shared penchant for infusing erudite scholarship into their poetry: 'The practice of Eliot's verse harks back to Browning, in its jumbling together of various arts and conditions of life. It would seem that the theory that scholarship should underlie creative writing comes also from Browning, by way of Pound.'[9] Eliot's later poetry, *Ash Wednesday* and *Four Quartets*, like Pound's later *Cantos*, moves far from the realistic dramatic monologues of Browning. That poetry, in its turn, has influenced much of English and American 'modernist' poetry in which the original impetus of Browning is nearly obscured.

Pound and Eliot, though American born, allied themselves early with British and European movements in the modern arts. More consciously 'native' American poets found that they also could learn from the example of Browning. The 'Browning craze' that began with the founding of the Browning Societies in the 1880s was particularly strong in New England and the American Middle West. Matthew Arnold on one of his lecture tours of the United States asked a resident of a small New England village how the people amused themselves. 'Well,' replied the resident, 'last week they had a lecture on Browning.' By the time Browning died in 1889, the ladies of St Louis, Missouri, had formed a Sordello Club. Across the river in Illinois, a young law student, Edgar Lee Masters, wrote an elegy on Browning and published it in the journal *Inter Ocean*. Masters would later transform Browning's dramatic monologue into a vehicle by which he could recreate the fabric of life in a small mid-western village in *Spoon River Anthology* (1915). In 1920 he published *Domesday Book*, his long poem creating a court inquest out of the conflicting testimony of dramatic monologues, legal documents, and letters. Highly conscious of his aims to write of regional themes in a regional idiom, Masters was somewhat distressed when reviewers like Padraic Colum saw *The Ring and the Book* behind his poem. The New Englander, Edwin Arlington Robinson, was also occasionally discontented with reviewers who insisted on the similarities of his poetry to that of Browning. Dramatic monologues like *The Clinging Vine*, *John Gorham*, *Ben Jonson Entertains a Man from Stratford*, and *Rembrandt to Rembrandt*, however, reveal strong affinities. To Ivor Winters, one of Robinson's most sensitive commentators, 'the obvious and important influence is that of Browning'.[10] The distinctively regional poetry of another New Englander, Robert Frost, also owes something to Browning's dramatic rendering of conversational phrasing and diction. The woman in *A Servant to Servants*, who gradually reveals her history of insanity, begins her monologue:

I didn't make you know how glad I was
To have you come and camp here on our land.
I promised myself to get down some day
And see the way you lived, but I didn't know!
With a houseful of hungry men to feed
I guess I'd find. . . . It seems to me
I can't express my feelings anymore
Than I can raise my voice or want to lift
My hand (oh, I can lift it when I have to).
Did you ever feel so? I hope you never.

In the monologue of *The Pauper Witch of Grafton* a Browninglike grotesqueness is given a realistic setting through colloquial language; in *Paul's Wife* even the tall tale of the legendary lumberjack Paul Bunyan takes on the form of a realistic dramatic monologue. In old age Frost echoed the common twentieth-century complaint that, in Eliot's phrase, Browning was 'tediously longwinded'. 'He never knew

when he had it,' Frost said, 'he got so facile he couldn't stop writing.'
One of the distinct qualities of modernist poetry has been its movement towards more compact, tightly patterned and economical utterance. There is a greater conciseness in the monologues of Frost than
those of Browning; even within Frost's carefully constructed lyrics,
however, there is a tone he caught from Browning. Joseph Warren
Beach, who visited Frost in 1915 just as Frost was beginning to be
recognized as an important new poet, has left this record of the younger
Frost's literary tastes: 'His favorite poets were Chaucer, Shakespeare,
Wordsworth, and Browning. For in their verse he could hear the
inflections of the voice speaking.'[11] Many of the poems written by the
generation of poets coming into their own immediately before and
after the First World War share Browning's practice of dramatic
utterance in a language that is close to ordinary human speech. Those
poems have, as Amy Lowell said hers had, a 'very marked cousinship'
with the poetry of Robert Browning. Few of these modernist poems
are 'imitations' of Browning in the manner of Hardy or the early
Pound. Though Browning could offer a starting-point, each poet
developed his own distinctive style and mode. The poetry of another
member of that generation, John Crowe Ransome, might well illustrate the role that Browning has played in much modernist poetry.
Ransome's carefully patterned 'metaphysical' poetry is quite distinct
from that of the more voluble Browning. Yet Ransome has testified:
'It is a fact that Browning started me on my own, and no other poet
did.'[12]

The direction Browning gave to poetry has persisted among more
recent generations of poets. Auden's prose monologues *Herod* and
Caliban to the Audience owe something to the older poet; Edwin Muir
has been a sensitive commentator and has said of the poetic variety of
Browning that 'he is second among English poets to no one but
Shakespeare and Chaucer'.[13] Edward Lucie-Smith notes a stylistic 'debt
to Browning' in poems by Donald Davie and George MacBeth.[14]
Ransome's student, Robert Lowell, has consistently practised the form
of the Browningesque monologue, although in his earlier poems the
style is more heightened and intense, the diction more allusive. The
monologues of *Lord Weary's Castle* (1946) and *The Mills of the Kavan-
aughs* (1951), however, 'diminish in violence and resemble the model
that Lowell himself has named, the Robert Browning of "My Last
Duchess" and of "Sordello"'.[15] Browning's mode is nowhere more
alive in recent poetry than in Lowell's *After the Surprising Conversions*,

a monologue by the eighteenth-century New England divine, Jonathan Edwards:

> *September twenty-second*, Sir: today
> I answer. In the latter part of May
> Hard on our Lord's Ascension, it began
> To be more sensible. A gentleman
> Of more than common understanding, strict
> In morals, pious in behavior, kicked
> Against our goad.

Among the diverse movements within the newer poetry of the 1950s and 1960s has been a tendency away from the dramatic creation of character and narrative and towards a new mode of 'confessional' poetry in which poets speak in their own voices about their own experiences. Browning is not among the acknowledged forefathers of the new confessional poets; they look more to Whitman, Blake, Rilke, Rimbaud, or Lorca. In *Life Studies* (1959), Lowell blended the Browning monologue with the personal, confessional mode in poems about his childhood and youth:

> At Beverly Farms, a portly uncomfortable boulder
> bulked in the garden's center –
> an irregular Japanese touch.
> After his Bourbon "old fashioned", Father,
> bronzed, breezy, a shade too ruddy,
> swayed as if on deck duty
> under his six-pointed star-lantern –
> last July's birthday present.

The rough colloquial phrasing and the infusion of prosaic detail, exhibited here by Lowell, are elements that much contemporary poetry holds in common with Browning. 'Browning is a kind of quarry,' Lucie-Smith has said, 'from which modern poetry continues to be hewn.'[16] He has not influenced twentieth-century poetry in the manner, say, that his contemporary Marx influenced political economy or Darwin biology or Fraser anthropology. Browning was, in a partly obscured way, an interpreter of the life of the nineteenth century. Readers who recognize something 'modern' in the themes, forms, and above all in the varied voices of Browning are, perhaps, recognizing the modernity of the experience of Robert Browning and of the nineteenth century.

STIRLING COUNTY LIBRARY

Notes

Chapter 1 A Context for Browning's Early Life

1 *Robert Browning and His World: The Private Face, 1812–1861* (1967), p. 14.
2 *Robert Browning: A Portrait* (1952), p. 14.
3 M. D. George, *London Life in the XVIIIth Century* (1926), p. 18.
4 *Victorian England: Portrait of an Age* (1952), p. 14.
5 See Morse Peckham, *Victorian Revolutionaries: Speculations on Some Heroes of a Culture Crisis* (1970), pp. 84–129.
6 *In Bluebeard's Castle* (1971), p. 16.

Chapter 2 The Eighteen-Thirties

1 William C. DeVane, *A Browning Handbook* (1955), p. 42.
2 See J. Hillis Miller's chapter on Browning in *The Disappearance of God* (1965), pp. 81–156.
3 *The Early Literary Career of Robert Browning* (1911), p. 92.
4 Lionel Stevenson, 'The Key Poem of the Victorian Age' in *Essays in American and English Literature Presented to Bruce Robert McElderry, Jr*, ed. M. F. Schulz (1968), pp. 260–89.

Chapter 3 The Eighteen-Forties

1 Elizabeth Barrett expressed a similar dissatisfaction with older literary forms in a letter written to Browning early in their courtship: 'I am inclined to think that we want new *forms*, as well as thoughts. The old gods are dethroned. Why should we go back to antique moulds, classical moulds, as they are so improperly called?' *The Letters of Robert Browning and Elizabeth Barrett Barrett, 1845–1846* (1899), I, p. 45.
2 For a history and description of the dramatic monologue see Park Honan's chapter 'The Solitary Voice' in *Browning's Characters* (1961), pp. 104–28.
3 Robert Langbaum in his *The Poetry of Experience: The Dramatic Monologue*

in Modern Literary Tradition (1957) is particularly interested in Browning's genius for evoking the reader's sympathy for morally eccentric characters.
4 *A Browning Handbook*, p. 125.

Chapter 4 The Eighteen-Fifties

1 *Portrait of an Age*, 149.
2 See William Whitla, *The Central Truth: The Incarnation in Browning's Poetry* (1967).
3 *Browning: The Critical Heritage* (1970), p. 12.
4 Roma A. King, Jr, *The Bow and the Lyre: The Art of Robert Browning* (1957), p. 136.
5 'Historiography and *The Ring and the Book*', *Victorian Poetry*, VI (Autumn–Winter 1968), 247.
6 *Ibid.*, 243.
7 Donald Smalley, *Browning's Essay on Chatterton* (1948), p. 88.
8 Langbaum, p. 146.
9 King, p. 51.
10 *A Browning Handbook*, p. 219.

Chapter 5 The Eighteen-Sixties: I

1 *A Browning Handbook*, p. 282.
2 William Cadbury analyses the differences between fully dramatic poems and those in which Browning's own personality and ideas are more evident in his essay 'Lyric and Anti-Lyric Poems: A Method for Judging Browning', *University of Toronto Quarterly*, XXXIV (October 1964), 49–67.

Chapter 6 The Eighteen-Sixties: II

1 *The Poetry of Experience*, p. 109.
2 Miller, *The Disappearance of God*, pp. 81–156.
3 E. D. H. Johnson, 'Robert Browning's Pluralistic Universe: A Reading of *The Ring and the Book*', *University of Toronto Quarterly*, XXXI (October 1961), 20–41.
4 Peckham, 'Historiography and *The Ring and the Book*', 247.
5 Park Honan, 'The Murder Poem for Elizabeth', *Victorian Poetry*, VI (Autumn–Winter 1968), 215–30.
6 'A Note on the Lawyers', *Victorian Poetry*, VI (Autumn–Winter 1968), 305.
7 *Ibid.*, 307.
8 'The Disappearance of God in Victorian Poetry', *Victorian Studies*, VI (March 1963), 219.
9 *Ibid.*, 217–18.

Chapter 7 The Eighteen-Seventies and Eighties

1 See Max K. Sutton, 'The Affront to Victorian Dignity in the Satire of the Eighteen-Seventies', in *The Nineteenth-Century Writer and His Audience*, eds. H. Orel and G. Worth (1969), pp. 93–117.
2 J. M. Hitner, *Browning's Analysis of a Murder: A Case for The Inn Album* (1969).
3 See William S. Peterson, *Interrogating the Oracle: A History of the London Browning Society* (1969).
4 *The Poetry of Robert Browning* (1970), p. 409.

Chapter 8 Browning among the Modern Poets

1 *Modern Verse in English, 1900–1950*, eds. D. Cecil and A. Tate (1958), p. 35.
2 *A Choice of Browning's Verse* (1967), p. 12.
3 'Donne in Our Time', in *A Garland for John Donne 1631–1931*, ed. T. Spencer (1931), p. 15. For one of the earliest and best discussions of Browning's influence on Eliot and Pound see G. Robert Stange, 'Browning and Modern Poetry', in *Browning's Mind and Art*, ed. C. Tracy (1968), pp. 184–97.
4 Carl Weber, *Hardy of Wessex* (1965), p. 48.
5 See Marvel Shmiefsky, 'Yeats and Browning: The Shock of Recognition', *Studies in English Literature*, X (Autumn 1970), 701–22.
6 Horace Reynolds, 'Introduction' to W. B. Yeats, *Letters to the New Island* (1934), p. 35.
7 Shmiefsky, *ibid.*, 718.
8 See Christoph de Nagy's chapter 'Pound and Browning' in *The Poetry of Ezra Pound: The Pre-Imagist Stage* (1960), pp. 105–32.
9 *The Time of Yeats* (1937), p. 11.
10 *Edwin Arlington Robinson* (1946), pp. 22–3.
11 'Robert Frost', *Yale Review*, XLIII (December 1953), 210.
12 Quoted by Stange, *ibid.*, p. 197.
13 *Robert Browning: A Collection of Critical Essays*, ed. P. Drew (1966), p. 71.
14 *Ibid.*, p. 11.
15 Donald Hall, 'Robert Lowell' in *Contemporary Poets of the English Language*, ed. R. Murphy (1970), p. 673.
16 *Ibid.*, p. 29.

Bibliography

Browning, who was so intensively studied during the last two decades of his life, still lacks a 'definitive' edition of his poems and correspondence as well as a detailed and critical biography. Under the general editorship of Roma A. King, Jr, the Ohio University Press edition of the poetry and prose is under way; Philip Kelly has announced plans for an edition of the complete correspondence; Park Honan and William Irvine will soon publish a new scholarly biography. Scholarly and critical inquiry into the life and work of Browning has been particularly active in recent years. *Victorian Studies* annually lists scores of essays and books on Browning, reflecting a continuing trend that worried Andrew Lang in 1888: 'This later generation is in danger of forgetting the real poet in the multitudes of dissertations about poems which need explaining.' This bibliography is a selection, beyond the basic texts and reference works, of those books on Browning that might have a greater interest for the general student of nineteenth-century culture; those books will, in their turn, direct the reader to more specialized studies.

Editions

The Complete Works of Robert Browning (Florentine Edition), eds C. Porter and H. Clarke, 12 vols (1898, 1910, 1912). Along with the Kenyon edition (below) one of the standard editions from which Browning scholars draw their texts.

The Complete Works of Robert Browning, eds R. King, P. Honan, M. Peckham and G. Pitts (1968 —). Three volumes of a projected thirteen have now (1972) been published. They include important annotation, variant readings, and will become the standard texts.

The Works of Robert Browning (Centenary Edition), ed F. Kenyon, 10 vols (1912). Useful material introduces each volume of this edition most frequently cited by Browning scholars.

The Complete Poetical Works of Browning, ed H. Scudder (1895). Still in print, this is the only single-volume 'complete' edition; it includes the *Essay on Shelley*.

Letters

The Letters of Robert Browning and Elizabeth Barrett Barrett, 1845–1846, ed E. Kintner (1969).
Letters of Robert Browning, Collected by Thomas J. Wise, ed T. Hood (1933).
Robert Browning and Julia Wedgwood. A Broken Friendship as Revealed by Their Letters, ed R. Curle (1937).
New Letters of Robert Browning, eds W. DeVane and K. Knickerbocker (1950).
Dearest Isa, Robert Browning's Letters to Isabella Blagden, ed E. McAleer (1966).
Browning to His American Friends: Letters Between the Brownings, the Storys, and James Russell Lowell, ed G. Hudson (1965).
Learned Lady: Letters from Robert Browning to Mrs. Thomas FitzGerald, 1876–1889, ed E. McAleer (1966).

Reference Works and Essay Collections

Broughton, L., Northrup, C. and Pearsall, R. *Robert Browning: A Bibliography, 1830–1950* (1953). The most comprehensive listing of Browning's own publications as well as writings about him, anthologies, parodies, adaptations, etc.
Cook, A. *A Commentary upon Browning's 'The Ring and the Book'* (1920). Indispensable annotations to the highly allusive monologues of Browning's masterpiece.
DeVane, W. *A Browning Handbook* (1955). The single most complete and authoritative guide to the poetry.
Drew, P., ed. *Robert Browning: A Collection of Critical Essays* (1966). Essays by Mill, James, Santayana and Lubbock as well as more recent studies.
Litzinger, B. and Smalley, D., eds *Browning: The Critical Heritage* (1970). An extremely useful selection of contemporary reviews and comments by other Victorian authors.
Tracy, C., ed. *Browning's Mind and Art* (1968). A representative selection of essays on Browning since the 1950s.

Biographies

Griffith, W. and Minchin, H. *The Life of Robert Browning* (1938). An early standard life first published in 1910 and revised in 1938.

Miller, B. *Robert Browning: A Portrait* (1952). Draws upon previously un-published materials and aims at a psychological portrait.

Ward, M. *Robert Browning and His World: The Private Face* (1967) and *Two Robert Brownings?* (1969). The fullest biography to date. It places Browning well within the life of the nineteenth century.

General Studies

Chesterton, G. K. *Robert Browning* (1903). Remains one of the most readable and provocative books on Browning.

DeVane, W. *Browning's Parleyings: The Autobiography of a Mind* (1927). A study of the poet's ideas and reading, centring on his late poem *Parleyings With Certain People of Importance in Their Day.*

Drew, P. *The Poetry of Robert Browning: A Critical Introduction* (1970). A general survey of the poetry, discussions of the 'surface difficulties' the poems present to modern readers, and an assessment of twentieth-century critical attitudes.

Honan, P. *Browning's Characters: A Study in Poetic Technique* (1961). A thorough discussion of the technical aspects of the dramatic monologue: speaker, auditor, syntax, imagery, etc.

King, R. *The Focusing Artifice: The Poetry of Robert Browning* (1968). Brief critical assessments of most of Browning's poems by one of his most astute commentators.

Langbaum, R. *The Poetry of Experience: The Dramatic Monologue in Modern Literary Tradition* (1957). Acute insights into Browning's practice of the monologue form, as well as the practice of his predecessors and successors.

Miller, J. *The Disappearance of God: Five Nineteenth-Century Writers* (1963).

Peckham, M. *Victorian Revolutionaries: Speculations on Some Heroes of a Culture Crisis* (1970).

Raymond, W. *The Infinite Moment, and Other Essays in Robert Browning* (1951). Contains especially valuable essays on 'Browning and Higher Criticism' and a review of Browning studies from 1910 to 1949.

Smalley, D. *Browning's Essay on Chatterton* (1948). An important essay on Browning's development of the monologue form introduces an edition of one of the two extant essays Browning wrote.

Symons, A. *An Introduction to the Study of Browning* (1906). A revised edition of Symons's appreciative study of 1886.

Index

186

Index